Contemporary Approaches to Group Treatment

Traditional, Behavior-Modification, and Group-Centered Methods

Ronald A. Feldman

John S. Wodarski

CONTEMPORARY
APPROACHES
TO GROUP
TREATMENT

 Jossey-Bass Publishers
San Francisco • Washington • London • 1975

CONTEMPORARY APPROACHES TO GROUP TREATMENT
Traditional, Behavior-Modification, and Group-Centered Methods
by Ronald A. Feldman and John S. Wodarski

Copyright © 1975 by: Jossey-Bass, Inc., Publishers
615 Montgomery Street
San Francisco, California 94111
&
Jossey-Bass Limited
3 Henrietta Street
London WC2E 8LU

Library of Congress Catalogue Card Number LC 74-27913

International Standard Book Number ISBN 0-87589-249-3

Manufactured in the United States of America

JACKET DESIGN BY WILLI BAUM

FIRST EDITION

Code 7501

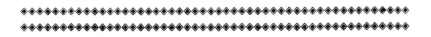

The Jossey-Bass
Behavioral Science Series

Preface

Group treatment has been found useful in a variety of helping professions, including social work, psychology, psychiatry, and guidance counseling. And many therapists who do not clearly identify themselves with a given profession view themselves as expert within the confines of one group treatment approach, such as transactional analysis or sensitivity training. Countless paraprofessionals and subprofessionals too, including street club workers, youth group leaders, and camp counselors, have applied group treatment methods in their work. Few group treatment methods, however, have been analyzed comprehensively in terms of their theoretical bases, practice implications, and measurable results. Some approaches, such as transactional analysis, have generated much theory but relatively little experimental research. Others, such as sensitivity training, have been researched without producing much theory and concomitant practice prescriptions. Most practitioners apply a broad variety of group treatment methods, which often results in a mixture of theory and practice most prudently described as eclectic.

Our intent here is to provide a relatively comprehensive overview of the theoretical bases for three currently used group treatment methods: the traditional social group work, group level behavior modification, and group-centered ("no-treatment") methods. The presentation is based not only upon the work of others but also upon theoretical and practical extensions which we have developed expressly for *Contemporary Approaches to Group Treatment*. Where appropriate, we note the presence or absence of relevant empirical support and suggest directions for future work. Even more important, we indicate how the three approaches might be made to complement and strengthen one another. In brief, then, the book provides a comprehensive statement of three treatment methods that currently are of interest to both group therapists and small group researchers.

A careful review of *Contemporary Approaches to Group Treatment* will reveal practice guidelines for many client problems, whether the client is viewed as the individual or the group. For all three methods, the interrelationships among diagnosis, treatment, and evaluation are discussed in detail, and, in many cases, relevant explications of these interrelationships appear in print for the first time.

We hope that *Contemporary Approaches to Group Treatment* will provide helping professionals with an opportunity for reflection, critical examination, synthesis, and the development of practical insights. We present it solely as a benchmark in knowledge development—one that endeavors to collate, synthesize, occasionally prescribe, and point to future directions.

In large part, *Contemporary Approaches to Group Treatment* describes methods actually utilized in a service-research project devoted to the study of group treatment, group integration, and behavioral change among antisocial and prosocial youth. The group treatment methods discussed here and the theories behind them are therefore elaborated with an eye toward their applicability to young people. Data from the research project currently are being analyzed and will be presented in a future volume that will focus primarily upon our research design, data analysis procedures, and relevant findings. We hope that our research will stimulate more vigorous empirical evaluation of the three methods than has thus far been attempted.

For support and assistance with the project and, consequently, with *Contemporary Approaches to Group Treatment* we are deeply indebted to a number of individuals and agencies. These include The Center for Studies of Crime and Delinquency of The

National Institute of Mental Health and, most particularly, its deputy chief, George H. Weber. Likewise, The Jewish Community Centers Association of St. Louis, Missouri, has been of assistance in providing resources and staff assistance, particularly through William Kahn, executive director. Administration and staff at Washington University (St. Louis) and The George Warren Brown School of Social Work have provided support and assistance. We are especially appreciative of aid from Mortimer Goodman, who helped to conceive and implement the original project, and from Norman Flax, who participated in the formulation and execution of many facets of the project, particularly those pertaining to the group-centered method. Stephen Pedi and Wallace Gingerich provided outstanding service as research associates, and Margaret Rosen, Mabel Degenhardt, and Patricia Golden offered expert research assistance as well as superb secretarial service. Among the many students who helped to bring the project to fruition were Kimm Dittrich, Donald Goldstein, Richard McQuiston, David Portowicz, Shelley Natkow, Robin Axelrod, Ronald Hursh, Robert Davidson, Ghassan Rubeiz, Judith Upham, Timothy Caplinger, Arthur Gilbert, Richard Green, Richard Hallam, Lawrence Hutchins, Douglas Shine, Frank Williams, and Jay Finesilver.

We dedicate this book to those group members who are dearest to us—to our wives, Dina and Lois Ann, who have provided inestimable supportive treatment, and to our children, Danny, Debbie, and Chrissie, who have served occasionally as subjects but more often as models.

Omaha, Nebraska RONALD A. FELDMAN
Knoxville, Tennessee JOHN S. WODARSKI
January 1975

Contents

Contemporary Approaches to Group Treatment

Traditional, Behavior-Modification,
and Group-Centered Methods

Group Treatment
in Social Work

The following chapters describe three group-treatment methods that have attracted large numbers of advocates within the social work profession. An effort is made to present each formulation in a more comprehensive and unified manner than has the current literature. Although these methods are used extensively by social workers, they have not been developed exclusively by that profession; like social work itself, each formulation draws upon allied professions and disciplines, including psychiatry, psychology, social psychology, and sociology. In line with the applied nature of the social work profession however, we put these methods into operation in our research primarily to test their differential effectiveness, particularly among groups which comprise antisocial youth.

Each of the three treatment methods was applied over a three-year period within a totally open community agency—The Jewish Community Centers Association of St. Louis, Missouri. During this period more than four hundred antisocial boys, ranging in age from nine to sixteen, were referred to the center by a variety of social agencies, including juvenile courts, public school guidance offices, residential treatment centers for antisocial youth, family and children's service agencies, and a school district created especially to deal with the behavioral and learning problems of exceptional children. All the boys were referred because, in the judgment of the agency, they had engaged recently in frequent or serious displays of antisocial behavior, including fighting, temper tantrums, and theft. Full details of the study, including pretest, posttest, and follow-up measures and behavioral data, will be presented in a separate volume currently in preparation. The main purpose of this volume is to describe the three methods in full detail and to explicate their historical backgrounds, underlying assumptions and rationales, modes of operation, and the elaborations of them which we introduced. Thus, only the major parameters of the larger study are discussed here.

Although each of the three methods can be implemented with ease in closed correctional or rehabilitative institutions such as prisons, reformatories, mental hospitals, or residential treatment centers, the St. Louis Experiment was conducted in an open community agency for a number of reasons. Initial behavioral modifications are somewhat more difficult to achieve in open environments (including outpatient clinics, halfway houses, and community centers) since these settings tend to be more turbulent and changing than closed institutions. Correspondingly, both the therapist and the group members can exert less control over variables that may influence the treatment process. Nonetheless, behavioral changes effected in such settings probably are more readily stabilized in the larger community than are those achieved in closed institutional settings.

After a comprehensive review of the relevant literature (Feldman and others, 1972, 1973a), we concluded that virtually all treatment programs conducted in closed institutions for antisocial youth had demonstrated serious deficiencies or high failure rates or both for a variety of reasons. One of these is the fact that multiple goals are often espoused by staff members. This espousal of many goals tends to foster serious intraorganizational conflicts over custodial versus therapeutic objectives and practices (Cressey, 1959; Grusky, 1959; Ohlin, 1958; Ohlin, Piven, and Pappenfort, 1956; Piliavin, 1966; Piven and Pappenfort, 1960; Prentice and Kelly, 1966; Street, Vinter, and Perrow, 1966; Vinter and Janowitz, 1959; Weber, 1957; Weber and Haberlein, 1972; Zald, 1962). However, although clients may suffer unduly as a result of staff conflicts, some data suggest, contrariwise, that treatment institutions characterized by such conflict may be far more progressive and flexible than those marked by excessive stability and staff harmony (Street, Vinter, and Perrow, 1966). As a result, clients may be subjected more readily to advanced and relatively contemporary treatment methods in such institutions. Nevertheless, excessive conflict over goals can be harmful to clients if it extends over long periods of time.

Closed correctional institutions also have been characterized by serious client overpopulation. For example, in eleven states with programs housing 9,165 children (the only ones for which statistics are available) the average daily inmate population of correctional institutions was 10 percent or more above capacity (National Council on Crime and Delinquency, 1967). Overpopulation leads not only to fragmentation of rehabilitative endeavors but to control problems which often are resolved at the expense of treatment objectives. Custodial staff, for example, may bargain with inmate leaders in order to retain ultimate control over all inmates. In effect, staff frequently delegate control to highly antisocial inmates in order to protect their own positions, thus legitimizing and reinforcing deviant behavior among the inmate population (Barker and Adams, 1959; Clemmer, 1958; Grosser, 1958; Polsky, 1962; Rolde and others, 1970; Schrag, 1954; Street, 1965; Sykes and Matza, 1957; Tittle, 1969). Overcrowding may lead also to the segregation of the most incorrigible individuals, thus making it additionally difficult to evoke therapeutic change. Likewise, early offenders may be refused admission or treatment because of overcrowding—a practice which contributes to the maintenance of deviant behavioral patterns that may be proportionately more difficult to treat at later stages of a delinquent career.

The foregoing factors are closely associated with what may be the most pervasive and debilitating variable contributing to the high failure rate in closed correctional institutions, namely, the peer composition of available treatment groups. Most role models within the inmate's environment are antisocial. His peers exhibit seriously antisocial behavior, reinforce and reciprocate such behavior, and, to some extent, have demonstrated an inability to function within acceptable limits in the open community. Such factors necessarily deter efforts to rehabilitate inmates and to prepare them for effective prosocial functioning beyond the walls of the institution (Clemmer, 1958; Hindelang, 1970; Jesness, 1965; Street, 1965; Sykes and Messinger, 1960). Moreover, they may foster more frequent or more serious deviant behavior patterns among inmates who were relatively prosocial prior to incarceration.

Since the two environments are so dissimilar, behavioral changes manifested within a correctional institution may be quite different from those required for effective social functioning in the larger community, and so behavioral changes wrought in the closed institution may be of negligible long-term significance. In brief, then, the marked differences between closed and open environments and the differing skills necessary for successful functioning within each point to the likelihood of low transferability or stabilization of behavioral changes learned in the correctional institution.

Another problem is that regardless of the adequacy of the services the requisite financial expenditures for care in closed correctional facilities tend to be inordinately high. In 1967 the average per capita operating expense for such institutions was $3,411, equivalent to tuition and living expenses for one year at a top-quality liberal arts college (National Council on Crime and Delinquency, 1967). No doubt per capita costs will continue to spiral upward in concert with accelerating inflation.

A final problem pertaining to closed correctional institutions and, to a lesser extent, to all institutions defined primarily as treatment or rehabilitative agencies is the adverse labeling and stigmatization of their inmates and former inmates. Numerous investigators have described the process whereby relevant others stigmatize former inmates, thus limiting their opportunities to engage in prosocial behavior and, in effect, creating the necessary conditions for continued deviance (Akers, 1968; DeLamater, 1968; Erikson, 1962; Gibbs, 1966; McSally, 1960; Piliavin and Briar, 1964; Schur, 1971; Schwartz and Skolnick, 1962; Sheridan, 1967; Simmons, 1965; Wheeler and Cottrell, 1966).

Although community-based treatment programs may entail somewhat less stigmatization than those conducted in closed institutions, the many failures noted for community-based treatment (Berleman and others, 1972; Empey and Rabow, 1961; Empey

and Lubeck, 1971; Kantor and Bennett, 1968; Klein, 1965; J. Mc-
Cord and W. McCord, 1959; W. McCord and J. McCord, 1959;
Meyer and others, 1965; Miller, 1970; Powers and Witmer, 1951;
Stephenson and Scarpitti, 1969; Warren, 1970)' may be due in
large part to the serious stigmatization still encountered by individuals who are subjected to treatment within any kind of treatment
agency. Just as mere processing by the police may label a juvenile
adversely (Piliavin and Briar, 1964), association with presumably
innocuous rehabilitative agencies, such as a juvenile court (Cicourel,
1967; Platt, 1969; Werthman, 1967; Williams and Gold, 1972;
Wolfgang and others, 1972) or a special public school class (Schafer,
1967), may stigmatize a child. In order to minimize the stigmatization associated with rehabilitative efforts, we believe it necessary
to locate such programs within institutions that are not viewed primarily as treatment agencies and, consequently, where stigmatization is not transmitted in part from institution to child—hence the
location of the St. Louis Experiment in a community-center setting.

Given the above considerations, one of the major objectives
of the St. Louis Experiment was to examine the differential effectiveness of the three group treatment methods in an open setting.
More particularly, the experiment examined differential incidences
of prosocial, nonsocial, and antisocial behavior exhibited by the
subjects at varying points in time (Feldman and others, 1973b)',
including: the time prior to the subjects' referral to the program,
during a six- to eight-week baseline period prior to the implementation of treatment, at five separate junctures during the thirty-week
treatment period, and during follow-up tests conducted a year or
more after the termination of treatment. Requisite behavioral data
were recorded throughout the experiment by trained nonparticipant
observers utilizing a systematic time-sampling procedure. Corresponding inventory data also were obtained from group leaders,
referral agencies, the subjects' parents, and the subjects themselves.
Additional data included subjects' scores on the Jesness Inventory,
designed to gauge tendencies toward manifest aggression and social
maladjustment, and data regarding variations in group integration,
including normative, functional, and interpersonal integration
(Feldman, 1968, 1969a, 1969b, 1973)'.

In addition to analyzing the differential effectiveness of the three group treatment methods, the St. Louis Experiment was designed to evaluate the effects of another major variable, differential group composition. Specifically, three different treatment groups were studied: those consisting solely of boys referred because of their antisocial behavior, those consisting solely of boys not referred because of antisocial behavior (regular agency members), and those consisting solely of boys not referred because of antisocial behavior plus one or two boys who were referred for such behavior. Respectively, these were classified as antisocial, prosocial, and mixed, or integrated, groups. Approximately twenty to thirty such groups were studied each year. A 3 × 3 experimental design was devised, resulting in the creation of groups that were subjected to one of the three modes of group composition and to one of the three modes of treatment.

Differing modes of group composition were investigated primarily because we posited that certain major deficiencies associated with the treatment of antisocial youth might be ameliorated through ongoing group therapy among prosocial peers. In particular, these deficiencies are the stigmatization associated with treatment among antisocial peers and the dysfunctional peer-group composition of the treatment milieu. The stigmatization resulting from the antisocial-peer composition of a treatment group may present barriers to rehabilitation that are entirely independent of the peers' direct influences upon one another. And these direct peer influences in a solely antisocial-children group also may be serious impediments to rehabilitation. In such groups the treatment milieu continues to present the basic conditions that militate against adaptive and sustained behavioral change. These include deviant role models and maladaptive systems of reward and punishment. Hence the composition of the treatment group, as well as the way in which it is perceived by others, may adversely influence treatment efforts.

Given the problems of composing effective treatment groups, why not treat antisocial children individually? Many rationales obtain for the provision of group-treatment programs for clients who manifest serious behavioral problems. Most of these rationales apply with special emphasis to antisocial youth. As one of its major objectives, social work frequently cites enabling clients to engage in "more adequate social functioning" (Boehm, 1959). By definition, social functioning is behavior that takes place with or among other persons—the reciprocal interactions among human beings.

Contemporary theoretical formulations regarding the antisocial behavior of youth tend to be set forth within predominantly social rather than individual frameworks. For example, existing formulations refer to the availability of legitimate and illegitimate social opportunities and opportunity structures (Cloward, 1959; Cloward and Ohlin, 1960; Merton, 1959; Schrag, 1962), differential association with delinquent peers and socialization among deviant subcultures (Cressey, 1960; Hindelang, 1970; Lerman, 1968; Miller, 1958; Reiss and Rhodes, 1961; Short and others, 1965; Short, 1957; Spergel, 1967; Voss, 1969), and the effects of deviant situational inducements (Briar and Piliavin, 1965).

Similarly, formulations exist regarding the neutralization of prosocial norms (Matza, 1964; Matza and Sykes, 1961; Sykes and Matza, 1957), reaction formations against middle-class values and success standards (Cohen, 1955, 1965), adverse labeling by peers and others (Akers, 1968; Becker, 1963; Eisner, 1969; Simmons, 1965), and the development of deviant self-concepts as a result of maladaptive social affiliations (Backman and others, 1966; Eynon and Simpson, 1965; Fannin and Clinard, 1965; Kinch, 1962; Reckless and Dinitz, 1967; Schwartz and Tangri, 1965; Tangri and Schwartz, 1967). Many if not all of these formulations point to the efficacy of diagnosing and treating delinquent individuals within social contexts, rather than as isolated cases.

In contrast with the usual one-to-one therapeutic situation, any treatment group composed of more than two persons is likely to present a broad variety of social stimuli, behavioral patterns, and reinforcement mechanisms. To the extent that these represent the "real world" or, more specifically, the client's typical social environment, they are likely to provide the preconditions for an accurate diagnosis of his true difficulties in social functioning. Each client is likely to be confronted with a wide array of social problems, peer relationships, and task responsibilities that inevitably are lacking in the typical one-to-one therapeutic encounter. Consequently, in a group the therapist has many opportunities and referents for diagnosis of the client's behavioral difficulties in the "real world."

Moreover, unlike the dyadic treatment relationship, the

group setting provides the therapist with a unique opportunity for longitudinal, or ongoing, social diagnosis. He is therefore able to gain an understanding of the developmental nature of each client's sociobehavioral problems and to perceive how these problems result from the client's interrelationships with others. The therapist also can ascertain the scope of each client's behavioral problems, particularly with reference to the social situations in which these problems occur or are exacerbated.

Correspondingly, group treatment affords multiple foci for therapeutic interventions. The therapist's activities may be directed toward a broad variety of social situations or behavioral problems, oriented toward the interactions between a client and his peers. Skilled therapy, moreover, may draw upon the capacities of other clients within the group. In contrast with the dyadic therapeutic relationship, cohesive groups of three or more persons are likely to produce greater mutual trust among members, more frequent efforts of peers to influence one another, and enhanced susceptibility to peer influence (Cartwright, 1968; Frank, 1957; Thomas, 1967b). Hence peer-group pressures and group behavioral contingencies (see Chapter Five) can be utilized with great effectiveness in the treatment context. In addition, treatment groups necessarily provide many actual and potential role models for each client. The skilled therapist can draw readily upon this resource in order to provide effective treatment. Because of the many social resources available within the group context, the client has numerous occasions to test new insights and behavioral skills as soon as they are developed and before the watchful eyes of the therapist, thus affording further opportunities for immediate feedback, correction of maladaptive behaviors, and shaping of adaptive behavior.

To the extent that the treatment group accurately represents the client's social environment, behavioral changes achieved within it are likely to be transferred to that environment and to be readily stabilized within it. This is no small accomplishment in social treatment since, as noted earlier, numerous programs have reported significant client changes within the treatment environment, but have ended as abject failures because such changes could not be transferred to or stabilized within the client's natural environment.

Finally, the per capita costs of group-treatment programs

are likely to be far less than those for individual-treatment programs, particularly if client change takes place at the same or at a more rapid pace. Relative speed of change, however, has not yet been sufficiently studied.

Clearly, there are also a number of distinct liabilities to group-treatment modalities. Although they hardly appear to countervail the many assets, the liabilities are significant nevertheless. The therapist's diagnostic and treatment efforts necessarily are fragmented in both their focus and their chronology. He must attend simultaneously to a myriad of diagnostic cues, interventive opportunities, and monitoring responsibilities. On occasion, he must cope with unanticipated peer-oriented obfuscations posed by clients, and, therefore, he may be forced to lose continuity in diagnosis or treatment. In contrast with the dyadic situation, in a group the therapist is less able to control all the variables relevant for influencing clients' behavior. However, by forgoing some control he is able to draw upon countless opportunities unavailable in the typical one-to-one therapeutic situation. These considerations are discussed in detail in subsequent chapters.

The three group-treatment methods discussed here have been selected, in large part, because they fall within the mainstream of contemporary social group work. Each has a significant number of advocates, has been the subject of considerable writing by group workers and allied professionals, and has been applied to a large variety of client populations. Yet, rather surprisingly, none has been subjected to systematic and rigorous empirical research. Furthermore, few, if any, efforts have been made within social work to collate and synthesize the variations thus far propounded for each approach and to set forth a coherent and integrated explication of each.

The first of the three methods to be discussed is traditional social group work. The appellation *traditional* has been used primarily for two reasons. First, the method probably is the predominant mode of group work used by contemporary social work practitioners. Since the latter part of the 1950s, various facets of this approach have been taught at The University of Michigan School of Social Work. This school currently has the largest M.S.W. program in the United States. Moreover, for the greater part of the

1960s it had the largest Ph.D. enrollment of any school of social work in the world. Consequently, its graduates have disseminated its basic group-work perspective to many other schools of social work. The second reason for denoting this treatment modality as traditional is that its concepts and principles are drawn heavily from the social science disciplines (including sociology and social psychology) upon which social workers have relied since the inception of the group-work specialization.

The traditional group-work method envisions therapists as highly directive, especially during the early phases of treatment. The therapist engages in diagnoses, at both the individual and group levels, continuously throughout the course of treatment. He also formulates both short-term and long-term treatment objectives for individual members and for the group as a whole, and he engages in a series of systematic, direct interventions to attain these objectives. Effective utilization of this method requires the group worker to be well acquainted with certain theoretical formulations of sociology and social psychology, such as role theory and social-exchange theory. Similarly, he must be well grounded in group dynamics, including knowledge of group structures, group development, and deviant group processes.

The principal features of this treatment modality as set forth by its main proponents are presented in two collections of readings (Vinter, 1967; Glasser and others, 1974) which are the major sources for practitioners. Chapters Two, Three, and Four supplement the original sources by explicating the underlying assumptions of the approach, delineating its relationships with other kinds of group treatment, and presenting a description of the method that incorporates its variations in a common framework. In addition, we highlight practical implications, especially with reference to antisocial youth. Finally, the method is described as one base for the St. Louis Experiment.

The second treatment method to be discussed is group-level behavior modification. This framework draws primarily upon the knowledge base of experimental psychology, especially social-learning theory and behavior-modification theory. Behavior modification was first introduced to the social work literature in the middle of the 1960s. However, virtually all the early literature focused solely upon the treatment of individuals in therapeutic encounters that were similar to the traditional social casework relationship. Only recently have attempts been made to apply this knowledge base to therapeutic work with small groups. Interestingly, most of these applications have been devised by present or former faculty members of The University of Michigan School of Social Work. Yet, little of the total literature pertaining to behavior-modification group treatment has been produced by social group workers. The great bulk of the literature is by sociologists, social psychologists, and experimental psychologists.

Chapter Five delineates many of the underlying assumptions and concepts of a behavior-modification approach to treatment in small groups. Again, the particular focus is upon work with anti-social youth. Although many of the basic concepts are identical to those used in all behavior-modification endeavors, the discussion proceeds beyond most others through its detailed explication of group contingencies and through the illustration of their application to group-work practice. Without question, the discussion is only an initial step in the continued elaboration of knowledge regarding the use of group contingencies in small-group treatment. Nevertheless, we expect this knowledge base to expand rapidly, and it may eventually lead to a coherent synthesis of behavior-modification techniques and components of the traditional group-work method.

The group-centered method is the final formulation discussed. Chapter Six had its origins in our desire to provide a contrast for evaluating the efficacy of the other two treatment modalities for the St. Louis Experiment. To do so, we had to find a group-work method which, in essence, resulted in the application of few, if any, interventions by the group leader. Although such a task may appear to be rather straightforward, the discussion in Chapter Six clearly reveals the critical conceptual and methodological difficulties involved.

In order to devise a group-work approach truly consonant with a no-treatment philosophy, it is essential to preclude, to the greatest extent possible, group leaders' predilections to diagnose, evaluate, and otherwise interact with group members in any manner that might be regarded as systematically providing treatment. Consequently, it has been necessary to conceptualize the requisite approach in a manner that has been rarely, if ever, fully detailed in the literature of social group work or, for that matter, in related literature concerning group treatment. Similarly, we considered it necessary to elaborate a series of guidelines for implementation of such a method. The discussion in Chapter Six most probably is one of the few that endeavors to delineate underlying assumptions of such an approach, to analyze its contributions to research methodology as well as to group-work treatment, and to organize operational guidelines within a concise framework.

But the group-centered method ought not to be viewed solely as a research instrument. In fact, a substantial body of literature covers the legitimate precursor of this method, namely, the client-centered therapeutic approach propounded by Carl Rogers and his colleagues. Elements of this method also can be found in the social work literature and in much of the contemporary literature concerning group treatment based upon sensitivity training, encounter experiences, personal growth, and existential therapies. The efficacy of such an approach has until now seldom been rigorously tested at the individual level and only rarely has been validated as a result of rigorous small-group research.

In the discussions which follow, the multidisciplinary roots of the three methods are reflected in a diversity of labels. Thus, for example, the primary therapeutic agent is denoted as the group worker or, more concisely, as the worker. Yet the appellation is used interchangeably with therapist, group leader, and practitioner. Similarly, in accord with traditional social work argot, the primary target of therapeutic interventions is called the client. However, in line with the terminology of other professions and with the research framework of the St. Louis Experiment, other terms such as patient and subject are utilized when appropriate.

II

Traditional Social Group Work: Group Development

Several social group work methods might be appropriately termed *traditional,* having been in use since World War II. During the first two postwar decades, social workers made use of small groups mainly to help individuals develop skills in democratic living (Coyle, 1947, 1948; Klein, 1953) or to promote social growth among group members (Phillips, 1957; Trecker, 1955; Tropp, 1965; Schwartz, 1961, 1962, 1963; Wilson and Ryland, 1949). Small groups were also used in the early postwar period for therapeutic, corrective, and rehabilitative purposes (Konopka, 1954, 1963; Redl and Wineman, 1951)' but to a much lesser extent. The trend seems to be reversing itself; although some current social work writers still have primarily democratic and social-growth orientations (Klein, 1970; Shulman, 1968; Tropp, 1971)', the late 1960s and early 1970s witnessed a pronounced tendency for social workers to use small groups for treatment purposes (Bernstein, 1970; Feldman, 1968, 1969c; Glasser and Garvin, 1971; Maier, 1965; Northen, 1969; Papell and Rothman, 1966; Rose, 1969; Spergel, 1966; Vinter, 1967).

The majority of contemporary group workers can be differentiated in another way from their predecessors of two decades earlier. Rather than focusing upon the group as a context for the treatment of malfunctioning individuals or social systems, contemporary social workers consider the group primarily as a means for treating individuals. Hence the group is viewed in current social work practice not only as a place where individuals express their critical concerns, hopes, and social inadequacies but also as an interpersonal environment in which members actively modify each other's social behavior in order to improve social functioning. This important distinction has been overlooked by contemporary theorists in other areas, including many with a behavior-modification orientation. In the latter area particularly, little cognizance is taken of members' capacities or inclinations to influence one another; group members are programed to respond to interventions of the worker alone rather than to contingencies set forth or sanctioned by their peers.

Contemporary group workers also are singularly distinguished from their predecessors and from non-social work colleagues by a strong emphasis on sociological and social-psychological knowledge. Whereas many psychiatrists and psychologists continue to conceptualize group interaction in terms of id (Freud, 1922), ego (Berne, 1964; Harris, 1967; Thelen, 1954; Durkin, 1965), or libidinal states, the social group work literature displays a strong interest in group-level constructs such as group integration (Feldman, 1968, 1969a, 1969b), group cohesiveness (Cartwright and Zander, 1968; Klein and Crawford, 1967; Lott and Lott, 1961, 1965), and group structure (Blum, 1962; Dunphy, 1963; Glasser and Navarre, 1965; Jansyn, 1966; Luchins, 1967; Northen, 1969; Short, 1967). This broad conceptual framework has enabled social group workers to justifiably contend that their diagnostic and treatment frameworks (1) are relatively more comprehensive than the formulations of other professions, (2) focus to a greater extent upon social desiderata, (3) examine a variety of interpersonal processes that clearly emerge as a consequence of ongoing interaction in the treatment group, such as scapegoating (Burke, 1969; Feldman, 1969b; Shulman, 1967), rejection (Feldman, 1969d; Schachter, 1960), aggression (Burke, 1966; Sabath, 1964; Wiggins, 1965), contagion (Kerckhoff and others, 1965; Lippitt and others, 1952; Wheeler and Levine, 1967), and conflict (Bernstein, 1965; Forman, 1967; Theodorson, 1962),

(4) focus on components of small-group interaction that often are excluded from consideration by other group treatment methods, such as nonverbal interaction (Middleman, 1968), (5) utilize play activities and recreational activities, in addition to discussion techniques, in order to induce therapeutic change (Feldman, 1967, 1969b; Maier, 1965; Spergel, 1966; Vinter, 1967), and (6) provide services to certain categories of clients that are typically neglected, such as the mentally retarded (Klein, 1967), the aged (Forman, 1967; Klein and others, 1965; Margulies, 1966), the indigent (Feldman, 1969c; Glasser, 1963; Schwartz, 1968), and street corner youth (Austin, 1957; Spergel, 1965, 1966).

These features have both positive and negative aspects. Although they have permitted therapeutic and remedial efforts to reach previously neglected client populations, they also have contributed to fragmentation of effort and have hampered the development of a unified, coherent theory. In effect, the diversity of client populations has generated a multiplicity of subtheories for social group work, each geared to the unique attributes and needs of a particular client population and linked to the rest only at the most general conceptual levels.

The traditional group work method to be outlined here is predicated primarily upon the approach developed by Robert D. Vinter and his colleagues at The University of Michigan School of Social Work. An early statement of the treatment method developed by Vinter and others was set forth in *Readings in Group Work Practice* (1967). A more current and comprehensive formulation is found in Glasser and others (1974). The present explication draws heavily from both discussions. Additionally an early review of the method, denoting it as "remedial social group work," is provided by Papell and Rothman (1966); they contrast it with two other methods commonly used by social workers—the "social goals" model and the "reciprocal" model. A more recent review, albeit brief, is found in Garvin and Glasser (1971).

In the traditional group work approach, the group is viewed as a small social system whose influences can be purposefully guided to modify client behavior. This perspective allows the use of many bodies of substantive knowledge about the assessment and alteration of group behavior. General systems theory, role theory, social-exchange theory, communications theory, and so forth are all relevant for the group worker. So is information about social processes such as social judgment, attitude change, coalition formation, and decision making. Whatever disciplines or sciences he draws on, the group worker with this approach acknowledges that potent change forces are generated within small groups. He seeks to marshal these forces by controlling the size, composition, and developmental processes of the group, in order to achieve selected treatment goals.

In the traditional approach the social worker is concerned with developmental processes within the group that may affect the behavior of individual group members. Four major dimensions of group development are of special concern: the social organization of the group, with its pattern of participant roles; the activities, tasks, and operative processes of the group; the culture of the group, including norms, values, and shared purposes; and the group's relations to the external environment. Most groups pass through a series of developmental phases in which each of the foregoing major dimensions is affected. Through influencing these broad dimensions—sometimes by his interventive efforts with only one or two group members—the worker may exert an important effect upon the entire group. The essence of group work rests, then, on the worker's skill in improving the social functioning of group members. In order to do this the worker must develop competence in the assessment, or diagnosis, of individual and group malfunctioning; the formulation of appropriate treatment goals for individual members and for the entire group; the execution of interventive strategies that effect desired behavioral changes within the group and among individual group members; and the evaluation of subsequent behavioral changes among group members. To complement the foregoing skill areas, the worker must be adequately educated in normal and deviant processes of group development, techniques of group work intervention, and phases of the treatment process.

The present chapter extensively discusses normal and deviant processes of group development. It provides the framework for our explication, in Chapters Three and Four, of group work intervention and treatment phases. The discussion here focuses primarily upon the group development model set forth by two of Vinter's colleagues,

Rosemary C. Sarri and Maeda Galinsky. In many respects, their discussion of group developmental phases is the most significant in the social work literature. Moreover, their model is a central component of the traditional group work method, especially as elaborated by the Michigan school. We highlight the particular role of their model within the traditional method by contrasting it with important antecedent and subsequent models and, moreover, by pointing to its particular assets and liabilities in group work practice.

Bales and Strodtbeck

Perhaps the most widely reported series of group development studies was performed by Bales (1950a), Bales and Strodtbeck (1951), and Bales and Slater (1955). This work focused primarily on group problem-solving. Utilizing an observational technique called Interaction Process Analysis, Bales (1950a) and his colleagues analyzed interpersonal behavior in twenty-two problem-solving groups composed of Harvard University students. For the most part the students were asked to work toward group solutions for hypothetical problem situations concerning chess strategies, party planning, and interpretations of projective stories. The investigators observed the participants' behavior throughout each group session and classified it according to whether the members displayed (1) positive socioemotional behavior (showing solidarity, raising others' status, giving help or rewards, showing tension release, joking, laughing, showing satisfaction, agreeing with peers, showing passive acceptance, understanding, concurring, complying), (2) negative socioemotional behavior (showing antagonism, deflating others' status, defending or asserting one's self, showing tension, asking for help, withdrawing, disagreeing, showing passive rejection or formality, withholding help), (3) task behavior involving attempted answers (giving suggestion or direction; implying autonomy for others; giving opinions, evaluations, or analysis; expressing feelings or wishes; engaging in orientation; giving information; repeating; clarifying; confirming), or (4) task behavior involving questions (asking for suggestions, direction, possible ways of action, opinion, evaluation, analysis, expression of feelings, orientation, information, repetition, clarification, confirmation).

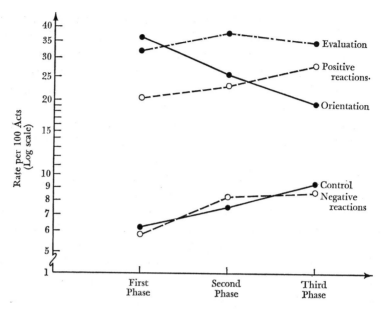

FIGURE 1. Relative frequency of acts by type and phase, based upon twenty-two sessions. (From Bales and Strodtbeck, 1951.)

As indicated in Figure 1 Bales and Strodtbeck concluded that groups move sequentially from a relative emphasis upon orientation, to evaluation, and, subsequently, to control. Hence they inferred the existence of three general phases of development through which groups progress. However, Bales and his colleagues studied each group meeting as a separate unit of analysis; the three phases were observed only within single group sessions. Bales and Strodtbeck made no claim that groups progress through the three phases longitudinally, that is, over a continuous series of meetings.

To date, however, few persons have fully interpreted Bales and Strodtbeck's data. For example, these data indicate that there were more orientation acts, or behaviors, during the first phase of group development than during any other phase, more evaluation acts during the second phase than during any other, and more control acts during the third phase. This does not mean, however, that control acts predominated within the group during the third phase, a common, but incorrect, representation of the Bales and Strodtbeck data. Although there were more control acts during this phase than during the two preceding phases, a close review of Figure 1 shows that there were still far more evaluation and orientation acts than control acts. The data suggest, then, that a worker's expectations regarding inordinate amounts of control behavior during the final phase of group development would be unwarranted, even for problem-solving groups. Conversely, some control acts may be expected during the first phase of group development although they might be relatively fragmented or premature.

An analysis of the positive and negative behaviors displayed by group members during the Bales and Strodtbeck study also is of special interest. Throughout all three phases of group development, positive reactions occur about three times as frequently as negative ones. The former increase steadily throughout the three phases and tend to peak as the group approaches attainment of its goals. Numerous studies have shown that the relationship between liking behavior and movement toward goal attainment is a positive and reciprocal one (Feldman, 1968). Positive socioemotional relations enable members to work cooperatively and productively; successful goal attainment, conversely, contributes to heightened satisfaction and interpersonal attraction among group members.

Figure 1 indicates that negative interpersonal behavior peaks during the second (evaluative) and third (control) phases of group development. Presumably, during these phases members' frustrations and tensions are at a maximum since the participants have expended considerable effort but have not yet witnessed clear-cut results from their labors. The absolute difference in rate between positive and negative reactions is lowest during the middle phase. Therefore, not only do negative reactions approach a peak, but they tend to be least effectively countervailed by positive reactions during the second phase. Clearly, then, this phase can be regarded as a period of maximum tension in group development, a conclusion not readily noted in the Bales and Strodtbeck discussions. In contrast, the rate difference between positive and negative reactions is greatest during the third phase, with the positive behaviors far outpacing negative ones. This phase appears to be one of minimum tension. Or, as has been suggested in a different context, it may be considered a period of "optimum benefit" during which there occurs an amount of mutual facilitation that maximizes the speed of movement for group members and minimizes emotional tension for them (Thomas, 1957). The particularly strong showing of positive behaviors readily countervails the negative behaviors, also at a maximum in this phase.

Negative behavior is observed to some extent throughout all three phases. Therefore, even in "well-adjusted" groups working on concrete problems, some negativism may be expected during problem-solving activities. A somewhat continuous increase in negativism should be a routinely expected correlate of problem-solving behavior. Obviously negativism and conflict must be held within acceptable limits if a group is to sustain itself over time. But moderate levels of anxiety, frustration, and tension appear to several motivation theorists to be normal concomitants, if not preconditions, of problem-solving behavior (Atkinson and Feather, 1966; Brown, 1961; Dibner, 1958; Thomas, 1957). Whereas unduly high anxiety interferes with goal-attainment efforts, particularly for complex tasks, unduly low anxiety produces little impetus for effective goal-attainment activity. Applying these findings to treatment groups might help diminish group therapist bias against conflict, hostility, and negativism (Frank, 1957; Goldstein and others, 1966). Negative behavior could be expected and welcomed as functional for therapeutic change. Indeed, its absence might be more symptomatic of maladaptive social functioning of the group than its presence. It need not be regarded as an indication of individual pathology, but rather as socially mediated and as an indicator of forward movement by the group. It should be viewed as dysfunctional only when it severely deters positive social functioning and prevents movement toward control behaviors and ultimate goal attainment.

Caution is warranted in applying this material to group treatment endeavors however. The particular problems studied by Bales and Strodtbeck lend themselves readily to evaluation and control endeavors, to concrete solutions, and, therefore, to the succession of phases observed. Likewise, although the study was successfully replicated with a different sample and a different problem focus (Phillips and Dunphy, 1959), the all-male sample of Harvard students is not especially representative of the larger society in general or of most treatment groups in particular. And, whereas all three phases were rarely observed for any particular group, Bales and

Strodtbeck's conclusions were based upon the averaging of observations for all groups, thus raising serious questions regarding the ability of their findings to be generalized to discrete small groups. Perhaps of greatest concern is the possibility that their conclusions regarding the existence of three developmental phases may be an artifact of their data-collection techniques. The data were analyzed separately for each of three distinct and different time periods, which could, in turn, have predetermined the behavioral variations presumably associated with each of the three phases. Finally, the data for each group were gathered for one session only. In group therapy, by contrast, it is rare to witness closure during a single session. Hence many observers might question whether the relatively long-term, open-ended problems associated with group treatment are sufficiently analogous to those studied by Bales and Strodtbeck to warrant extrapolation of their data to treatment situations. Fortunately, however, at least two investigators have addressed this question.

Talland and Psathas

Talland (1955) replicated the Bales and Strodtbeck observational procedure in a study of four mixed-sex groups undergoing analytic group psychotherapy. Each group was composed of six to eight members, ranging in age from twenty-three to forty-five. All the subjects were diagnosed as suffering from psychoneuroses. Data were analyzed for eighteen meetings, each lasting ninety minutes, during the first eight weeks of therapy. Talland did not find evidence that groups passed sequentially through orientation, evaluation, and control phases during any given meeting. In contrast, there was a pronounced emphasis upon orientation behavior and positive reactions throughout each meeting. Talland attributed these findings to the different problem focus of therapy groups, assuming that such groups were characterized by the continuous emergence of new problems, relatively superficial discussions of such problems, and comparatively few efforts toward total control, or problem solving. Moreover, a high level of positive behaviors was deemed necessary to encourage continuous revelation and discussion of member concerns.

Psathas (1960) did another replication of the Bales and

Strodtbeck study with therapy groups. Psathas correctly noted that Talland's study suffered from several key deficiencies. For example, Talland coded only verbal behaviors. Nonverbal acts were totally excluded. Talland omitted tension and tension-release (positive) behaviors and excluded the therapist's actions from his analysis. In contrast, Psathas viewed the therapist as an integral group member actively involved in evaluative, control, and tension-release behaviors. Moreover, he correctly posited that a typical phase sequence was highly improbable during the course of a single meeting in therapy groups but, instead, ought to be expected over the total course of group sessions observed.

Consequently he replicated the study with two groups exposed to analytic group psychotherapy. There were four patients in each group; most were suffering from asthma or from rheumatoid arthritis. Utilizing Interaction Process Analysis, the researchers observed nine sessions of each group over a period of one year. Equal numbers of sessions were chosen from early, middle, and late periods in therapy. Data included the therapist's tension and tension-release behaviors, as well as nonverbal acts, all missing from the Talland study. In further contrast with Talland, the phase-sequence hypothesis proposed by Bales and Strodtbeck was confirmed rather than rejected. The sequence was observed, however, only for the total series of group meetings. Only two single meetings conformed to the phase sequence described by Bales and Strodtbeck.

Psathas also noted that negative acts increased over the three phases. He concluded, however, that this increase does not occur because of a concomitant increase in control acts, but because of tension arousal, emotional involvement, and disagreements that occur as problems are discussed. Positive acts remained relatively high throughout all phases, most likely in order to encourage patients to disclose their problems before the group. These two observations suggest that the overall climate of interpersonal attraction (positive acts minus negative acts) may deteriorate during the course of group therapy. However, this tendency may be countervailed by the benefits that accrue to members from their cumulative progress toward goal attainment and improved social functioning.

Although Psathas' findings confirm the phase-sequence hypothesis, the small number of groups studied must give us pause in unduly generalizing from his data. Moreover, other researchers have found it fruitful to inquire whether group development entails more than the three phases.

Tuckman

In contrast to the foregoing experimental approach, Tuckman (1965) derived a model of group development based on a comprehensive review of fifty publications dealing with stages of group development in therapy groups, T-groups, natural (task) groups, and laboratory groups. He distinguished between interpersonal (or social) stages of group development and task (or instrumental) stages and concluded that within each realm four analogous phases occurred. Bales and Strodtbeck also observed two major activities during the course of group development: interpersonal (or socioemotional) and task (or instrumental) activities. Moreover, in approximately 90 percent of their groups two different specialists, or leaders, emerged within each group to perform these functions: the task leader and the socioemotional leader. Their data indicated, in addition, that the task leaders seldom were among the most liked group members (as determined by postexperimental ratings made by the group members) and that the socioemotional leaders rarely were considered effective in the task realm (as determined by peer ratings). In the relatively few instances in which one person was able to perform both functions effectively (in approximately 10 percent of the groups studied) that individual was labeled the "great man leader" (Bales and Slater, 1955). Presumably, then, the role requirements associated with task and socioemotional activities tend to be incompatible. The individual who continually urges the group to greater activity may do so at the expense of friendship with his peers. Conversely, the person who expends great effort upon friendship may have relatively little time or ability to perform instrumental activities.

Elaborating on this duality of behavioral requirements, Tuckman adduced the existence of four general phases of group development. In the interpersonal, or social, realm groups passed through the following sequence: testing and dependence (phase 1), intragroup conflict (phase 2), development of cohesion (phase 3), and functional role relatedness (phase 4). In the task, or instrumental, realm groups passed through analogous phases: orientation and testing (phase 1), emotional response to task demands (phase 2), expression of opinion (phase 3), and emergence of solutions (phase 4). Emotional responses to task demands (phase 2) occurred much more frequently among treatment groups than among task groups. In therapy groups phase 3 focused primarily upon discussions of self and others. The solution associated with phase 4 usually was interpreted as the emergence of insight. Tuckman calls the four sequential processes that are more or less characteristic of all small groups, regardless of the nature of their main concerns or tasks, *forming, storming, norming,* and *performing.*

Orientation, testing, and dependence constitute the group process of *forming.* As Tuckman notes, "Groups initially concern themselves with orientation accomplished primarily through testing. Such testing serves to identify the boundaries of both interpersonal and task behaviors. Coincident with testing in the interpersonal realm is the establishment of dependency relationships with leaders, other group members, or pre-existing standards" (1965, p. 396). *Storming,* the second phase in the sequence, is characterized by conflict and polarization around interpersonal issues, with concomitant emotional responses in the task sphere. Resistances during this period tend to be overcome during the process of *norming,* which predominates in the third developmental phase. During the third phase in-group feeling and cohesiveness develop, new standards evolve, and new roles are adopted. In the task realm intimate and personal opinions are expressed. Finally, the *performing,* or fourth, phase of group development is characterized by the emergence of flexible and functional roles addressed to achievement of the group's tasks. Structural issues have been resolved and the group's interpersonal climate and functional structures can become supportive of task performance.

In essence, then, Tuckman's model proceeds slightly beyond that of Bales and Strodtbeck through the inclusion of an additional stage oriented primarily toward the emotional relations among group members (that is, Tuckman's phase 2). Otherwise, the developmental processes posited by Tuckman (forming, norming, and performing) are remarkably similar to the respective developmental phases suggested by Bales and Strodtbeck (orientation, evaluation, and control).

The treatment utility of Tuckman's slightly expanded model is rather questionable, however. Presumably group treatment should involve a series of discrete, differentiated therapeutic interventions. It is highly doubtful that such interventions can be collapsed into only three or four types of therapist behavior that can be differentially applied to a similar number of group developmental phases. A better differentiated model of group development would seem to be more conducive to the diagnostic, evaluative, and interventive activities of group therapists. Consequently such a model will be discussed, with particular reference to its place in traditional social group work.

Sarri and Galinsky

The essential components of the traditional group work method can be best explicated within the context of the group development schema set forth by Sarri and Galinsky (1967). A prerequisite for the formulation of systematic group work practice theory is a frame of reference which (1) anticipates discrete phases in group development, (2) suggests their antecedents, consequences, and correlates, and (3) elaborates basic practice considerations that correspond with small-group developmental phases. As their point of departure, Sarri and Galinsky note that the analysis of group development rests upon certain basic assumptions, the foremost being that the group is a potent influence system that can be used as an efficient vehicle for individual change. A corollary is the assumption that group development can be controlled and influenced by the worker's actions. Group work efforts are guided by the principle that the group is not an end in itself. The aim of social group work is to maximize the potential of the group for individual change rather than to create an enduring small social system.

Like Tuckman's model, the one set forth by Sarri and Galinsky is based upon a comprehensive review of the available literature concerning group development. As will be shown below, their paradigm tends to expand the three- and four-phase models described previously into a seven-phase model of group development.

In effect, the orientation, evaluation, and control phases posited by Bales and Strodtbeck are differentiated into subphases, making it possible to describe key elements of group development with greater specificity and to formulate relatively discrete treatment interventions that correspond with each phase.

Sarri and Galinsky define group development as "changes through time in the internal structures, processes, and culture of the group" (p. 74). Consequently their model focuses primarily upon three dimensions of group development: social structure, or social organization, of the group (power, affect, friendship, leadership, communication structures, and other patterns of role relationships); activities, tasks, and operative processes of the group (changes in decision-making processes); and culture of the group (norms, values, and shared purposes). What distinguishes the foregoing as dimensions of group development is that they change over time, and that there are certain regularities that may be noted in their manifestations at different periods in the life of the group. These regularities purportedly can be delineated and categorized as occurring in certain phases. Although the authors assert that the foregoing dimensions include most of the group phenomena that can be observed and manipulated, it is clear that they cannot be considered mutually exclusive.

Certain aspects of a group's culture may be viewed as structural features of the group, such as its normative structure or value structure. In general, the structural features of small groups are static representations of social behaviors or activities manifested by the group members. Whereas group structure usually refers to the *static* pattern of relationships among group members (in terms of power differentials, friendship relations, and so on) group processes refer to the *dynamic* pattern of relationships among the group's members. Although both constructs refer to the *patterning* of relationships, the latter refers to the actuated modality of the former. Process is the essence of a living group. However, in order to best analyze group process it is usually necessary to view the group at a given isolated moment in time. In effect, the analysis of group structure is analogous to viewing one frame of a movie reel that has been temporarily halted, thus facilitating a thoroughgoing and, presumably, more accurate assessment of the members' interpersonal relations. As will be noted below, such assessment is an integral part of group work diagnosis. However, as with a temporarily halted movie reel, one must be wary of the possibility that ongoing events will alter the patterned relationships previously noted. Hence the assessment, or diagnosis, of group structure constitutes an ongoing and continuous responsibility of the professionally trained group worker.

The seven group developmental phases cited by Sarri and Galinsky (1967, pp. 76–84) occur in the following sequence: (1) origin phase, (2) formative phase, (3) intermediate phase I, (4) revision phase, (5) intermediate phase II, (6) maturation phase, and (7) termination phase. The first two are analogous to the orientation phase posited by Bales and Strodtbeck, the next three are roughly analogous to their evaluation phase, and the last two are somewhat analogous to their control phase. Based in large part upon Sarri and Galinsky's original discussion, a detailed explication of the seven phases follows. The major purpose of the discussion is to highlight the importance of their model for diagnostic and interventive activities associated with the traditional social group work method.

Phases of Development

Phase 1, *origin,* essentially refers to the group worker's activities associated with group composition. It is distinguished primarily for analytic purposes since events that occur during group composition create crucial preconditions for subsequent group development. Major variables to be examined in the origin phase are size of the group, members' characteristics and initial orientations, and the environmental location of the group. Group size has determinate effects upon the development of group structural properties, patterns of individual participation, and individual members' satisfactions (Thomas and Fink, 1963). Member characteristics influence subsequent activities, tasks, operating procedures, and aspects of the group's culture. And environmental location, which denotes the community and/or organizational context within which the group exists, is of concern because it may influence the norms and values espoused by members or may set limits upon the goals, activities, and tasks available to the group.

The worker's awareness of such factors necessarily alerts him to a multitude of variables that can be utilized in his diagnostic and treatment endeavors, enhancing his effectiveness as a professional change agent. However, the worker should know that group developmental processes are influenced by such a complex interplay of factors that specific predictive efforts regarding these processes are fraught with hazard. A developmental model that is generally applicable to most groups—even to most treatment groups—can be valid only at relatively general and abstract levels. The predictive limitations of most group development models are one of the major obstacles to the elaboration of a systematic practice theory for group workers. A favorable interpretation of this paradox would, perhaps, be based upon the assumption that "negative" knowledge is nonetheless valued knowledge. That is, the mere awareness of various contingencies and complexities that may bias the developmental pattern of a group places contemporary practitioners in a position superior to their predecessors, who may have proceeded blithely upon the assumption that all groups invariably follow a fixed and universal sequence of developmental phases. The reader's cognizance of these qualifying factors should guide him to a circumspect interpretation of the developmental phases set forth by Sarri and Galinsky. These phases are neither invariant nor inevitable since they, too, are influenced by unique antecedent conditions. Fortunately, however, many of the major features of small group treatment are relatively common to most treatment professions. For instance, in evaluating origin factors, it is useful to know that group size typically ranges from five to eight members for virtually all modes of group therapy. Organizational contexts are often remarkably similar. And the most common sources of variance found in the origin phase are due to the background characteristics and presenting problems of the client population itself, factors that can be subjected to substantial worker control and that may prove to be of immense therapeutic value.

During Phase 2, *formation,* the group members' initial activity is oriented towards seeking similarities, common values, and mutuality of interests. Initial commitments to group purpose emerge and interpersonal ties begin to develop among group members. Quasi-structures develop wherein leadership roles are played by the more assertive and aggressive individuals. Tentative prestige and status structures may emerge and rudimentary norms tend to develop, based primarily on common values and attitudes that the members bring into the group from the external world. Akin to the "exogenous determinants" of group behavior cited by Thibaut and Kelley (1959), these structures are determined by initial goals defined for and/or by the group and by constraints imposed upon the group by its social and material environment. The simple and tentative operating procedures characteristic of the formative phase will be of decreasing importance as the group progresses toward the elaboration of new goals and explores the opportunities and demands available within its environment. However, if the members do not experience sufficient gratification from participation during this phase it is unlikely that the group will survive the demands of subsequent phases, especially if group membership is voluntary and other attractive groups are readily available (Rosenblatt and Mayer, 1966).

During Phase 3, *Intermediate Phase I*, group members develop stronger and more extensive interpersonal ties. Consequently a moderate level of cohesion occurs in the group. Although group cohesiveness usually is defined in terms of members' friendship or liking relationships (Lott and Lott, 1965), the concept also may refer, in part, to the emergence of norm structures and functional interdependencies among the group's members (Feldman, 1968). Therefore, during this phase the group's purposes are clarified and there is increasing involvement in goal-directed activities. These frequently are accompanied by emergent role specializations among the members in order to facilitate the group's task performance efforts. Members also may form tentative subgroups or cliques in accord with their task responsibilities and/or affiliative needs derived from a myriad of developmental experiences. Likewise, deviations from the group's emerging normative structure are likely to result in negative sanctioning by peers, although not to the extent observed in the later phases. Members' participation may be somewhat guarded; similarly, certain deviant behaviors may not be negatively sanctioned pending further development and/or recognition of norm consensus among the group's members. In essence, then, the group begins somewhat warily to build common traditions, sentiments, and values. The group leader must be aware of the many cues that indicate the pace with which such developments occur within the group. And he must be able to help clarify and define group norms and traditions as they emerge or, should his treatment goals so indicate, deter them.

Sarri and Galinsky posit that a fourth phase, *revision,* can be identified in group development and that this occurs either prior to or following Phase 3. This is one of the most interesting and crucial of developmental phases because it refutes a misconception prevalent in many other formulations, namely, that groups proceed through a series of phases in a smooth and unidirectional manner characterized by constantly increasing levels of group cohesiveness and strengthening of interpersonal ties. To the contrary, the appearance of this phase suggests that interpersonal conflict and/or retrogression may be expected for the majority of groups that survive Phases 1 and 2. Frequently there may occur a challenge to, and revision of, the group's leadership structures and operating procedures. Sarri and Galinsky note that this phenomenon is most likely if leaders in the earlier stages are aggressive individuals who attempt to prevent other members' participation in leadership activities. More important, perhaps, a situational or interactional perspective regarding leadership (Cartwright and Zander, 1968; Gibb, 1968) would suggest that leadership behaviors conducive to the early phases of group development, such as aggressiveness and innovativeness, may be far different from those required for later phases of development, such as coordinative and task skills. Should a given leader be unable to perform all of the foregoing activities with a high level of competence it is probable that new leaders will emerge as the group progresses from one phase to another. Even if the same individual should have the capacity to execute such a broad range of behaviors, this perspective would suggest, nonetheless, that he would be likely to alter his predominant leadership activities, resulting in subsequent alterations in members' norms, task behaviors and, perhaps, friendship relations.

As a group assumes more task responsibilities and explores

more areas of interest, new leadership functions and opportunities are likely to evolve. No one member or subgroup is likely to exert effective control in all areas of group functioning. Consequently more members can be expected to assume leadership functions and increased role differentiation is likely to occur in the group. At least temporarily, this is likely to result in competition for resources and allegiances and to contribute to a further revision of earlier group structures and traditions. As members come to feel more secure in their specialized roles, and as they develop greater interpersonal dependencies for various satisfactions, there is likely to be continued growth of positive affect toward one another. At the same time, however, as pressures for goal attainment mount there is likely to be a corresponding increase in negative reactions (Bales, 1950a). The concurrent increment of both positive and negative reactions, though seemingly paradoxical, can be realistically anticipated during this phase of group development. This is especially so since early goal attainment efforts may lead to the development of task and friendship liaisons, forward locomotion toward the goal and, at the same time, to conflicts of interest, competition for resources, and a number of role ambiguities. In later phases of group development, however, the incidence of negative reactions is likely to decrease substantially, given the proper longitudinal development. Changes in the norms, values, and traditions of the group may occur in varying degrees, depending upon the extent of the revision. If norms do not change it is possible that they will be at least clarified and strengthened. Further clarification of group purposes also can be expected during this phase and, most probably, following the various anticipated revisions.

During Phase 5, *Intermediate Phase II,* as noted by Sarri and Galinsky, a significant proportion of groups appear to manifest characteristics which resemble the earlier intermediate phase. However, a higher level of group integration is expected along with greater stability in goal-directed activity and in group structure. In effect, the group is expected to approach a more balanced state of equilibrium than in any of the earlier phases. In addition, because the participants have been together for a relatively long period of time, there are more traditions, clearer norms, and more stable functional interdependencies which can be expected to increase members' liking for one another and, in turn, the influence which they are capable of exerting upon one another (Thomas, 1957). Should the latter situation lead to more effective goal attainment by the group the former conditions are more likely to be strengthened, thus leading to a type of spiraling or mutually reinforcing effect that is highly conducive to effective group-work treatment. Since many of the problems from earlier phases have been resolved, greater attention can be paid to specific goal-required activities and to higher levels of interdependence and cooperation.

Although not all groups experience a clearly discernible re-vision phase, it is nonetheless probable that modifications in group structure will ensue, if only from the increasingly complex division of labor that develops as members become more competent and con-fident and assume responsibility for a variety of new tasks. As leader-ship roles become more widely diffused, there are likely to develop substantial changes in the group's operating procedures, most typically toward efforts to simplify and coordinate the group's various task demands.

Attainment of Phase 6, the *maturation* phase, represents a major goal of social group work activity. At this phase group mem-bers are expected to function relatively autonomously and maturely, thus obviating the need for further active intervention by the group worker. Should the group sustain this phase for a long period of time, the worker may be able to quit the group for new challenges, or terminate one or more group members in accord with some of the considerations set forth in the next section. During this phase, group structures are well developed, although not overly rigid. The structures are characterized by clear ranking, specialization, inter-dependent roles, formalized patterns of interaction, and the full proliferation of positive interpersonal ties. The evolution and routin-ization of various operating procedures permit broad member par-ticipation in decision-making and the development of effective techniques for decision-making and the implementation of decisions. Successful groups reach and maintain this phase when they are able to cope with both extra-group and intra-group change pressures. In essence, the group develops effective mechanisms for adaptation which permit it to operate within a dynamic, or moving, equilibrium rather than a static one. In accord with the basic requisites for a viable social system, noted by Parsons (1951), groups that attain this developmental stage are capable of attaining essential goals, adapting effectively to both internal and external stresses, maintaining relatively consistent and harmonious social relationships among members of the group, and interacting in a productive and regularized manner with the members of other social groups, organizations, or communities.

It is important to note that many, and perhaps most, treatment groups do not reach the maturation phase. Typically, well-functioning members may be discharged early, leaving less able ones in the group. Although highly desirable for the former persons, such an event prevents the group as a whole from attaining the maturation phase. Likewise, when discharged members are replaced by new clients, this not only impedes movement toward the maturation phase but poses the distinct possibility that the group will retrogress to earlier phases—to reexplore commonalities, redefine norms, and reestablish leadership, communication, and other key structures. This possibility in Phase 6 offers another warning against viewing group development as a unidirectional process, suggesting rather that it is subject to retrogression and stagnation as well as substantial forward movement.

Phase 7, *termination*, may or may not be prearranged. The duration of existence for some groups is defined a priori or according to certain time limits or specified objectives set forth by the worker or his agency. Thus, for example, participants may contract with a group worker for a given period of weeks or, as is often the case with student workers and/or clients, for a period of time equivalent to the school year. Some groups are formed only for as long as it is necessary to diagnose group members or to acquaint them with agency objectives or practices. The members are then referred to other groups. Time limitations are highly undesirable in group work practice since the group's existence is contingent upon a variable (time) that may be totally independent of members' treatment progress. The preferred criterion for judging a group's readiness for termination is the progress that the members have made toward the treatment goals that they or the worker originally designed.

For various reasons mentioned above, it is desirable for the entire group to be terminated together. However, since the simultaneous attainment of treatment goals occurs rarely, most workers must make a difficult decision—to retain normally functioning members in the group until others have approximated their level of social functioning, to discharge improved members, thus losing valuable role models and change agents for the remaining members, or to add new members to the group, thus risking at least a temporary retrogression to earlier phases of group development.

In some situations the worker may have to terminate the group or certain of its members because of a pronounced maladaptation or lack of integration of the group. Thus, for instance, a group may not be able to develop or sustain effective means for responding to environmental pressures. Or it may have developed adaptive mechanisms, effective during previous developmental phases, that have since become too rigid or institutionalized to adapt to new social conditions. Similarly, groups may be unable to achieve basic member consensus concerning goals or means for obtaining goals, high levels of interpersonal attraction, or effective operating procedures. In these instances and others it may be necessary for the group worker to subgroup the larger unit, to regroup it, or to terminate one or more members while bearing in mind certain of the practice suggestions to be noted below.

Overview and Discussion

The foregoing conceptualization of developmental phases is an essential one for any group-work practice that focuses upon the traditional method. As will be discussed below, the varying phases of development are associated with analogous phases of the group-work treatment process. Consequently any discussion regarding the essential practice processes of diagnosis, treatment, and evaluation must be interwoven with anticipated developmental phases. Although the posited developmental phases are consonant with the available small-group literature and compatible with conceptualizations of the treatment process to be detailed below, they must be considered within the context of a number of important qualifications. And it is important to note that these qualifications are likely to characterize virtually all models of group development and, therefore, are likely to represent necessary concerns for all group therapies at this early juncture of theoretical and experimental development.

Perhaps the most important qualification pertains to the extreme difficulty in clearly distinguishing any one of the seven developmental phases from the others. In effect, the seven phases of development may represent relatively arbitrary distinctions. Perhaps the total number of developmental phases elaborated by Sarri and Galinsky could have been set at six, eight or, perhaps, virtually any other discrete number of phases. This concern poses implications for practice as well as for purely intellectual analysis. In large part, the problem of clearly differentiating various phases is due to the fact that the particular attributes associated with each are both manifold and multidimensional. While there may be substantial positive change along a given dimension, such as members' friendship relations, progress along a different dimension, such as task attainment, might not occur at the same rate. Likewise, movement along one dimension might produce countervailing and/or retrogressive tendencies along another. Consequently, it is most difficult, if not impossible, to define clear-cut junctures between one phase and another. In and of itself, however, this observation does not totally vitiate the analytic and practice utility of a model of group development phases.

Similar problems occur to the extent that key group structures remain undefined or otherwise ambiguous. Sarri and Galinsky, for example, frequently refer to concepts such as "group cohesiveness" and "group integration" as important analytic and interventive foci for group development. However, in recent years there has been a substantial tendency to break down these broad concepts into particularized terms. "Group integration," for instance, may be more meaningful in terms of subreferents such as normative integration, functional integration, and interpersonal integration (Feldman, 1968). The latter approach permits the group worker to become cognizant of the manner in which various modes of integration tend to countervail, or correspond with, one another and, therefore, to delineate particularized treatment plans and specific foci for group work intervention.

Among the most common targets for analysis and intervention in the traditional group work method are the power, friendship, communication, task, leadership, norm, and formal structures of small groups. The latter represent the arrangement of formal offices, such as secretary, treasurer, and so forth, that may be evolved by certain groups. Group-work treatment frequently is oriented towards alteration of the foregoing structures in order to make the group a more effective means for treatment and for the attainment of individual members' treatment goals. Likewise group-work practice frequently consists of efforts to relocate individual members within certain of the above structures in order to promote movement toward the attainment of treatment goals.

Closer examination of merely one of the foregoing group structures will shed further light upon the complexity of group-development models and their utilization for diagnosis and treatment. In some cases, for instance, a group worker's treatment goals may suggest the wisdom of strengthening or weakening the group's overall power structure. On other occasions the worker's treatment plan may suggest the efficacy of merely enhancing or diminishing a given member's power within the group. A sophisticated assessment of group power structures would lead the worker to the conclusion that social power itself is a general concept worthy of differentiation into its various components or bases. Although power typically is defined as the ability of person(s) A to exert influence over person(s) B (Lippitt and others, 1952), most investigators now concur with French and Raven (1959) that at least five varying bases of social power can be distinguished. These are *reward power* (where person A's ability to exert influence over person B is based upon his capacity to provide rewards for the latter), *coercive power* (where A's ability to influence B is based upon his capacity to punish the latter), *expert power* (where A's ability to influence B is contingent upon his capacity to provide needed or desired knowledge or skills for the latter), *referent power* (where A's ability to influence B is contingent upon the latter's attraction to A, usually because A possesses certain attractive or liked attributes), and *legitimate power* (where A's ability to influence B is based upon the formal delegation of rights and responsibilities to each). Each of the foregoing types of power not only has differing antecedents and correlates, but their consequent effects upon members' behavior frequently vary. Again, therefore, it is necessary to differentiate a relatively general construct, such as group power structure, into particularized sub-referents in order to enhance the worker's ability to analyze and intervene within the group. Moreover, it should be noted that this requirement does not necessarily represent a unique deficiency of the foregoing model of group development. Instead, it reflects deficiencies in theoretical and experimental work that are characteristic of virtually all developmental models that focus upon group structure.

Any treatment model that focuses upon the longitudinal development of interpersonal relationships among group members must be regarded as a tentative and incomplete one, appropriate only to the current state of the art. Future efforts will no doubt lead to better models for analysis and treatment, but the above paradigm represents a concise and serviceable version of current group development models. It can sensitize the group worker to the fluid and interrelated set of variables that influence group members' behavior and, in turn, serve to determine his own interventive efforts.

Summary

This chapter has presented several major features of the traditional social group work method. Following an historical overview, antecedents of the main group development models utilized in conjunction with the method were discussed. These models included those set forth by Bales and Strodtbeck, Talland, Psathas, and Tuckman. In addition many features of the traditional method are based upon a particularly comprehensive group development model set forth by Sarri and Galinsky. This model posits the existence of seven separate phases of group development which are considered to be correlates of seven discrete phases of the typical group work treatment sequence. This model was discussed in detail, with particular emphasis on its relevance for group work interventions.

III

Traditional Social Group Work: Treatment Sequence and Diagnosis

In the traditional group work method, certain phases of treatment parallel phases of normal group development. As with all social behavior, group work treatment represents a developmental process. Consequently, effective group work requires diagnostic, or evaluative, activities to take place throughout the course of treatment, especially since the processes of treatment and diagnosis are interrelated. In this chapter we highlight the similarities and differences of treatment phases and normal developmental phases. Diagnosis is then explicated within this context.

Treatment Sequence

Concomitant with the seven phases of group development discussed in Chapter Two, Sarri and Galinsky postulate a series of discrete phases associated with the treatment process. Because these are stated at a relatively broad level of abstraction, it is assumed that they apply with equal validity to many types of groups, including both adult groups and children's groups. These are: (1)

intake, selection, and diagnosis, (2) group formation, (3) building a viable and cohesive group, (4) maintaining the group through revision, (5) guiding group processes toward treatment goals, (6) maintaining the group, and (7) terminating the group. Although all of these phases will be explicated below, certain of them, particularly those pertaining to diagnostic and interventive behaviors, will receive separate and extensive attention.

Phase 1: Intake, selection, and diagnosis. Intake, selection, and diagnosis correspond to the origin phase in group development. Typically these processes occur *prior* to the first group meeting. Worker activities at this point include interviewing, preparation of a preliminary diagnosis, and the formulation of tentative treatment goals. Unless the client has been diagnosed on the basis of observations in other groups, any evaluation at this phase of the treatment process must be strictly tentative. Such diagnoses are likely to be based primarily upon interviews with the client and upon information from secondary sources, including written records. However, a more accurate assessment of the subject's interpersonal behavior can be best obtained through observations of his actual interaction within the context of the treatment group. Frequently the worker's observations of such behavior contribute to a substantial revision of whatever diagnoses were made primarily upon the basis of indirect reports.

During this phase the worker may establish a "contract" with individual members in order to specify the particular type of social work service to be provided. Additionally, mutual expectations may be clarified and/or confirmed regarding such matters as the type of group treatment to be offered, reciprocal responsibilities and obligations concerning the treatment program, the frequency of meetings, time and place for meetings, projected length of service, and so forth. The worker also may engage in initial efforts to determine the group's overall purposes and objectives, once it is possible to ascertain and synthesize the various members' individual treatment goals. Again, however, the elaboration of such purposes must be regarded as highly tentative in this early phase of group development. Indeed, there exists a strong likelihood that individual members' capacities and treatment goals will shift over time, thus altering the total group's purposes and objectives.

Phase 2: Group formation. A number of empirical studies indicate that nearly 60% of social work clients quit casework treatment during the first two or three weeks of treatment (see, for example, Aronson and Overall, 1966). Although comparable data are not available for social group work, it is obvious that the early phases of treatment are crucial not only for client continuance, but for the emergence of therapeutic interpersonal relationships among the group's members. This stage corresponds to the formative phase of group development and is one wherein the worker is absolutely essential as a central person for the group. The members may identify to some extent with the worker's objectives and behaviors. The worker most probably will assume a more directive role than during subsequent phases of group development and may very well assign particular functions to members, explicate key norms, or help the members to explore common values and to establish the grounds for development of positive interpersonal relations.

During this phase it is essential for the worker to help members develop a high level of attraction to the group and to one another. This may be done in a variety of ways, including the use of valued reinforcers, such as refreshments, expert knowledge, and prestige, that are distributed frequently and relatively equally among all members. The worker must help the group define and engage in activities or tasks that are highly attractive for all the members.

In the formative phase of group development, workers often seek to expose the members to common and unifying experiences as well as to determine the extent to which their past experiences bear similarities to one another. Thus, for example, a group worker may help the group to develop a name, motto, or symbol that expresses the members' common interests and goals, or he may help them to share in the performance of a given task or activity, such as a group trip. Frequently the worker arranges for all of the group's members to share in refreshments during or following the group's meeting. Although the latter may represent a seemingly mundane type of unifying group experience, it has proven to be a real and rewarding one for countless groups of all types. The continued utilization of this mode of group sharing experience over the years attests to its efficacy for the enhancement of group functioning and interpersonal attraction. Once the group's positive features have been established, it will be much easier for the members to participate over increasingly longer periods of time with relatively little reinforcement and, likewise, to temporarily provide satisfactions for their peers while forgoing their own immediate gratification.

In view of his previous acquaintance with the members and his participation in the intake process the worker may be in a favored position to help each member explore what he has in common with the others. This may entail movement toward shared recognition of members' common difficulties and problems, as well as their unique and idiosyncratic difficulties. Similarly, the worker may be better able than others to provide the members with sufficient security and reassurance to guarantee continued participation during this early and ambiguous phase of treatment. Through his assistance to group members, and by helping to develop firm bases for interpersonal attraction between each member and himself, the worker lays the groundwork for the further development of interpersonal attraction among the varying members. Where appropriate, special emphasis is placed upon values and objectives related to treatment goals. The worker motivates members not only toward activities that they enjoy, but toward those which are therapeutically beneficial.

Sarri and Galinsky observe that group norms that emerge during this phase of development not only shape future norms but, in addition, may prove extraordinarily resistant to change. Consequently, it is important for the worker to stress norms of flexibility and openness to change. Moreover, he should initiate and support other norms in accord with his treatment objectives. At the same time, he may wish to deemphasize and/or suppress norms that may have negative implications for treatment, although this must be done with sufficient skill and caution to avoid jeopardizing good working relationships with the members. During this phase the worker also elaborates and further defines the general purposes of the group and reinforces the contracts established in initial interviews. In so doing, he helps to clearly define the limits within which members may strive toward the attainment of improved social functioning.

A number of problems may be properly anticipated by the worker during the formation phase. Substantial role ambiguity will exist for the members. Moreover, it is possible that members' initial role expectations for the treatment group will not be congruent with their first experiences. Consequently, it is necessary for the worker to preclude as many ambiguities as possible and to clearly define the expected behaviors and outcomes of the first group sessions. It is likely that certain group members will exhibit strong tendencies toward dependency upon the worker at this time. The worker must deal with such behavior in a manner which is supportive but nonetheless lays the groundwork for development of the client's autonomy. For example, the worker may wish to focus attention upon attractive features of the group experience while at the same time minimizing the client's efforts to develop undue dependency upon him. During this phase the members may severely "test" the worker in order to evaluate his acceptance of them, his reliability, and his tolerance for their behavior.

Another problem may involve the tendency for certain groups to develop initial leadership structures in which unduly aggressive or irresponsible members predominate. As Sarri and Galinsky note, the prestige of these members may arise initially from their external status, but is likely to be based, in the long run, upon the members' intragroup performances. During this phase the worker should endeavor to influence the group so that persons assuming initial leadership functions will be supportive of treatment norms and values. He should be careful not to provide positive sanctions for leaders who hinder the treatment process. He may wish to forestall premature crystallization of the leadership structure and to provide opportunities for a number of members to perform key leadership functions. In part, the worker also can facilitate this objective by stressing the norms of equal and active participation by all group members and, concomitantly, of acceptance of each member's functional contributions to the group.

Phase 3: Building a viable and cohesive group. During this stage in the treatment sequence, the worker facilitates the growth of friendship and functional relationships among the group's members. As such relationships evolve, the participants are likely to attempt increasingly to exert influence upon one another, to accept such influence efforts more readily, and to severely sanction members who reject influence (Feldman, 1968; Frank, 1957; Goldstein and others, 1966; Lott and Lott, 1965; Schachter, 1960). Utilizing the direct and indirect means of influence cited below, the worker attempts to influence group norms and to shape group structures that are conducive to the attainment of treatment goals. In large part, this is done through the elaboration of a sequence of carefully planned group activities and/or discussions. Program activities that promote cooperation and the elaboration of norms conducive to treatment are likely to catalyze development of the group as an effective vehicle for treatment. Since various cliques or subgroups may develop during this phase, the worker must be cognizant of their emergence and/or dysfunctional effects. Moreover, he must be capable of supporting those that have positive implications for group functioning and treatment, while neutralizing or fragmenting those that may hinder treatment. Depending upon his assessment, he can support the leadership structure developed in the preceding phases or he can facilitate efforts toward revision of that structure during subsequent developmental phases. In any event, as the group progresses he will wish to expand the number of leadership functions available within it in order to afford each member with greater opportunities for experimentation with adaptive behavior. While striving to effect desirable changes for certain group members, however, the worker must be careful not to create conditions that will be harmful to the therapeutic progress of other group members. In any kind of group therapy this consideration is an essential one and, moreover, one that entails extraordinary intellectual and cognitive demands for the therapist.

In order to maximize the group's potential as a treatment vehicle, the worker should encourage its efforts to develop appropriate control and sanctioning procedures during this phase. However, he must be prepared to moderate tendencies toward undue excesses in these developments since they can result in extreme rejection or scapegoating of nonconforming members. Should such behavior be permitted, the worker, in effect, not only tacitly supports actions that are countertherapeutic for an individual client but, additionally, acknowledges his inability to control the group and/or a lack of concern for individuals' welfare that is likely to reduce *all* the members' trust in him.

As the group proceeds toward the elaboration of a larger range of role specializations, there are likely to be more frequent struggles over individual domains. Likewise, role conflicts may occur as members are expected to perform a variety of different functions. Consequently, a greater level of overall conflict may develop within the group. This is especially likely if stresses such as the foregoing should temporarily forestall the group's movement toward the attainment of treatment goals or other common objectives. Therefore the stage will be set for movement into the revision phase and for the implementation of corresponding worker interventions. Each such development will present the worker with a plethora of information that may alter his earlier diagnoses of each member, and of the group as a unit. Consequently he should be prepared to continually revise his treatment goals as the need becomes manifest.

Phase 4: Maintaining group through revision. To some extent, a group's progression through the earlier developmental phases may reflect the cautious and wary behavior of group members that typically is associated with a honeymoon period. However, as the members become more secure with their positions in the group, they may be readier and more able to react against various sources of actual or perceived dissatisfaction within it, including power, task, or communication structures that may be considered undesirable or counterproductive. Should such thrusts toward revision be anticipated and/or facilitated by the worker, movement through the revision phase may be gradual and continuous, rather than abrupt and disjunctive. Although there may be alterations in various group structures, it is essential for the worker to create and/or sustain conditions that will enable all members to derive continued satisfaction from their participation in the group. Individuals who are removed from previously gratifying positions should be helped to secure other such positions within the group and to appreciate hitherto unrecognized assets of the small group experience. At the same time, they should be encouraged to assess the considerations that resulted in such changes.

Concomitantly, the worker should strive to assure that new leaders will be oriented toward norms and operating procedures that are conducive to the attainment of treatment goals. Since the revision stage is rather fluid, it presents the worker with an opportunity to modify group norms and procedures that he might not have been able to influence earlier. In any event, he will endeavor to support those changes that are likely to provide for increased participation and for more mature and socially effective approaches to group and individual problem-solving.

Phase 5: Guiding group toward treatment goals. Following the revision phase significant progress toward treatment goals is expected. The worker's actions during earlier stages should have resulted in the emergence and crystallization of norms, social control mechanisms, and operating and problem-solving procedures based upon a higher level of self-direction by the group. Consequently, fewer direct interventions are necessary by the worker and there will be a strong thrust toward the use of indirect interventions if, indeed, any are necessary. Interventions primarily will be directed toward reinforcing and implementing previous changes so that the varying group structures will be able to provide all members with a multitude of opportunities for sampling and shaping new behaviors. As the group expands its interests and concomitant task structures, there will be many more occasions for the display of leadership skills than before. Similarly, as members learn to cope with increasingly complex problems, the group's effectiveness as a treatment vehicle will be enhanced.

Noting the relatively great progress anticipated during this phase, Sarri and Galinsky caution that the worker must remain alert to the possibility that the group will move toward a static equilibrium rather than a dynamic one. That is, problem-solving procedures may become institutionalized and inflexible or, even worse, the members may become unduly apathetic. Therefore, the worker must guard against viewing the group as an end itself rather than as a tool for effective treatment. On occasion, the worker's interventions may be oriented toward disrupting the group in a manner that is consonant with continued movement toward treatment goals. The foregoing possibilities are especially germane if the group has passed through the revision phase with relatively few major changes.

On the other hand, if the group experiences a series of major changes during the revision phase, the worker must help it to sustain them in a manner that serves to stabilize the modified group structures. New norms should be clarified, put into effect, and closely aligned with treatment objectives. Alterations in the group's governing and operating procedures should allow for greater self-direction among the members and, in effect, the worker should consciously and gradually diminish the frequency of his interventions.

Finally, of course, even at this stage of development the group's movement cannot be viewed solely from a unidirectional perspective. Periodic conflicts and retrogressions may occur but, as before, these may constitute evidence of a dynamic equilibrium rather than a static one. Likewise, they may provide opportunities for further challenges, experiences, and insights that may lead to greater client improvement. As with every facet of group development, all such changes should be scrutinized constantly for their theoretical and practical implications for individual members' treatment goals.

Phase 6: Maintaining group. The maturation phase should be among the most gratifying of all phases, and should call for the least amount of active intervention. The worker should be able to view the fruits of his labor firsthand while actually exerting only a minimum of influence upon the group. However, this state of affairs probably will be short-lived since economic exigencies and treatment considerations are likely to limit the worker's presence during this phase. The worker may make himself available for assistance in the event of unanticipated crises but he need not be present constantly in order to monitor the group's performance. Additionally, it is important to note that many, if not most, groups never attain this stage. As discussed earlier, since treatment goals for some clients may have already been reached the group may have been terminated prior to the maturation phase, or an influx of replacements may have caused a retrogression to earlier developmental phases.

Sarri and Galinsky suggest that groups in the maturation phase are characterized by a high level of integration, stabilized group structures, consensus and directionality with respect to goals, customary operating and governing procedures, an expanded group culture, and effective mechanisms for change. If such characteristics are observed it can be assumed that the members by and large are functioning in a mature and autonomous manner and, therefore, are in little need of professional group-work service, at least compared with other needy groups.

Phase 7: Terminating group. The worker's approach to termination of a group is dependent upon the particular reasons for that termination. Thus, for instance, if termination has been set in accord with a previously fixed time limit, the worker's interventions during any phase must take cognizance of the particular restrictions imposed by that limit. Some members may have progressed considerably and will face few, if any, problems due to the termination process. Others may have experienced little progress and may require close attention from the worker, including the possibility of a gradual transfer to other treatment groups or resources. Similarly, if the group is terminated due to lack of integration or continued maladaptive functioning, the worker may wish to recompose it with certain of the same members, to refer the entire group for treatment elsewhere or, of course, to reassess his entire treatment approach and competence. In some instances the most promising foci for intervention may be external to the treatment group per se, such as in the family environment, the school system (cf., especially, Vinter and Sarri, 1965), or the neighborhood (see Feldman and Specht, 1968). Regardless, the worker must evaluate the anticipated effects of termination for each and every member. Should the process be considered harmful for any given member, the worker must make special efforts to afford that individual with sufficient support and/or alternative resources to make the process a welcome one.

Preferably, termination should take place because the worker has attained the treatment objectives for all, or nearly all, of the group's members. In addition, it is desirable for the members to be engaged in the evaluative and planning process that leads to termination. In part, this process may be based upon the original worker-client contract and upon any subsequent revisions that have been mutually agreed upon. The termination process always should be a gradual one. In order to avert unduly abrupt transitions, clients should be afforded sufficient opportunities to experiment with, and to apply, their newly learned skills in social environments other than the treatment group. For the most part, these environments should be the regular family, neighborhood, and community settings within which the client or other members of the larger society are located. Since behavioral changes established in the treatment group should be transferred and stabilized beyond the treatment group per se, it is advisable for the client to test his capabilities in such settings.

In addition, it may be desirable for the group worker to actually treat clients within those contexts in order to facilitate adjustment to the open community. However, it is essential that treatment be done in a manner that does not stigmatize or otherwise adversely label the client. Persons in the environment should be able to accept the client readily and to provide him with responsibilities and privileges that are consonant with the full range of his capacities. Indeed, as some investigators have noted, to do less is likely to perpetuate a level of social functioning that is markedly below the capacities of the discharged client (Dinitz and others, 1962; Freeman and Simmons, 1958; Parsons, 1951).

Overview and discussion. In effect, the foregoing phases of the treatment process represent an expanded and highly differentiated version of the customary social work activities denoted as study, diagnosis, and treatment. Similarly, the seven developmental phases posited by Sarri and Galinsky represent an extension and further elaboration of the three-phase model postulated by Bales and Strodtbeck (1951). By further specifying discrete phases of group development and concomitant stages of the treatment sequence, Sarri and Galinsky have attempted to provide social workers with a greater capacity for the straightforward identification of varying foci for group-work intervention. In addition, they have attempted to provide some degree of precision and longitudinal predictability to the sequencing of interventions. Although the actual phasing of group developmental processes should still be considered an unresolved empirical question, the seven-phase model presents a contemporary framework and reference point for the analytic and interventive efforts of social group workers. As long as the developmental progress of each and every therapy group is individually assessed, the model can be considered a useful aid in providing an efficient structure for the worker's evaluative efforts.

It is relevant to note that a number of other group development models have appeared in the social work literature over the years. Thus, for example, Garland and others (1965, 1970) have posited the following five developmental phases: (1) preaffiliation, (2) power and control, (3) intimacy, (4) differentiation, and (5) separation. During each phase of group development a considerable array of member behaviors are posited. These are supplemented with a variety of observational and behavioral foci for the group worker and corresponding program activities suggested for worker use. Similarly, Maier (1965) has suggested four phases of group development: (1) locating commonness, (2) creating exchange, (3) developing mutual identification, and (4) developing group identification. Earlier, Kindelsperger (1957) and Trecker (1955) each identified six phases of group development. Kindelsperger denotes the following phases: (1) approach-orientation, (2) relationship negotiation, or conflict, (3) group role emergence, (4) vacillating group emergence, (5) group role dominance, and (6) institutionalized group roles. Trecker, more broadly, posits the following: (1) beginning stage, (2) emergence of a group "feeling", organization, and so forth, (3) development of bond, purpose, and cohesiveness, (4) strong group feeling and goal attainment, (5) decline in interest and diminution of group feeling, and (6) an ending stage. And, finally, in an excellent effort to integrate and synthesize all of the foregoing perspectives, Whittaker (1970) has indicated the manner in which the various phases posited by each of the above can be juxtaposed in accord with the five developmental stages delineated by Garland and his colleagues.

In summary, then, it is clear that the varying phases of group development denoted by group work investigators tend to share a number of essential attributes. To some extent these attributes are to be found in most, if not all, developmental phases. What differentiates one phase from another, however, is the extent to which a given attribute, or cluster of attributes, predominates in that phase compared with others. Furthermore, none of the developmental models offer guidelines regarding the expected duration of any given developmental phase, relatively or absolutely. Although knowledge development in these areas still is in a rather rudimentary form, progress has been made nonetheless. In the following sections of this chapter the various elaborations and explications thus far set forth by Vinter and his colleagues will be discussed.

Diagnosis

Rosemary Sarri and certain of her colleagues (Maeda Galinsky, Paul Glasser, Sheldon Siegel, and Robert Vinter) consider many disciplines to be relevant for diagnosis in social group work, noting that social work practice principles are derived primarily from several behavioral sciences, including dynamic psychology, social psychology, sociology, and cultural anthropology. Economics, political science, anatomy, and physiology are also deemed of diagnostic relevance.

The worker may well need every discipline at his command in order to distinguish between the client's self-defined behavioral difficulties, his problems with functioning in the group, and his conflicts with the larger environment. The actual diagnostic process involves the interrelationship of these factors as they manifest themselves in the small group context. In short, the worker wants to identify his client's problems, how they are defined, by whom they are defined, and what aspects of the personality and environment are involved. Problems may be differentiated according to the client's experience of stress or dissatisfaction in role performance, the client's ineffective role performance as viewed by individuals such as his parents, spouse, teachers, employers, co-workers, or others, and the practitioner's overall judgment of the client's role performance problems.

Such a broad range of variables provides more foci for the therapist's interventions than many other frameworks. Interventions may be directed toward the individual client, the small group environment, or relevant others within the larger social environment.

There is some attendant risk that an overabundance of interventive possibilities may cloud the therapist's judgment; the worker can experience serious difficulties in assigning priorities to the varying types of diagnostic information and the differing interventive foci derived from them. Sarri and her colleagues present no guidelines for the selection of priorities. While it is conceivable that no definitive guidelines should be expected at this stage of knowledge development, the inclusion of an unduly broad range of diagnostic data would seem to impede not only the effective synthesis of that information by the worker but also the development of an in-depth understanding about more than a few components of the total data base. Consequently, the accuracy of diagnostic judgments may vary considerably, depending upon the expertise of the worker and the particular components of the data base most frequently used. Similar problems afflict practitioners utilizing any framework. Nonetheless, one would expect such problems to increase with the breadth of information deemed appropriate for diagnosis and intervention. Perhaps such difficulties will be overcome in the long run by more efficient data retrieval systems and the development of advanced computer systems that will be able to synthesize and codify various bodies of information for the worker's and researcher's use. Until such time, however, the above-cited difficulties associated with the scheme of Sarri and her associates must be considered as extant and valid. Moreover, as noted below, Sarri offers several differing diagnostic statements to help cull out various longitudinal components of the diagnostic process.

Those practitioners who use the traditional group-work method probably would concur with the widely accepted assertion that social work seeks to assure "the enhancement of social functioning wherever the need for such enhancement is either socially or individually perceived" (Boehm, 1959). In accord with this definition, social workers presumably focus to a large extent upon the social functioning and dysfunctioning of clients. Since the client's behavior, or role performance, constitutes the main diagnostic and treatment focus of the worker, theoretical frameworks that focus upon such phenomena constitute the major bases of social group-work knowledge. Prior to the present decade, social *role* theory clearly constituted the primary knowledge base for group work. That body of knowledge currently is substantially complemented by knowledge derived from social *learning* theory, even though the latter is still at a relatively early stage of development. Both theoretical frames of reference are far superior to most earlier ones in that they take cognizance of clients' social interaction with others in their environment. Additionally, both permit the treatment group itself to be viewed as an important medium for the diagnosis of clients' dysfunctioning, thus affording a major and distinctive advantage over most therapies based upon the practitioner's treatment of a single client.

Rather than rely solely, or even primarily, upon the client's sometimes skewed statement of his social functioning problem, the practitioner can avert possible errors associated with inaccurate interpretation or inference through direct observations of the client's behavior in the treatment group. In the group situation, the client's behavior can be viewed and diagnosed within a social context that is markedly more representative of his actual social world than is the therapist's office. In addition, the therapist can view the client in interaction with other individuals, can observe the client's efforts to execute a variety of relevant social behaviors and, even, can prestructure certain tasks or behavioral assignments so that he can selectively observe and diagnose the client's social capabilities (Churchill, 1959, 1965). This diagnostic strategy is especially helpful to the extent that the worker can structure the group experience to simulate social situations encountered by the client in the larger society. The small group, as a diagnostic medium, permits the worker to observe the reciprocal interplay between the client's behavior and those stimulus or response conditions presented by peers, and by the worker himself, which may contribute to the client's social dysfunctioning. Diagnostic observations will suggest treatment plans and, though the ultimate target of intervention may be the malfunctioning individual, may be directed at his peers as well.

Following the client's presentation of his social problem(s), at least five clearly distinguishable processes can be identified throughout the treatment sequence of traditional social group work: (1) formulation of a preliminary diagnosis, (2) information gathering, ordering, and analysis, (3) formulation of a working diagnosis and treatment goals, (4) treatment through direct and indirect worker interventions, (5) formulation of a terminal diagnosis.

The *preliminary diagnostic statement* can be developed by the worker as a result of one or more contacts with the prospective client or significant others. It includes descriptive information regarding the individual's presenting problem(s) and the treatment organization's decision to accept, reject, or defer the client for group work service, as its resources dictate. This statement also may report on the client's motivation, suggested service recommendations, and the worker's experience with the client. Particularly now, as in later phases of treatment, it is important to guard against mislabeling the client or his behaviors in any manner that could adversely affect the treatment process. Although the preliminary diagnostic statement may establish a framework for the collection of additional diagnostic data and, therefore, for the derivation of future treatment plans, all conclusions voiced therein should be regarded as tentative and as subject to revision pending the accumulation of additional data. Each diagnostic datum must be evaluated independently with reference to its validity and reliability. This is not to suggest that each datum be considered in isolation from its relationship to other data. The most adequate diagnostic endeavors will strive to juxtapose and synthesize varying bits and pieces of data in order to create a concise, comprehensive, and accurate diagnostic evaluation, while avoiding information that can prejudice the collection and elaboration of subsequent diagnostic data.

Completion of the preliminary diagnostic statement marks the point at which the worker may accept the client for treatment and begin the *systematic accumulation of additional and more comprehensive diagnostic information*. The worker is likely to obtain detailed information from the client's own reports about his problematic situation, his motivations, and his potential for change. Additionally, he may find it useful to obtain reports concerning the client's behaviors and attitudes from professionals and significant others in the client's environment. Most important, perhaps, he will wish to observe the client's behavior in the treatment group. And, finally, through a series of home visits he may wish to observe the client engaging in social interaction with peers and relatives who are not members of the treatment group.

A number of difficulties are associated with home visits. They are time-consuming and therefore expensive, for the therapist and perhaps for the client as well. Moreover, the client and relevant others may be seriously inhibited when they realize that their behavior is being observed, particularly during the early stages of observation. The above concerns notwithstanding, it seems probable that the worker's firsthand observations are likely to be more valid than inferences derived from his conversations with the client and others. Indeed, the observation of clients' behavior is a common occurrence in the daily social interaction of individuals, as, for example, when persons interact in classroom or work situations. Moreover, a number of techniques can be used to reduce the visibility and obtrusiveness of the observer (see Reiss, 1971). And it appears that, after the initial difficulties in orienting themselves to an observer, the overwhelming majority of clients become accustomed to observation and revert to behavior that is more or less natural. Perhaps such a conclusion represents a commentary upon the frequency with which individuals' social behavior is observed in contemporary society and the readiness with which observations are accepted. Indeed, during the course of the St. Louis Experiment observers trained by the present writers and their colleagues systematically observed all the meetings of more than 100 groups of children that met for periods ranging from three to thirty weeks. The clear consensus of observers, group leaders, and reports from the children themselves was that the presence of observers did little or nothing to inhibit the children's behavior.

The validity of diagnostic data is likely to be strengthened as the number of independent informational sources is enlarged. Moreover, firsthand data regarding individuals' behavior is less likely to be in error than data obtained from secondhand sources or data based upon inferences concerning comparatively unobservable phenomena such as client motivations, attitudes, or other internal processes. Likewise, diagnostic statements are likely to avoid error to the extent that they omit generalizations from incomplete data and avoid unverifiable assumptions concerning causes of problematic behaviors.

Following the gathering and ordering of diagnostic information, the worker can collate such data in written form and elaborate *treatment goals* directly from the data. In order to refine earlier diagnostic formulations, Sarri and Feldman coined a term with a unique meaning: *working diagnosis*. The term was utilized in order to connote the notion that group-work diagnosis constitutes an ongoing process subject to continual revision. Since the behavioral capabilities of clients constantly fluctuate, particularly as treatment progresses, it is necessary to revise one's diagnostic statement continually and to formulate updated treatment plans based upon the client's newly developed behavioral skills. In essence, the working diagnostic statement is an analysis and summary of the client's problems, his resources and potential for change, the barriers or constraints that might impede change, and concomitant treatment goals and plans.

Certain strategies for organizing diagnostic information are clearly superior to others in assuring the comprehensiveness, systematization, and validity of data collection. Gauron and Dickenson

(1966), for example, suggest that diagnosis can be organized in at least six ways: intuitive-adversary, diagnosis-by-exclusion, over-inclusive-indecisive, textbook, bibliography, and flexible-adaptable. Gauron and Dickenson favor the diagnosis-by-exclusion approach over all others since it is both highly structured and has an inductive-logical base. Except for the textbook approach, the others are relatively unstructured or have an intuitive-alogical orientation. The hallmark of the diagnosis-by-exclusion approach is its reliance upon the gathering of all relevant diagnostic information and the subsequent winnowing out of alternatives until a single, clear-cut diagnostic statement remains.

There are few reliable guidelines for the collection of differing types of diagnostic data. Although Sarri and her colleagues suggest that many kinds of information are useful, they also acknowledge that the particular types of information sought will depend upon the nature of the presenting problems, the resources and barriers influencing the client's social functioning, the worker's particular resources, and the agency's goals and policies. It is neither necessary nor possible to know everything about the client. And, as Gauron and Dickenson (1966) note, the collection of an overabundance of irrelevant or inappropriate information may obfuscate accurate diagnosis. Attributes of the information itself, along with the conditions under which it is collected and processed, will differentially influence its reliability and validity (Bieri and others, 1966; Miller and Tripodi, 1967; Tripodi and Miller, 1966).

Basic types of diagnostic information collected for social group work, as well as for other treatment approaches, concern the client's social and personality attributes, characteristics of his family situation, his community of residence, and his cultural and socioeconomic background. Information concerning the client's age, sex, physical health and handicaps, and intelligence is pertinent, as is information regarding the client's parental or conjugal family—the number of siblings and the client's ordinal position, marital status and relationships of parents, patterns of childrearing, and relationships with other relatives. It is useful to know about the client's neighborhood, especially the adequacy of housing, education, social service resources, and the availability of desirable membership groups or voluntary organizations. Similarly, information regarding the client's occupation, income, education, religious affiliation, ethnic background, and opportunities for social mobility may be relevant. It may be useful, also, to obtain information regarding any previous contacts with health and welfare agencies. Finally, it is usually advantageous to learn about certain of the client's personality characteristics, such as his past processes of growth, development, and self-actualization, his attitudes toward himself, perceptual capacities, environmental mastery, interpersonal adequacy, and psychosocial integration (see Jahoda, 1958).

Obviously the predictive and explanatory potencies of the foregoing factors vary considerably. Presumably each is of some utility insofar as it permits proper diagnostic generalizations from the corpus of knowledge associated with it. Again, however, it is essential to be wary of premature or unwarranted generalization. Unfortunately, the foregoing factors are highly disparate and, to some extent, so unquantifiable or poorly quantified that predictive efforts are at best hazardous. Moreover, in some cases empirical evidence regarding the generalizations derivable from a given knowledge base is rudimentary or contradictory. In essence, then, given the present state of knowledge development, diagnostic information such as the foregoing may be obtained more for its heuristic value than its predictive validity. To this extent, perhaps, group treatment in social work must retain its identification as more of an art than a science and, likewise, as more of a semi-profession than a profession (Toren, 1969).

The type of diagnostic information that most uniquely distinguishes group work from other therapeutic approaches is that which is derived from observations within the treatment group itself. Sarri and associates point to a wealth of information that can be obtained from such observations. The worker, first of all, can identify the client's orientation to the treatment group, including the bases of his attraction to the group and his personal goals for the group. Most important, perhaps, he can observe the client's position in varying group structures, including the power, task, communication, friendship, leadership, and formal structures. During the course of his observations the worker also can obtain valuable diagnostic information regarding areas of program interest to the client and his differential reactions to programs that involve cooperative, competitive, or parallel activities. Information may be obtained concerning the types of activity preferred by the client, his mode of participation, ranging from passive to active, his attention span, and his skills in varying activities. Through observations of the therapy group the worker also can gauge the client's differential contributions to varying group functions, his adherence to group norms, and the frequency, stability, and normalcy of certain role behaviors. And, of course, he will be able to judge the type and quality of the relationship between the client and himself.

In order to maximize the utility of the working diagnostic statement, the worker also assesses the gifts, skills, and external resources of the client that can facilitate his movement toward effective social functioning. The diagnosis must take into account the accessibility of those resources and indicate the degree to which they are expected to facilitate movement. Likewise, having identified any significant barriers or constraints, either internal or external, that impede the client's effective social functioning, the worker should indicate which of these can be modified and how much improvement can be expected from such modification. It is especially helpful if the worker can ascertain the differential efficacy of direct interventions with the client and of indirect interventions geared toward the client's environment but which, in turn, are expected to modify key conditions or constraints affecting his progress. In addition, the worker may attempt to prognosticate those levels of more adequate role performance that can be reasonably expected as a result of group-work treatment or with the aid of other types of treatment.

Treatment goals for the client are derived directly from the working diagnostic statement that has been prepared. Such goals must be directly related to the problems identified as a result of the diagnosis. They must be as specific as possible and, preferably, should focus upon role performances or behaviors that are clearly observable and identifiable. Obviously treatment goals must be realistic and demonstrable, and they must focus upon those changes that can be realized through group-work service. Treatment goals may be either short-term or long-term. It is most beneficial for the worker to formulate a graduated series of short-term goals that will eventuate in the attainment of his long-term goals for the client. For example, in order to achieve the long-term objective of elimination of a child's temper tantrums, the worker may wish to formulate a sequence of short-term goals that will limit the client to ten temper tantrums at a certain meeting, only five temper tantrums at a subsequent group meeting, two such tantrums at the next meeting, and none thereafter.

Perhaps most important, it is absolutely essential for the group worker to establish treatment goals that can be transferred and stabilized beyond the treatment group itself, that is, within the open community. The extraordinarily high recidivism rates associated with group therapy and other treatment modalities clearly indicate that objectives attained within the treatment group have not been readily transferred and stabilized within the open community. In part, this state of affairs necessarily is due to the experimental nature or inadequate conceptualizing of most current helping therapies. But, also, it is largely attributable to a myriad of related conditions, including the ineffective composition of treatment groups and the disparity between the social conditions of the treatment group and those of the open community, particularly if treatment is conducted behind the walls of a correctional or "rehabilitative" facility. Virtually all group therapies have perpetuated the basic error of composing treatment groups exclusively of dysfunctioning individuals—except, perhaps, for the therapist himself. The failure potential of this strategy is inherent in the fact that such groups consist largely of individuals who have adopted deviant or maladaptive patterns of social functioning, who display and model deviant or dysfunctional role behaviors for one another, and who reinforce or positively sanction deviant or maladaptive social behavior. Perhaps, then, treatment might be most efficacious in groups composed primarily of individuals who accept and display adaptive modes of behavior except, of course, for one or two selected clients. Although such a step would mark a drastic departure from traditional approaches to group therapy, it is entirely conceivable that it would afford substantial therapeutic advantages and, moreover, that it could be done within present institutional structures, at low cost, and with a minimum of disruption to current community resources (Feldman and others, 1972).

Finally, it is relevant to note that Vinter, Sarri, and their colleagues emphasize that treatment goals should seek a reduction of the particular stress or difficulty as experienced by the client. Although this constitutes a most desirable objective for group-work treatment, it is doubtful that it is altogether necessary or, even, particularly feasible at all times. Thus, for example, following an empirical study, Kelman and Parloff (1957) reported that there is no discernible relationship among three criteria of improvement in group therapy: insight, comfort, and effective social functioning. They conclude that it is entirely possible for certain clients to considerably improve their level of social functioning while still experiencing substantial stress. And, conversely, it is possible for a client's experienced stress to diminish substantially without any concomitant enhancement of his social functioning.

Following the formulation of treatment goals for a client, the worker may proceed to the preparation of a *treatment plan.* The latter indicates a sequence of direct and indirect interventions that may take place either inside or outside of the treatment group. Such interventions are discussed in detail in Chapter Four. At this juncture, however, it is most pertinent to reemphasize that any treatment plan must be predicated upon the gradual shaping of a client's behavior. Drastic changes cannot be expected immediately. Indeed, abrupt behavioral changes are not only difficult to achieve but may result both in a serious failure for the client and in a serious lowering of his self-confidence and self-esteem. Therefore, the worker should evolve a treatment plan that requires realistic client role performances and that entails a gradual and continuous improvement in the client's role performance capabilities (Oxley, 1966).

The *terminal diagnostic statement* serves as the final evaluation of the client's treatment progress. It denotes behavioral and attitudinal changes that occurred during treatment and defines the client's current level of functioning with reference to variables once considered problematic. The client's presenting problems, those problems noted on the working diagnosis, and the treatment goals elaborated for the client constitute the main bases for the assessment of change. The worker prepares this statement when he determines that essential long-term treatment goals have been obtained and, therefore, that no further treatment is required. Such a statement also may be prepared when the worker determines that his service is no longer useful, and when he considers it necessary to refer the client to another worker or agency. As Sarri and colleagues note, a description of the worker's treatment goals should be included in this statement along with a description of the treatment provided, the client's response to it, and a prognosis concerning the transferability and stability of the changes that have been observed. Preferably, a series of final observations should be performed in social environments beyond the treatment group, such as the client's family, school, or work environment. Such observations are desirable in order to verify whether or not intragroup treatment changes have been transferred and stabilized within the open community.

Thus far our discussion has focused primarily on diagnosis of the individual client's social functioning. In social group work, however, it is both feasible and desirable to conduct *diagnosis and intervention at the group level* as well as at the individual level. By ascertaining the various ways in which the group's members interact as a unit, it is possible for the worker to enhance the group's efficacy as a treatment medium. Therefore, virtually the entire diagnostic process denoted above can be replicated at the group level. The worker may cite various resources and/or impediments affecting the group's efficacy as a treatment vehicle. He may identify varying performance problems of the group as a unit, such as its difficulties in attaining key goals, developing appropriate levels of group cohesiveness, or elaborating a coherent norm structure. And, consequently, he may formulate treatment goals uniquely focused at the group level. He may, for instance, endeavor to increase cooperation and subsequent attraction among group members through the presentation of a carefully selected series of activities. The ultimate aim of such activities, however, is to develop the group's utility for treatment purposes or, more specifically, to strengthen the group as a medium which enables members to exert more frequent and potent positive influences upon one another. In effect, then, the worker should prepare working and terminal diagnostic statements for the group in which he describes the patterning of various group structures (power, leadership, friendship, task, communication structures, and so forth) and their implications for the elaboration of treatment goals and a coherent treatment plan. To the extent that he does so with diligence and skill he avails himself of a potent source of influence that is seldom available to therapists engaging in one-to-one therapeutic approaches.

From a group level perspective, the greatest difficulty lies in the preparation of treatment goals for individuals and the group that are *compatible* with one another. Thus, for example, if a given treatment goal for member A calls for greater opportunity to engage in aggressive behavior, whereas one for member B calls for a reduction in such behavior, the worker will be hard pressed to develop group interventive strategies that will satisfy both objectives simultaneously. Consequently, it may be necessary to forgo both treatment objectives, to satisfy only one of them at one time while satisfying the other later, or to subgroup the larger unit, at least temporarily, so that the treatment goals for both members can be met at approximately the same time. Should treatment goals for two or more members be seriously incompatible for a prolonged period, it may be necessary, of course, to remove one or more members from the group, to recompose the group, or to enlist the aid of additional group workers who can attend to the differential needs of the various group members.

Synthesizing a variety of differing objectives may require a certain amount of bargaining between the members and the worker (Galinsky and Schopler, 1971; Schopler and Galinsky, 1974). The individual members may have varying goals that may or may not be related to their own conceptions of the treatment process. To some extent these must be clarified and synthesized in order to define members' common purposes for the group as a treatment vehicle. Likewise, it would be desirable to establish and to assure member consensus regarding other purposes and attractions of the group, such as its capacity to afford opportunities for learning, developing friendships, enjoying new activities, and gaining prestige. At the same time, the worker is likely to have certain general goals for the group that are closely related to his own conception of it as a useful means for the treatment of individuals. Consequently, he should elaborate specific purposes for the group that will be shared with the members and, most importantly, that will be congruent or compatible with the members' commonly defined purposes for the group. It is important that the purposes be communicated in a manner relevant to the interests and developmental level of the group members and compatible with the mutual treatment interests of worker and client. The worker's specific purposes for the group, as stated to the members, may not clearly reveal all of the treatment goals that he envisions. But they will constitute clear-cut and, presumably, valued objectives that the members share in common and, moreover, that they will be able to use as referents in order to assess their progress in a systematic and accurate manner. If, for instance, the worker's general goal for the group is to enhance its utility as a treatment vehicle, he may formulate important subgoals that will contribute to that objective, such as increasing the group's level of normative integration or functional integration. In order to achieve those goals he may present the group's purpose to the members as problem exploration, the development of cooperative relationships or, merely, as having fun through a variety of activities.

Summary

This chapter described seven phases of the typical group work treatment sequence consonant with the seven-phase group development model presented in Chapter Two. Following a discussion of treatment sequence phases and concomitant group developmental phases, diagnostic procedures and processes were described. The discussion focused on diagnosis at both the individual and the group levels of analysis. An effort was made to critique and to extend the respective models as well as to describe their essential components.

IV

Traditional Social Group Work: Intervention and Programing

The basic modalities of worker interventions associated with the traditional group-work method were first set forth nearly fifteen years ago in a seminal manuscript by Vinter. Although few basic revisions have been introduced since (Vinter, 1967), the original formulations have been extended somewhat by certain of Vinter's colleagues (Glasser and Garvin, 1971; Glasser and others, 1974; Rose, 1972).

Unlike many others, Vinter always has endeavored to view the small group not only as a *context* for treatment but also as a *means* for treatment. That is, whereas a number of earlier group-work formulations focused solely upon the manner in which a *worker* interacts with and influences each individual group member, Vinter stresses the importance of fostering conditions whereby each *member* exerts a therapeutic influence upon the others. The treatment group is viewed as a deliberately structured influence system in which improvements in social functioning come about through social interaction with others. Such changes may involve the acquisition of new behavioral skills, changes in one's attitude toward

63

himself or others, or a multitude of other positive changes. Through influencing the group's activities, programs, and key structures, the worker may promote these important interactions. In essence, while the group itself may foster a given member's more effective social functioning to a degree that proceeds considerably beyond the direct interventions of the worker himself, the group's capacity to influence does not represent a random state of affairs. To maximize the group's change potential, the worker executes certain interventions directed at the group as a unit and these, in turn, exert a determinate effect upon the target individuals who are participants in the group. This, in brief, is the essence of what Vinter has described as indirect means of influence.

More specifically, Vinter has posited three basic modalities of group-work intervention, which he prefers to define as *means of influence*. These are (1) direct means of influence, (2) indirect means of influence, and (3) extra-group means of influence. *Direct means of influence* are those interventions utilized to effect change through immediate interaction with one or another group member. *Indirect means of influence* are those interventions utilized to effect modifications in group conditions which subsequently affect one or more members. *Extra-group means of influence* refer to those worker activities conducted outside of the treatment group but on behalf of the clients.

Direct Means of Influence

Worker as central person. In elaborating one basic direct means of influence, that is, utilization of the worker as a central person, Vinter has drawn heavily upon the writings of Fritz Redl (1955). This mode of worker influence is based primarily upon the presumed tendency for certain of the group's members to focus upon the worker as an object of identification, drive satisfaction, and ego support. Members, for instance, may identify with the worker on the basis of love or fear. The worker may become an object of love drives or aggressive drives. And the worker may provide ego support for members by offering a means for drive satisfaction or by dissolving conflict situations through the assuagement of guilt and anxiety (Redl, 1955).

Frequently the worker may exert this type of influence over members without consciously endeavoring to do so. Group members may copy his style of dress, processes of decision-making, or other behavioral patterns, for instance. Consequently it is essential for therapists constantly to evaluate the many ways in which they may exert influence over group members, particularly if such influence could be counterproductive for the attainment of therapeutic goals. On certain occasions the worker may wish to take purposeful advantage of his capacity to influence the group directly. Therefore, he might attempt to heighten the visibility of some desired behaviors or attributes by increasing the frequency with which they are displayed, by drawing members' attention to them, or by reinforcing members who simulate such behaviors in the presence of their peers.

The various members within the group also may exert this type of influence upon one another. But, as Vinter notes, the worker's position of preeminence within the group is likely to enhance his capacity to apply this particular mode of influence. In part, this preeminence is due to his role in initiating the group, and is associated with the legitimacy and authority vested in him by the agency and the community. It also may be attributable to varying personal resources, such as his particular competencies and personality characteristics, some of which may have been shaped during the course of professional education. As the members develop an identification with the worker, it is important to note that this shared behavior also may strengthen interpersonal ties among themselves: clients may identify with each other as they experience the similarity of relationships with the worker. In general, positive identification with the worker is likely to increase as the worker expresses warmth and sensitivity to the clients and as he structures the group meeting, sustains communication, and otherwise decreases the clients' level of tension (Thomas, Kounin, and Polansky, 1967).

Although the worker's efforts to reduce the clients' tension may increase the group's identification with him, it is important to note that for certain types of social dysfunction, such as severe depression, they may only serve to sustain the clients' problems and, possibly, to reinforce them (Stuart, 1967). Consequently, as with his entire repertoire of interventions, the worker must scrutinize each possible intervention for its therapeutic efficacy with reference to the client's particular behavioral difficulty, his level of progress, and its possible effects upon other persons within the treatment group.

Worker as symbol and spokesman. In order to effect critical changes within the group, the worker sometimes may wish to create, clarify, revise, or eliminate certain behavioral norms shared by the group's members. Indeed, as Vinter has noted, many of the clients served through social group work manifest difficulties with respect to the norms and values that they have internalized and, for some, these difficulties may comprise the crux of their social functioning problems. In some cases resocialization through social group work is a relatively simple and straightforward process that meets with the wholehearted acceptance of the client. Pertinent examples might include group work with immigrants from foreign countries or with persons moving into new social, economic, or cultural environments.

In other instances, such as street work with delinquent gangs socialized toward "deviant" subcultural norms, the worker is afflicted with certain value dilemmas that may hinder his treatment effectiveness (Klein, 1967; Spergel, 1965, 1966). These pertain to the ethicality and efficacy of imposing his values, or even those of the larger society, upon a "deviant" subgroup. In such instances group workers tend to take a variety of stances, including the refusal to provide service in situations that are untenable or overly ambiguous. In some instances group workers will provide service only if the clients voluntarily request it and enter into the treatment program with clearly defined expectations, outlining both their rights and obligations. In other instances, workers focus upon only clearly deviant behaviors, such as assault, theft, and so forth, and refrain from intervening in behavioral areas less clearly defined as deviant. And, in still other instances, workers serve as agents of reform or rehabilitation because they have been authorized to do so by an agency that has been entrusted with such functions by the larger society, such as juvenile courts and correctional institutions. Here the service function can become rather tenuous especially if the agency should attempt to legitimize practices of dubious ethicality such as "midnight visits" to clients suspected of receiving fraudulent welfare payments or the unwarranted use of electroshock therapy.

Thus group workers—like many other therapists—sometimes are placed in situations where the values of a deviant subculture may appear more justifiable than those of the larger society. In some such situations, action may be taken more appropriately against malfunctioning components of the larger society (see Feldman and Specht, 1968) than against the values of clients in the treatment group. Where this strategy is tactically unsound (or, indeed, contrary to the agency's job definition for the worker), the worker's professional judgments and objectives may be seriously limited, prompting some observers to suggest that all therapeutic service should be offered within the context of private practice (Piliavin, 1968). However, for certain therapeutic endeavors the bureaucratic context obviously affords advantages as well as liabilities.

When the worker deems it desirable, in the light of all the foregoing considerations, to alter the members' norms to any significant degree, it is usually wise to share this decision with the group members, or their guardians, insofar as possible and to explain the implications and effects of the new norms in contrast with those that prevailed earlier. If the group is engaged in treatment voluntarily and if the worker's reasoning is clearly expressed in favor of such changes, the group is likely to agree to new norms.

One emphatic note of caution: *Premature* efforts of therapists to impose their norms and values upon treatment groups are fraught with hazard, especially if the group has met as a unit prior to inclusion of the therapist, or has achieved strong consensus regarding social norms clearly not espoused by the therapist. As Merei (1949) has shown in experimental studies of children's leadership behavior, new members of a group—even those with evident leadership skills—are likely to be rejected by a group until they are considered tolerant of, and receptive to, the group's norms. Only after newcomers have been accepted by the group, largely upon the basis of their adherence to group norms, is it possible for them to gradually introduce their own norms in a manner acceptable to the majority. In treatment groups, then, the worker's ability to alter behavioral norms is largely contingent upon his acceptance by the group members and this, in turn, may depend largely on the amount of time that the worker has spent with the group. It follows that new norms and values should be introduced gradually and with great care.

As Vinter notes, a group worker also may influence a group's norms in other ways. Thus, for example, he may personify, or model, key norms in his own behavior. Bandura and McDonald (1963) have shown this mode of influencing behavior to be as potent as more widely accepted reinforcement techniques and/or combinations of the two (compare also Bandura and Kupers, 1964; Bandura, Ross, and Ross, 1961; Ullmann, 1969). The worker also may act as a spokesman for legitimate norms and values. That is, he may verbalize, explicate, or otherwise urge the acceptance of norms considered appropriate for the group. In addition, he may subtly clarify or heighten the visibility of certain latent or covert norms and urge the development of consensus regarding norms that may be disputed or unclarified; he may formally or informally assist the group in creating new norms and at the same time reinforce norms conducive to strengthening the treatment efficacy of the group, such as those pertaining to openness, candor, and cooperation. In these efforts, the overwhelming majority of current empirical literature recommends the use of positive, rather than negative, techniques, and inducements and rewards rather than deprivations or punishments (Collins and Guetzkow, 1964; Wodarski, Feldman, and Flax, 1973).

Worker as motivator and stimulator. Within the context of a group situation, workers can encourage members to confront experiences that they may wish to avoid, but which are conducive, nonetheless, to the attainment of treatment goals. As Cloward and Ohlin (1960) have noted, individuals can make substantial forward strides if they learn about social opportunities that had previously escaped their attention or, indeed, had been closed to them. The worker may train clients to develop the requisite skills for discerning such opportunities or for availing themselves of them. Or he may suggest, encourage, or otherwise reinforce members' initial explorations of new social roles. He may stimulate such efforts through setting appropriate expectations for members (Dinitz and others, 1962; Feldman, 1968; Lefton, 1962; Oxley, 1966; Strean, 1967) or, more directly, through skillful persuasion (compare Bettinghaus, 1968; Karlins and Abelson, 1970). As will be noted below, the worker's control over physical resources and group decision-making processes also will enable him to structure indirect interventions, such as certain group programs, that may motivate or stimulate members to experiment with new role behaviors.

Worker as executive. The last direct mode of influence cited by Vinter employs the group worker as an executive, or as one who specifically controls and defines certain roles for the group members. Interventions predicated upon this modality are derived largely from a role-theory perspective concerning small group structures. This perspective posits that all groups develop social structures consisting of interacting social positions and role performances. Interventions may be geared toward changes in a given group structure and, therefore, may be considered as an indirect means of influence. Or, as will be discussed in this section, a given member's position(s) within such structures may be changed through the worker's assistance or advisement, thus constituting a direct means of influence.

Depending upon the worker's particular treatment goals for a client, he may attempt to alter that client's position in one or more group structures, such as the group's power, leadership, friendship, communication, or task structures. Thus, if one of his treatment goals calls for a higher level of client self-esteem, the worker might temporarily place that client within a position of power in the group. Prior to such placement the worker may prepare the client for the new position by coaching him in requisite skills or role performances associated with the position. Not only might such a change in itself enhance the client's self-esteem but, even more pertinent from a group treatment perspective, the other group members may at least temporarily alter their typical ways of interacting with the client and, in view of the powers associated with his new position, further contribute to bolstering of his self-esteem. Consequently the worker's interventive activity may set in motion a variety of forces that will contribute to attainment of his treatment goals for the client. Should such changes generalize to other client role performances, the worker will have tapped the core strengths of treatment situated within a small group context. However, it should be noted that any of the foregoing interventive modalities may be used in one-to-one therapies as well as in group therapies. Although their foci may be different and the opportunities for intervention may be somewhat reduced in one-to-one therapeutic situations, they are nonetheless direct modes of intervention and rely only upon the worker's direct interaction with a single client. In contrast, indirect modes of intervention are eminently and uniquely applicable to therapeutic practice in small groups. And it is these modalities of intervention that provide group treatment with special advantages not available within a one-to-one treatment context.

Indirect Means of Influence

Indirect means of influence are interventions designed to modify group conditions which, in turn, affect the members (Vinter, 1967, p. 29). More specifically, by structuring certain social situations that affect the entire group, or a portion of the group, the worker attempts to create conditions that will influence a given individual who is the actual target of his activities. Depending upon the worker's treatment goals, most or all of the group's members, on occasion, may be the targets for his activity. One common example is the goal of increased cooperative behavior, which the worker may consider to be relevant for each and every group member. By structuring program activities or group operating procedures that require mutual cooperation in order for members' needs to be gratified, the worker may enhance the probability of moving toward the posited treatment goal. Although there are innumerable indirect means of influence, Vinter cites six major ones: (1) group purposes, (2) selection of group members, (3) group size, (4) group operating and governing procedures, (5) group development, and (6) programing.

Purposes. Vinter interprets group purposes as the composite of members' objectives and motives as manifested in observable activity. This interpretation includes the worker's definition of the group's purposes—the specific aims that the group ought to pursue to achieve treatment goals set for the individual clients. It is a virtual truism that the best results are achieved when there is substantial compatibility between the members' and the worker's purposes.

In most instances, both worker and members realize and acknowledge that the main purpose of the treatment group is to facilitate their mutual efforts toward improved social functioning. Aside from this central purpose, however, they may establish a number of secondary purposes, for example, to develop friendships, to relax, and so forth. In some instances, especially with groups of young children, the group's purpose is presented in a manner that is more consistent with the interests and developmental levels of the members—as a means for having fun, engaging in sports activities, and the like. As a mode of indirect influence, the worker's selection of group purposes is especially important for a number of reasons. If purposes are carefully selected in accord with the members' needs, this factor alone can serve to attract the members to the group to an extent that may far exceed the personal capacities of the individual worker.

Initially, the worker's or agency's definition of the group's purpose is likely to preselect those who will become interested in the group or who will be permitted to join it. Thereafter members tend to develop a series of discrete goals that are designed to help them attain the group's purposes. Thus, for example, if a group's objectives entail the inculcation of religious values, it may devise a series of activities designed to meet this purpose. In effect, the goals devised by members serve as relatively clear and useful criteria for their assessment of the group's progress at any given time. If a worker helps members to select goals that are clear and realistic, the members are more likely to experience success and satisfaction with their group. Accordingly, they are likely to realize a number of beneficial side-effects, such as a higher level of self-esteem and a greater receptivity to experimentation. And, finally, the clear definition of group purposes permits ready and accurate assessment of progress by the members themselves.

The group's purposes also are likely to determine the various tasks engaged in by members, the distribution of possible roles and role performance opportunities within the group (such as instrumental roles and socioemotional roles), the sequencing of group activities, and group decision-making and operating procedures. It is important to note that group purposes—aside from the central purpose of maximizing the group's effectiveness as a treatment vehicle—frequently change over time, particularly as the group becomes more autonomous and self-regulating. Indeed, in accord with his treatment goals, the worker may wish to initiate various alterations in group purposes as the group develops. So long as the new purposes are introduced gradually, clearly, and with the members' consent, such alterations may not only reflect positive changes in the group but may, indeed, foster the development of subsequent positive changes.

Selection of members. Obviously the composition of a treatment group will have determinate effects upon the interaction of members within that group and, ultimately, upon the attainment of treatment goals. Yet relatively little progress has been made in social group work, or in any other mode of group treatment, toward the systematic composition of treatment groups. Some professionals, such as Eric Berne, have refused to select clients for their treatment groups in any systematic manner. Their attitude seems to be that since nothing is known about group composition anyway, it is best to make a virtue of random selection. This attitude reflects not only the difficulties and frustrations associated with the rather exiguous knowledge base concerning group composition, but also an abiding faith in the therapeutic value of heterogeneous group membership. Nonetheless, it would seem that virtually *any* clues regarding means for enhancing a group's therapeutic effectiveness through the systematic selection of members would, indeed, constitute a most welcome addition to the therapist's armamentarium.

Much of the debate concerning group composition has centered upon the rather global dichotomy between "homogeneous" and "heterogeneous" member attributes. For many years social workers assumed that it would be more effective to treat groups that are homogeneously composed with reference to a given presenting problem—alcoholism, drug addiction, unwed motherhood, and so forth. In fact, substantial data support this position so long as the therapist's basic task for the particular presenting problem involves *information-giving or education* rather than the exploration of interpersonal problems or experimentation with new role behaviors (Feldman, 1969c). Typical examples are groups of welfare recipients to whom eligibility requirements are to be explained, foster care applicants who receive information concerning licensing, and drug addicts obtaining information concerning methadone maintenance. As Litwak (1961) has clearly stated, problems that are uniform and repetitive for any particular population can be dealt with effectively through relatively standardized, uniform, and repetitive service procedures. For such groups homogeneous membership is highly desirable. But for groups in which the members' problems are highly unique or nonrepetitive, such as, for example, the deviant behavior of juvenile delinquents, the therapists' interventions must be individually tailored for each member. Given the necessity for unstandardized, unique interventions, homogeneous group composition may not be particularly productive.

Heterogeneous groups may be far superior to homogeneous ones when the treatment of choice requires group members to experiment with new role behaviors or to emulate the role performance of more proficient individuals. Spohn and Wolk (1966), for instance, have shown that chronic schizophrenics apparently benefit more from social participation in heterogeneous groups than homogeneous ones. The mixed groups presumably provide patients with role models for new and more positive modes of behaving. Indeed, groups of patients with similar social functioning problems may tolerate and reinforce each other's deviance more than has been heretofore expected (Eisenman, 1966). Similarly, experimental studies of problem-solving groups have shown that the *type of problem* with which a group is faced frequently determines the differential efficacy of homogeneous versus heterogeneous group composition. If the group's problem is a straightforward one calling for expertise, one should endeavor to compose the group solely of experts in the particular problem area and, therefore, homogeneously. If the group's problems are extremely complex, require considerable interchange of communication, or call for inspirational, rather than routine, problem-solving strategies, heterogeneous group composition is deemed to be more effective (Goldberg and Maccoby, 1965; Hoffman and Maier, 1961; Kelley and Thibaut, 1968; Shalinsky, 1969a, 1969b; Shaw, 1960; Stotland and others, 1960; Thompson and Tuden, 1959).

An extension of the foregoing considerations might involve the elaboration of new and more effective modes of group composition than heretofore utilized in the group therapies. It would be plausible, for instance, to compose groups primarily, or entirely, of individuals who function adequately except for a given client who, in fact, is the main target of the treatment. Group composition of this nature would be likely to maximize change pressures toward more effective social functioning by replacing deviant role models with positive ones, by locating the client within a social context that primarily reinforces adaptive behaviors rather than maladaptive ones and, perhaps, by more closely simulating the client's actual social environment, the open community. This mode of group composition might be particularly appropriate for clients with behavioral problems such as schizophrenia or autism. In order to enhance the economic feasibility of this approach, however, it might be necessary to locate treatment efforts within ongoing groups characterized by adaptive social functioning, such as groups of "normal" children meeting in community centers. Since only one or two clients would be included in each group, the economic feasibility of this approach might be enhanced through the utilization of subprofessional personnel.

Vinter has properly noted that the worker's goals and purposes for the group provide a general guide for group composition. So long as the group is viewed as a means for treatment, as well as the context for it, the worker should seek members who not only are likely to benefit from treatment, but who also are expected to exert maximum impact for positive change among their peers. Therefore, the selected members should be potentially capable of developing appropriate levels of group integration and requisite group structures for effective goal attainment. Since group goals may change over time, particularly as the group progresses or as it faces new challenges, differing leadership, task, and communication structures may be required at varying points. In itself, this observation points to the efficacy of relatively heterogeneous group composition. Additional considerations of relevance would be the members' similarity of interests, their potentiality for attraction to one another, their capacity to participate in the general types of activity planned by the worker, and their capacity to form viable functional and interpersonal relationships with the worker and with one another. Consequently, it is essential to focus on the members' potential *compatibility* with one another rather than their similarity. Although member similarities may augur well for compatibility on certain dimensions—for example, religious background—their complementary attributes may be critical for others, as in the case when a two-person group might function better with one dominant member and one submissive member, rather than both of the same kind. The notion of compatibility in group composition can successfully incorporate both similarities and dissimilarities along various dimensions, depending upon the particular items in question. Consequently the relative treatment efficacy of "homogeneous" versus "heterogeneous" groups is a far more complex question than thus far recognized. Moreover, it is one that requires the systematic differentiation of large clusters of variables in order to establish the manner in which member compatibility is enhanced by similar and/or complementary attributes. Great incompatibilities in members' ages, interests, pathologies, interaction styles, and maturation levels may make it extraordinarily difficult for the group to form social structures essential for effective treatment.

In summary, a number of broad guidelines for group composition have been elaborated by Vinter. First, the types of primary client attributes for which compatibility is desired depend upon the nature of the treatment group and its program. Second, compatibility is sought with reference to one's peers in the group, and not with reference to any absolute standards of behavior or personality. Therefore, clients need not be identical with respect to their personal characteristics but, at a minimum, they should be potentially compatible. Finally, it should be noted that there are situations in which the worker has relatively little autonomy with which to influence the course of group composition. This is particularly true should he be assigned to previously formed groups, such as a gang of juvenile delinquents or a given ward of a correctional institution. Nonetheless, even in such situations, movement toward the worker's treatment goals may be facilitated as he strives to alter the group's composition during the course of treatment. This may be done by forming the treatment group into subgroups, by discharging certain members, by adding new ones, or by merging the group with other groups.

Size. Group size represents a key facet of group composition that may be integrally related to the attainment of treatment goals.

The worker's main objective is to determine the appropriate group size with reference to the specific treatment effects desired for his clients.

Certain broad-range behavioral patterns are clearly associated with differences in group size. Smaller groups (six to eight members) tend to be characterized by high levels of interpersonal integration, or reciprocal liking, whereas larger ones are more likely to demonstrate high levels of functional integration, or task interdependence (Feldman, 1973). As groups grow in size it becomes more difficult for members to engage in face-to-face interaction and to explore the common factors conducive to the establishment of strong friendship relations. Also, as groups grow in size, the varying role performances required for effective group functioning tend to proliferate both quantitatively and qualitatively. Consequently, the group's social integration is likely to be based primarily upon the various task interdependencies that emerge within the group and that serve to link the members together. Beyond a certain size, perhaps ranging from fifteen to twenty members, integrative problems are likely to worsen substantially. To some extent, they may depend for their resolution upon the formation of subgroups and the development of various linkages or coalitions among them.

As Vinter has noted, large groups, of nine members or more, tend toward anonymity of participation, less norm consensus, lower rates of participation for all members except those occupying leadership positions, and higher demands for leadership abilities. On the other hand, they are likely to be more effective at tasks requiring a marked division of labor in which attainment is dependent largely upon the absolute number of participants, such as fund raising, apple picking, and so forth. Small groups tend toward higher and more equalized rates of participation among the members, toward greater individual involvement, and toward greater norm consensus (Hare, 1962, pp. 244–245; Thomas and Fink, 1963). Although Vinter suggests that small groups are likely to be characterized by increased constraints upon members, this depends largely upon the basis of the constraint pressures.

Any of the foregoing effects may be desired in order to attain the treatment goals elaborated for given members. More mature and adequate clients are better able to cope with the participation requirements of larger groups. Clients who require substantial individual attention, in contrast, are likely to accrue greater benefits from participation in smaller groups. And, of course, in some instances clients' behavioral problems may be such that participation in groups of varying size would be conducive to the attainment of treatment goals. In such instances, it may be advisable for the treatment group to be subgrouped at various points in time, for it to merge with other groups for certain activities, for new members to be added as the group progresses or, in fact, for the member to be involved in more than one treatment group. As noted earlier, the treatment goals for the various members in a group must be highly compatible with one another. Otherwise, a given group size might be conducive to the attainment of treatment goals for a certain cluster of members, but might hinder the progress of others. In such cases the worker may again wish to introduce activities or short-term goals that temporarily fragment the larger group into subgroups aligned more appropriately with members' developmental levels and concomitant treatment goals.

It is interesting to note that considerable investigation has been devoted to a search for an optimum group size. Bales and Slater (1955) report, for instance, that groups of five persons appear to be more satisfying for group members than groups of other size. Presumably this is so because the members' opportunities for active and equal participation tend to decline substantially in groups of larger size, whereas their ability to temporarily withdraw from active participation, when so desired, is highly visible and, therefore, unduly constrained in smaller groups. Groups of approximately five members are considered to afford the optimum conditions for both participation and avoidance of participation, depending upon the members' particular needs. Indeed, a number of studies have shown that control over their own opportunities for participation in small groups is one of the most important factors associated with client satisfaction with the group experience (Heslin and Dunphy, 1964; White and Lippitt, 1960).

However, members' satisfaction is not always the prime determinant of a treatment group's effectiveness. In fact, as Kelman and Parloff (1957) have observed, studies of group therapy show no clear-cut positive association between clients' personal comfort and their level of social functioning. Moreover, satisfaction in itself represents a highly complex construct. It is possible, for instance, that group members' varying needs and concomitant need-satisfaction behaviors are likely to cover an inordinately broad range despite the worker's best efforts to engage in selective group composition. Certain of these variant needs are more likely to be met effectively by groups of large size than small size, and vice versa. In other words, member satisfaction is dependent, at least in part, upon the attainment of tasks and goals defined for the group and its individual members. The performance of differing tasks, in turn, is partially contingent upon variations in group size and in group structure that are more or less appropriate for the particular task at hand. Consequently an evaluation of the complex interplay among numerous variables is important for a worker's predictive and interventive activities regarding any single variable. This consideration, like others, points to the immense complexity of therapeutic endeavors premised upon the traditional group work method. It also points to the rather low predictive potency of this model at the present stage of its development. And, more trenchantly, it reveals the variant and elusive nature of efforts directed toward a definition of "optimum" group size.

Operating and governing procedures. The types of operating and governing procedures implemented by group members and the worker exert determinate effects upon opportunities for, and modes of, member interaction. They also influence the extent of members' participation in group activities and the likelihood of goal attainment for various tasks. Thus, for example, a democratic decision-making structure adapts well to tasks that call for the sharing and exchange of information in order to solve a problem. Democratic structure and cooperative problem-solving are both appropriate for clients with relatively well-developed social functioning capacities. But for clients with severe decision-making difficulties, or related social problems, such tasks and/or decision-making structures may only serve as unnecessary sources of frustration, failure, and diminished self-esteem. In those cases, a more centralized decision-making structure, with greater power accorded to the worker or certain adequately functioning members, may be conducive to the attainment of treatment goals. Moreover, task and goal assignments requiring the group to create a centralized decision-making structure may be desirable.

In many instances the nature of group operating and governing procedures may be expected to change considerably during the course of treatment. During the early phases, when members may be more incapacitated, such procedures may be highly structured. During subsequent phases they may become more flexible and may entail the broad distribution of self-governing powers among the members.

As Vinter has noted, group workers ought to be aware of the potential operational and therapeutic distinctions among many seemingly similar phenomena. Democratic decision-making, for instance, cannot always be equated with equal participation by all the group's members. Nor can it be equated with unrestricted permissiveness. Moreover, parliamentary procedure is often mistaken for democratic decision-making, but may be as readily utilized to subvert it as to facilitate it. In effect, the worker should choose to strengthen or weaken any particular mode of group governing, including the democratic, primarily upon the basis of the particular treatment goals that have been formulated for the group's members. Goals may entail variations in autonomy for certain group members, or for the group itself, at given points in its development. In turn, such considerations will serve to determine the appropriate operating and governing structure. As with all other considerations, this one must not be viewed with undue simplicity or inflexibility. Member autonomy and the implementation of given operating procedures may vary in content as well as in degree. For certain decision-making areas the members of a treatment group may be eminently capable of operating with great autonomy and, therefore, should be permitted to do so. Within the same time period, they may be considerably less capable of autonomous decision-making in other areas and, therefore, may need extra assistance from the worker. At times it may even be necessary to delegate certain decision-making responsibilities entirely to the worker.

One of the most significant innovations in the recent work of Vinter's colleagues is an increasing utilization of token economies in order to systematize group operating and governing procedures (Rose, 1967, 1969, 1972). This approach represents a creative, but only beginning, effort to link social-learning and behavior-modification formulations with the perspective traditionally utilized by the Michigan school. Since a more detailed discussion of token economies will be set forth in Chapter Five, suffice it to say that the worker, in collaboration with the group's members, may devise certain reward or reinforcement schedules for the members that are formally stated in terms of the group's actual operating and governing procedures. Token economies may be used to support any one of a variety of governing procedures, ranging from those that are thoroughly democratic to those that are thoroughly autocratic. Token economies, by and of themselves, are not inherently autocratic, as has been contended by a number of practitioners. Rather, they merely provide an orderly assessment and interventive system that may be tailored to any particular group operating procedure and, more specifically, to the particular treatment goals elaborated for the group's members. Consquently, to the extent that they can be put into effect, they afford the worker with an additional means for implementing selected group operating procedures, and for assessing their effectiveness with reference to the attainment of the members' treatment goals.

Programing. Since its inception social group work has relied upon programing as one of its most distinctive and identifiable modes of intervention. However, despite the frequent usage of the term, the actual definition and referents of programing have remained rather vague over the years. In a seminal paper concerning program activities and their effects on participants' behaviors, Vinter (1967) probably has done more than any other writer to clarify the meaning of the term, to define its implications for group work intervention, and to refine it sufficiently so that it lends itself readily to further elaboration (for example, Trieschman and others, 1969) and empirical study by other investigators (for example, Rubeiz, 1972). Vinter utilizes the term "program" to denote a general class of group activities, each of which consists of an interconnected, sequential series of social behaviors. The social behaviors that constitute any particular activity tend to follow a rather typical pattern that unfolds in a rough chronological sequence.

Program activities serve a variety of purposes. They can be structured to induce certain member behaviors, including the establishment of desired interpersonal relationships among the members of the group. Likewise, they serve as clearly defined mechanisms for helping the members and worker to identify their progress, or lack of progress, toward a given goal, including treatment goals. It is important to stress that program activities refer to the *sequencing* of group activities. Any given program should not be viewed apart from antecedent and ensuing programs. And, of course, no program activity should be considered apart from the various treatment goals upon which it is based. Instead, each and every program formulated by a group worker should be considered in terms of preceding programs and its anticipated effects upon future ones. Or, more specifically, each program should be individually considered in relation to the members' antecedent social growth and the treatment results anticipated.

In accord with the foregoing, programing cannot be considered to exclude other interventive modalities. In fact, the term is sufficiently broad to incorporate virtually all modalities. However, in practice the term usually refers to indirect modes of intervention that are sequentially arranged by the worker in order to shape members' role performances and behaviors toward the attainment of treatment goals. Programing may incorporate a broad array of activities, ranging from those that are rigorously and specifically defined (such as tournament chess) to those that are virtually undefined, such as the types of verbal discussions that frequently are observed in sensitivity training groups and encounter groups. Many activities, such as swimming, arts and crafts, and sandlot sports, may vary widely along certain physical or behavioral dimensions, subject only to the mutual definitions and specifications imposed by the members and worker.

Virtually any activity may be considered of value by the group worker so long as it can be shaped to facilitate movement toward the particular treatment goals set for members. Vinter has defined three major components of activities: a physical field, constituent performances, and respondent behaviors. In large part his formulations have been drawn from the work of Redl (1959) and Gump and Sutton-Smith (1955a). The present description, in turn, draws extensively upon a revised statement set forth by Vinter (1967, pp. 97–101).

The *physical field* of an activity refers to the space or terrain where it is performed and to the material or social objects associated with the activity. Baseball, for example, is played on a relatively flat unobstructed field with a ball, bat, and a given number of players. *Constituent performances* are those behaviors which are required in order to participate. For baseball, these include throwing the ball, hitting and catching it, and running. *Respondent behaviors* are those individual participant actions evoked by, but not essential to, participation in the activity. In baseball, for example, running, cheering, and disputes are behaviors frequently displayed by participants in response to the process of the game.

The basic features of an *activity setting* are the physical field and the constituent performances associated with it. These partially determine the respondent behaviors that are considered consonant with movement toward the treatment goals set for members. Various forms and combinations of basic components of an activity setting (that is, the physical field and constituent performances) are distinctive to different activities. In order to evaluate the differential treatment efficacy of various activity-settings it is essential to identify basic dimensions that apply to all of them. Vinter has defined six basic activity-setting dimensions.

1. *Prescriptiveness of the pattern of constituent performances.* This dimension refers to the degree and range of rules or other conduct guides for those engaging in the activity. Holding all other factors constant, Vinter posits a number of relationships between respondent behaviors and the prescriptiveness of the pattern of constituent performances. Highly prescriptive activities, such as tournament chess, are likely to be less attractive than those which are less prescriptive, or which are likely to result in fatigue, satiation, or the channeling and constriction of behavior.

2. *Institutionalized controls governing participant activity.* This dimension refers to the form, source, and agent of controls exercised over participants during the activity. Controls usually are exercised by group members or special arbiters, such as referees. Even when controls are viewed as relatively impersonal, for example, norms regarding batting rotation in baseball, their implementation and monitoring are within the members' purview. Vinter posits that an emphasis on formal controls is likely to reduce innovation in rules and performance techniques. Similarly, as controls are in-

creasingly concentrated in the hands of one or a few persons, there will be relatively greater interaction with those members and dependence upon them. Conversely, the remaining members will interact proportionately less frequently with one another.

3. *Provision for physical movement.* This dimension refers to the extent to which participants are required or permitted to move about in the activity-setting. The movement may refer to parts of the body (for example, the whole body versus specific segments of the body) or to portions of the physical field (in football, for example, the playing field versus the entire stadium). With reference to this dimension, Vinter posits that the greater the bodily movement, the greater the likelihood of physical interaction and, perhaps, of aggressive behavior. He also suggests that highly restricted, specialized, and repetitive physical movements produce fatigue sooner than do freer forms of physical activity.

4. *Competence required for performance.* This dimension refers to the minimum level of ability required to participate in an activity. In many instances, group workers can alter the level of competence required for a given activity through slight changes in the physical field or constituent performances. In order to utilize basketball as a therapeutic activity for paraplegics, for example, requisite alterations have been made in the height of baskets, weight of the ball, configuration of the basketball court, and in rules concerning dribbling the ball, amount of time permitted in the "key" area of the court, and the utilization of wheelchairs for locomotion. The worker and members often can define the competence levels necessary for successful activity performance, or for winning an activity, in accord with their own skill levels. For example, selection of the winning entry in a clay modeling contest can be determined in accord with performance criteria that are differentially geared toward participants' age levels or amount of prior experience with the activity. In order to illustrate the pertinence of this dimension, Vinter posits that high minimum competence is likely to result in lower interaction among participants, and in the shifting of rewards to those of task performance, rather than interpersonal gratification.

5. *Provision for participant interactiveness.* This dimension refers to the way in which the activity-setting locates and engages participants so that interaction among them is required or induced.

As Vinter notes, in group discussions adhering to formal procedures most statements are directed to the chairman. In contract bridge, players oppose each other in teams of two, bidding and playing in accord with a strict order. In tournament chess, participant interaction is highly delimited whereas, in contrast, free swimming permits members to engage in, or withdraw from, social interaction virtually as they see fit. In accord with numerous small group studies Vinter posits that high interactiveness is likely to result in high involvement and effort. Interactiveness, however, may be of varying types, such as that in which members facilitate each other's efforts (football players engaged in blocking and running), hinder each other's efforts (bodychecking of opposing teammates in hockey), or interact with relative independence from one another (laborers picking fruit at an hourly rate). Vinter suggests that high facilitating interaction will lead to cooperation and friendly relations, whereas high hindering interaction will lead to competitiveness, rivalry, and hostility.

6. *Reward structure.* This dimension refers to the types of rewards available, their abundance or scarcity, and the manner in which they are distributed during or after the activity. The dimension is of special interest because it can be easily reconceptualized in terms of social reinforcement theories. Consequently it provides a strong bridge between traditional group work theory and more recent developments in social learning and behavior modification theories (for example, Rose, 1967, 1969, 1972). Since these linkages will be fully elaborated elsewhere, the present discussion will be restricted to the presentation of Vinter's basic ideas regarding activity reward structures. He observes, with reference to type of rewards, that some activities, such as bowling tournaments, formally provide rewards for those who "win" them, whereas other activities are assumed to be their own rewards—singing a song or composing an oil painting for instance. Many activities, moreover, are characterized by secondary rewards such as a release of tension, prestige, praise from others, improved performance competence, and so forth.

With reference to abundance of rewards, it is pertinent to note that the completion of some activities assures relatively equal and substantial rewards for all participants; examples are preparation for a camping trip, winning a baseball championship, building a log cabin, and so forth. However, for other activities, certain positions inherently provide more rewards for their occupants than do others, as, for example, the position of orchestra conductor, team captain, and the like. Frequently, though not always, inordinately larger rewards accrue to members who are the focus of communication for an activity (again, an orchestra conductor), who interact more frequently with the other participants (a football quarterback), or who perform their assigned functions with substantially greater competence than the others (a baseball batting champion). Vinter posits that the greater the range and variety of desired and expected rewards, the greater the likelihood of attraction for most participants; a scarcity of rewards is likely to result in competitiveness, rivalry, and an unequal distribution of power. In addition, the more broadly and evenly distributed the rewards, the greater the likelihood of cohesiveness, trust, cooperation, productivity, and responsibility. The more unevenly distributed the rewards, the greater the likelihood of rivalry, competition, conflict, factions, and distrust. The greater the discrepancy between expected and actually earned rewards, the greater the likelihood of frustration, dissatisfaction, and withdrawal (Vinter, 1967, p. 105).

To further indicate the efficacy of his schema, Vinter has compared the manner in which arts and crafts and swimming activities are differentiated along the six above-described activity-setting dimensions. Moreover, he has indicated how they lend themselves to predictions regarding the respondent behaviors associated with each. An even more comprehensive and impressive extension of the schema has been set forth by Whittaker (see Trieschman and others, 1969). In elaborating Vinter's work, Whittaker posited that three variables associated with individual clients are of key importance for group workers. These are the individual's skill, level of motivation, and capacity for self-control. By viewing any one individual as either high or low on each of these dimensions, Whittaker has derived eight possible "program types." By further juxtaposing each of the eight program types with Vinter's six activity-setting dimensions (prescriptiveness, controls, physical movement, participant interactiveness, competence required, and reward structure), he then develops an "activity scale" that provides a rough categorization system for numerous program activities, such as swimming, finger painting, origami, baseball, football, checkers, and so forth. These are arrayed in accord with their treatment suitability for given clients (Trieschman and others, 1969, pp. 113–117). Although this procedure could have been extended even further by analyzing the skill, motivation, and control variables in terms of "medium," as well as "high" and "low," Whittaker's extension of the original schema is a promising innovation and, moreover, one that attests to the viability of the original model. Nonetheless, future elaborations are likely to be even more quantitative than those described above. They are likely to be conceptualized in terms of interval scales, rather than simpler nominal or ordinal scales, such as the "high" and "low" categories used by Whittaker. Moreover, it will be necessary to devise common units of analysis in order to facilitate cross-comparison of varying program activities. To do so will require the development of smaller and more discrete behavioral measurement units than those used heretofore.

In summarizing the basic rationale for his formulations, Vinter (1967, p. 98) states the following assumptions: different activities require different behavior patterns, or participants; different activities evoke diverse behavior patterns, or respondent behaviors, from participants; both constitutent performances and respondent behaviors are determined by the activity-setting, relatively independent of the individual participants' personality characteristics; the resultant behaviors have important consequences for the individuals and group that are relevant to treatment objectives; and these behaviors may be deliberately achieved or modified by the informal selection or modification of particular activities. At the same time, Vinter (1967, p. 101) justifiably acknowledges certain deficiencies of his schema at its present stage of development. The six dimensions, for instance, are not mutually exclusive. At certain points they overlap substantially. Moreover, they may not be inclusive of all relevant activities or activity characteristics. It is difficult to rate activities systematically, notwithstanding the contributions of Whittaker, since there are no standard scales or units of measurement for the activity-setting dimensions. Additionally, it is difficult to predict the particular type of respondent behavior expected as a consequence of the activity-setting dimensions. It is also difficult to predict the intensity of behavior and other of its qualitative characteristics, including its sequencing in relation to other possible respondent behaviors. Finally, of course, it is difficult to estimate the extent to which a given activity-setting dimension, or cluster of dimensions, explains the variance in the particular respondent behavior(s) under consideration. Hostility, for example, may be more attributable to high prescriptiveness and little participant interactiveness than to an unequal reward structure, or vice versa. Without systematic and interrelated measurement scales it is virtually impossible to make evaluations such as the foregoing. Consequently the scheme's utility is highly limited. Its particular advantage inheres, however, in the fact that the referents, or indicators, of the main variables (activities) are behavioral phenomena, are highly visible, and are amenable to monitoring even though, as noted previously, the monitoring of interaction effects between two or more activities or behaviors represents a highly complex undertaking.

Development. The last major indirect means of influence discussed by Vinter is group development. Since this topic was accorded separate and extensive attention in Chapter Two, only a few pertinent points will be noted here. By influencing a group's development over time, a therapist obviously exerts indirect influences upon one or more selected group members. A group worker may endeavor to increase the speed of a group's development by encouraging more frequent group meetings, by revising the group's composition, or through other means. Conversely, if so desired, he may wish to retard the rate of a group's development. For example, in order to reduce the possibility of delinquent behavior a worker may seek to prevent norm consensus, especially regarding deviant norms, among the members of a delinquent gang. Although this action would retard the rate of group development in the usual sense of the term it could, nonetheless, mark a distinct forward step toward the attainment of a group's treatment goals. Consequently it is possible, and sometimes preferable, to distinguish between group developmental processes that are independent of treatment and those that refer to developments associated with the treatment process. Although Vinter has suggested that these are analogous, this need not necessarily be the case.

In addition to affecting the rate of group development, the worker can influence its direction (forward progress or retrogression) and various qualitative aspects of development. The worker also can differentially influence various group structures (such as the power, leadership, friendship, communication, and task structures), which, in turn, affect the type and rate of group development. Likewise, to some extent he can determine which group members occupy given positions within those structures. Finally, he must act both to effect treatment at any given moment and to assure the attainment of long-term treatment objectives. These actions require continuous attention not only to immediate events, but to the ultimate development of the group as a viable instrument for treatment.

Diagnosis and Intervention: An Illustration

Although many social functioning problems lend themselves readily to analysis and corrective action from a traditional group work perspective, one particularly good illustration is scapegoating behavior in small groups. This problem is especially germane since scapegoating behavior clearly involves social interaction between one or more individuals and their peers, has etiological components at both the individual and group levels of analysis, and provides useful interventive foci at both levels. The present illustration will draw in large part from portions of an earlier and more comprehensive discussion set forth elsewhere (Feldman, 1969b).

The literature of the social sciences and related helping professions reveals two basic perspectives regarding scapegoating processes in small groups and other social environments. On the one hand, scapegoating frequently has been posited as the result of a group's efforts to foster or maintain integration (Coser, 1956; Dentler and Erikson, 1959; Klapp, 1954; Shulman, 1967; Theodorson, 1962). Thus, for example, Vogel and Bell (1960) suggest that clinical observations of families with an emotionally disturbed child frequently indicate that the child's illness has been fostered and/or sustained by intense scapegoating by his parents. Among other reasons, they posit that such scapegoating behavior tends to provide the parents with an area of common agreement and behavioral orientation, noting that this is relatively common in marital relationships that otherwise might be highly fragile and easily subject to disruption. In marriages where the spouses maintain rigid and superficial communication patterns and, furthermore, in which their social relationships are extremely tenuous, this source of common agreement tends to give the partners an otherwise unobtainable bond. Nonetheless, though scapegoating behavior may stabilize the marital relationship, it obviously damages the scapegoated child.

In contrast, a number of other writers suggest that scapegoating behavior primarily represents the specific provocations, deviant behaviors, or ineptitude of the scapegoated individual (Bretsch, 1952; Commoss, 1962; Davids and Parenti, 1958). As is frequently true when extreme positions are advocated, it appears altogether plausible that a middle-ground position may be more defensible than a single-minded adherence to either of the others. Critical factors at both the individual and group levels of analysis may contribute to the emergence and perpetuation of scapegoating behavior. Since it may be impossible (or, if possible, probably useless) to discover the original causes of such behavior, it is suggested that the therapist focus upon the current conditions that sustain it at *both* the individual and group levels, and orient his interventions accordingly.

In diagnosing the client's problem, the worker should focus upon those aspects of the client's behavior and personality that indicate the manner in which he provokes, sustains, or reacts to scapegoating by peers. An individual's spontaneous reactions to scapegoating are often counterproductive and, in effect, may reinforce those group members who engage in the scapegoating behavior. Further, the worker should seek information regarding the ways in which the scapegoated individual, his peers, and relevant others in the environment view his problems. He may wish to obtain information regarding relevant background characteristics of the client and his family, school, employment, and other peer group environments. Since scapegoating, in large part, can be considered a group-level problem, it is germane also to gather similar information regarding the other individuals in the group.

Among the most important diagnostic information is that obtained from the worker's observations of ongoing social interaction within the treatment group. The worker, for example, desires data regarding the client's orientation to the treatment group and the bases for his attraction to it. Also, it will be essential for the worker to determine the client's positions in varying group structures, including the power, task, communication, affectional, normative, and formal structures. Similarly, he will wish to delineate key patterns of the client's role behavior, including areas of program interest, reactions to program process, contributions to key group functions, and so forth. Consonant with the group-level features of scapegoating behavior, the worker also will wish to accumulate similar information for the other group members. These data will permit analyses of the overall patterning of various group structures and, therefore, will serve as an invaluable complement to information concerning the particular client's position within such structures.

Once the therapist is armed with the necessary background material, the dynamic nature of those social forces involved in scapegoating behavior will be apparent. It should reveal the manner in which interrelationships among all the group's members tend to sustain and reinforce scapegoating, as well as the client's locations in various social structures relevant to his functioning. The therapist can then assess the conditions that impede positive change for the client and those that can facilitate desired change. Consequently it will be easier to formulate relevant treatment goals for both the individual and the group and, moreover, to focus interventions at both levels.

Although each individual case must be examined closely for its own particular idiosyncrasy, the remainder of this illustration will benefit from reference to one of the few empirical studies of scapegoating behavior in children's groups (Feldman, 1969a, 1969b). Since the data are based upon a broad sample, they may be generalizable to a variety of peer groups. The sample was comprised of 807 children, members of ninety children's groups at residential summer camps. There were 423 subjects in forty-nine boys' groups and 384 subjects in forty-one girls' groups. The members of each group roomed together, ate together, and frequently participated in recreational and work activities as a unit. The subjects ranged in age from eight to sixteen years, and group size varied from six to thirteen members. The average number of members per group was nine and the mode was ten.

As part of a larger study, the subjects answered questionnaires designed to assess the extent to which they adhered to the norms of their peer group, the extent to which they contributed to the performance of basic group functions, such as goal attainment, pattern maintenance, and external relations, the extent of social power, or interpersonal influence, that they exercised over their peers, and the extent to which they liked, and were liked by, their peers. In addition, each subject participated in a brief experimental test designed to assess his susceptibility to perceived peer group conformity pressures. Through the utilization of specially designed indices (Feldman, 1968, pp. 35–38) it was possible, also, to assess differential levels of *group* norm consensus, interpersonal liking, power dispersion, and distribution of responsibilities for the performance of key group functions, along with indications of the group's overall success at performing such functions. The foregoing measures refer to varying structural features of groups and, therefore, have been defined respectively as measures of group normative integration, interpersonal integration, power integration, and functional integration.

The data indicated that approximately 10 percent of the groups studied were characterized by the presence of an intensely disliked, or scapegoated, individual. Should this incidence be characteristic of other groups in the larger society, scapegoating may be considered a fairly pervasive social phenomenon. The incidence of scapegoating behavior was *not* found to vary according to subjects' sex, age, social class, camp auspices, or group size.

Analysis of the data revealed that both individual and group level attributes were integrally related to the occurrence of scapegoating. At the individual level, it was found that scapegoated group members attained significantly lower normative integration scores than their peers. That is, they clearly deviated from norms shared by the other members of their group. It was not possible to ascertain whether this occurred as a result of conscious choice or inadvertently, as, for example, from an inability to clearly perceive the group's norms for one reason or another. In addition, scapegoated group members received significantly lower functional integration scores than their peers, contributing significantly less than their peers to *all* three group functions analyzed: goal attainment (helping the group to attain its preselected goals), pattern maintenance (helping to maintain harmony among members in the group), and external

relations (helping the group to establish and sustain viable relationships with other individuals and groups in the immediate environs).
Once again, whether this was due to the scapegoated members'
conscious rejection of such roles or to their exclusion from such roles
by peers was impossible to ascertain and, moreover, of minor importance for treatment purposes. Once put into motion, it appears
that the foregoing considerations are mutually interrelated and, in
effect, contribute to the creation of a vicious cycle wherein peer
rejection contributes to withdrawal from key role performances, and
vice versa. Consequently, relevant treatment interventions may be
directed toward either or both foci of the problem.

The reciprocal and self-reinforcing nature of scapegoating
behavior was further illustrated by the observation that scapegoated
individuals obtained significantly lower interpersonal integration
scores than their peers. That is, their peers expressed very low liking
for them and, in turn, they indicated especially low liking for their
peers. Given either one of the foregoing social phenomena, it would
appear highly probable that the other will follow. And, finally, the
data also revealed that scapegoated members were characterized by
significantly lower social power—the likelihood of exerting social
influence—than their peers.

At the group level, it was found that groups with a scapegoated child tended to have significantly lower levels of functional
integration and interpersonal integration than groups without such a
child. This finding was corroborated even when the significantly
lower scores of the scapegoated child were excluded from all calcu-
lations. In other words, in groups with a scapegoated child the other
members tended to like one another less than did members in groups
without such a child. Similarly, groups with a scapegoated child
were relatively less successful at performing key group functions and
at distributing them relatively equally among the members. Once
again, a number of plausible interpretations suggest themselves. The
members' incapacity to cope with environmental pressures or attain
internally designated goals may have caused them to vent their
frustrations upon the scapegoated member and, to a lesser extent,
upon one another. Or, perhaps, because of the scapegoated member's particular ineptitude or lack of concern for the peer group's
interests, the group experienced significant failures at attaining

various goals and maintaining an adequate level of interpersonal liking. Once again, regardless of the initiating behaviors, it appears likely that each phenomenon reinforced and contributed to the exacerbation of the other. Consequently, effective group work interventions might be geared toward a variety of foci.

Additionally, it is pertinent to note that groups with scapegoated children were characterized by either extremely low *or* extremely high levels of normative integration, or norm consensus. Consequently, as suggested by Vogel and Bell (1960), it is possible that the members' efforts to develop at least minimal norm consensus eventuated in a shared disliking and rejection of the scapegoated peer. And, in the case of those groups with high normative integration, this may indeed have been a most effective means of bolstering the group's level of norm consensus.

Clearly, then, scapegoating behavior may represent the interplay between individual and group-level factors and, as such, constitutes a problem highly susceptible to social group work intervention. The deadly combination of low commitment to group norms, inadequate performance of important group functions, low liking for peers, and low social power practically ensures scapegoat status for a group member. Moreover, once relegated to the scapegoat position, related studies suggest that the individual is likely to encounter further impediments that will exacerbate his social functioning problem. Thus, it has been shown that group members tend to afford less latitude for deviant or undesirable behavior to low-status members than to high-status members (Hollander, 1958; Sabath, 1964) and to misjudge (Sherif and others, 1955) or fail to recognize (Pastore, 1960) the desirable or nondeviant behavior of low-status members. The latter tendencies occur in part, it has been suggested, because positive acts are less salient and compelling than negative ones (Pastore, 1960).

Such results suggest numerous opportunities for direct and indirect group work interventions oriented toward disruption of the afore-described self-perpetuating cycle. Thus, for instance, greater commitment to group norms can be fostered directly through the clarification or positive reinforcement of such norms for the scapegoated member or, conversely, by nonreinforcement or negative sanctioning of countergroup norms. In accord with the direct modes of intervention cited by Vinter, the group worker may attempt to make his own normative behaviors more visible to the scapegoated individual, thus establishing and reinforcing the legitimate nature of such behavior. By modeling normative behavior, the worker may induce the scapegoated member to identify with or emulate such behavior, thus drawing him closer to the group's accepted behavioral standards and, therefore, to acceptance by the other members. In addition, the worker may serve as a spokesman for legitimate group norms, if necessary, by verbalizing them and explicating them to the deviant member. Or, by drawing upon his capacities as a possible stimulator or executive controller of membership roles, he may urge the scapegoated member to assume positions in the group that require the performance of normatively prescribed behavior. In fact, he may at least temporarily assign the member to such positions within the group.

The group worker also may facilitate such endeavors through indirect interventions. He might attempt to diminish the group's size in order to foster the development of a more visible and highly integrated norm structure, should one have been lacking. Such an interventive strategy also would enable closer monitoring of normative behavior. Similarly, the worker may structure certain program activities and/or group operating procedures that will afford greater opportunities for the scapegoated member to observe and experiment with normative behavior should this be considered a desirable treatment goal. Once such behavior occurs, it is noteworthy that the scapegoated member's norm-sharing is likely to contribute to enhanced liking for peers, greater willingness to work toward group goals, increased legitimate power within the group, and greater esteem and liking *from* peers (Berger, 1952; Deutsch and Solomon, 1959; Dittes, 1959; Gouldner, 1960; Julian and Steiner, 1961; Kiesler, 1963; Maehr and others, 1962; McIntyre, 1952; Norman, 1953; Reese, 1966; Sherwood, 1965; Videbeck, 1960; Zelen, 1954). Consequently, the worker's direct and indirect interventions with reference to this single variable may provide several points of entry for disrupting the dysfunctional cycle of events associated with scapegoating behavior.

Workers can also intervene effectively by facilitating the scapegoated member's performance of important group functions.

In addition to the stimulation of proper normative motivation for such functioning, the worker can directly model or teach essential task or socioemotional skills to the members and can provide them with resources that will facilitate their goal attainment efforts. Workers can arrange program activities that will permit the visible display of skills and abilities already a part of the scapegoated individual's repertoire. As such members adhere more closely to group norms, exhibit valued skills, and contribute to the attainment of group goals, they are likely to be received more favorably by their peers and to be attributed increasing power within the group. Additionally, the worker may attempt to further the scapegoat's interpersonal integration into the group in at least two ways. On the one hand, he may endeavor to enhance the scapegoat's awareness and appreciation of his peers' positive attributes. On the other, he may exert influence to make the scapegoated individual more attractive to his peers. This may be facilitated indirectly by structuring activities that call for cooperative relationships among all concerned in order to achieve a valued group goal. Or, by utilizing direct modes of intervention, he may actually stimulate and encourage the other members to develop friendship relations with one another, may assert legitimate norms regarding the importance of friendship and liking relations for the group, or may actually assign members certain positions or functions that are conducive to the furtherance of friendship relations.

In order to augment the scapegoated individual's social power a number of additional interventions may be posited. It should be noted, however, that many of the foregoing worker activities themselves are likely to enhance the scapegoat's power. Reference to the five bases of social power (referent, expert, reward, coercive, and legitimate) cited by French and Raven (1959) is particularly illustrative at this juncture. For instance, by fostering friendship relations between the scapegoat and his peers, the former's *referent power* is likely to be augmented, that is, that mode of power based upon the group members' attraction to him. By coaching the scapegoat in skills necessary for the effective performance of essential group functions, the worker is likely to increase the client's *expert power*. Each of the foregoing is likely to enhance the client's capacity to help his peers and, therefore, to exert *reward power*. Conversely, the capacity to withdraw such resources, should they be valued, enables the client to exert *coercive power* over his peers. Although this latter form of social power is least desirable, since it oftentimes entails undesired side effects (such as distrust, hostility, and dislike), it may nonetheless temporarily reverse the scapegoating cycle by providing the individual with substantially more leverage to determine his fate than previously. Finally, through investing the scapegoated member with certain privileges and responsibilities within the group, such as a formal office or a clearly defined function to perform, the worker may enhance his *legitimate power* and, therefore, his acceptance by the other group members. The client's legitimate power also may be strengthened by the worker's modeling of acceptance of the client, especially when he displays positive behavior, and by the worker's reaffirmation of *each* member's legitimate rights and obligations within the group. Frequently the latter may take the form of a verbal explanation of the group's importance as a treatment vehicle and a statement of each member's responsibility to work assiduously toward that end.

The foregoing suggestions are set forth merely as illustrations of possible interventive strategies associated with the traditional social group work method. They represent but a few of many possible types of interventions. However, for the particular problem cited it is especially desirable to direct a number of critical interventions toward the group per se as well as toward the particular scapegoated individual. Since scapegoating is viewed in part as a response to maladaptive group conditions, including low functional integration, interpersonal integration and, sometimes, normative integration, the use of interventions affecting such group conditions may indirectly alleviate many of the underlying factors contributing to maintenance of the scapegoating behavior.

At the group level, for instance, worker interventions designed to facilitate greater social interaction and communication, the attainment of group goals, and a broader sharing of functional responsibilities may serve indirectly to improve members' attitudes toward one another and, additionally, toward the scapegoated individual. Program activities should be directed toward goals that are readily attainable by the group and permit all members to contribute to the group's program either conjointly or serially. Activities that present insurmountable or unduly frustrating barriers to goal attainment, or that demand an inordinately long time to complete, are likely to encourage or prolong the manifestation of interpersonal disliking within the group.

At the group level, members' dislike for one another may be reduced by revising group normative patterns. The worker may approach such revisions by one of two strategies: by enhancement of normative integration for groups initially characterized by low norm consensus or, conversely, by diminution of normative integration for groups in which the scapegoated member serves as a focus for the clarification and reinforcement of dysfunctional norms. In the former instance, norm consensus can be promoted by a variety of means, including direct positive and/or negative reinforcement by the worker or fellow group members, by the clarification and crystallization of ambiguous or latent group norms, and by the introduction of program activities that require the elaboration and retention of normative behaviors, such as cooperation and sharing, that are likely to prove useful beyond the group's immediate social environment. Support for deviant or dysfunctional group norms can be weakened through the introduction of program activities that provide negative sanctioning or, even more preferably, no reinforcement (that is, extinction) following their manifestation. The worker also can achieve this objective by executing interventions that stimulate the elaboration of additional, conflicting, or substitute group norms. In this manner he can systematically alter qualitative aspects of the group's normative integration and, consequently, exert influence upon those conditions that promote, sustain, or diminish scapegoating behavior.

Finally, it should be noted that social work efforts designed to cope with the powerlessness of scapegoated members ought to be directed toward the group as well as the individual level. Power is a relative social phenomenon that is exerted and measured primarily through the interaction between two or more individuals. A person cannot be powerless unless some other individual in his immediate environment is capable of exerting greater power than he can, nor can he be deemed powerful if there is no one in the environment over whom he can exert his influence. Similarly, his relative power position will be attenuated if others who are usually considered rather powerless are suddenly granted resources or skills that increase their capabilities for influencing one another. The diminution or fragmentation of other members' social power is likely to enhance the relative social position of the scapegoated group member. At the same time, however, this interventive tactic may diminish the group's overall capacity to achieve its goals and, therefore, may exacerbate some of the conditions leading to scapegoating behavior.

Activities that facilitate the redistribution or dispersion of important resources among group members and provide members with relatively equal reward and expert power are likely to enhance members' tendencies to like one another. Once again, however, depending upon the particular tasks confronting the group, such a redistribution of power may or may not be conducive to effective goal attainment and, therefore, to members' liking for one another and subsequent scapegoating behavior. If the group must perform complex tasks that require considerable coordination of effort, an egalitarian distribution of power may militate against effective goal attainment. But if the group's successful goal attainment depends upon uninhibited and creative contributions by virtually all of its members, such a power distribution may be the most desirable of all possibilities. From a long-term perspective, the relative social powerlessness of certain group members, and concomitant tendencies toward scapegoating, are most likely to be attenuated through the development and institutionalization of group operating and governing procedures that assure recognition and acceptance of the legitimate rights, responsibilities, and resources of all the members.

In summary, then, the scapegoating illustration points to the efficacy of a broad variety of interventive strategies directed toward the elimination of a single and discrete behavioral problem. Interventions may be direct or indirect, and may be geared toward the scapegoated individual or toward his peers. As in the real world, some modes of intervention may produce countervailing influences that can inhibit movement toward the worker's treatment goals for a given member. Optimally, a given mode of intervention produces a large number of positive effects upon the group's functioning and, in concert, they all will considerably enhance the group's effectiveness as a treatment vehicle. Although many theoreticians opt for more simplified and clear-cut formulations, in doing so they necessarily retreat from the complex interactions observed in the open community, considerably reducing the possibilities for treatment intervention. The foregoing formulation takes into account the multiplicity of etiological and sustaining forces influencing maladaptive behavior and, accordingly, the numerous interventive foci for group work practice. The immense complexity of such an approach prevents the elaboration of a thoroughly informed and systematic interventive schema at this point in its intellectual and empirical development. Nonetheless, the efficacy of the approach, even at this stage of development, represents a measurable empirical question and, moreover, one that necessarily must be examined in order to determine its utility in accord with the canons of professional therapeutic practice.

Summary

This chapter has discussed various modalities of group work intervention associated with the traditional method. Both direct and indirect interventive procedures were described. Among the former are the worker's utilization as a central person, as a symbol and spokesman, as a motivator and stimulator, and as a controller of membership roles. Indirect interventions include those that focus upon group purposes, the selection of group members, the group's size, group operating and governing procedures, and programing. Application of many of the above procedures was illustrated through the discussion of scapegoating behavior in children's groups.

V

Group Level
Behavior Modification

During the past decade social workers have shown heightened interest in behavior modification for the development of conceptual and practice principles (Thomas, 1967a, 1968; Gambrill, Thomas, and Carter, 1971; Thomas and Carter, 1971). However, there have been few efforts to apply this knowledge to the practice of social group work (see Rose, 1967, 1969, 1971, 1972; Aronowitz and Weinberg, 1966; Lawrence and Sundel, 1972; Wodarski, Feldman, and Flax, 1973). Moreover, virtually all such endeavors have shown a pronounced tendency to reiterate behavior modification concepts at the individual level of analysis rather than to extend them to the group level. And, as with earlier efforts to develop practice theory, such endeavors have viewed the group more as a *context* for the application of interventive techniques than as the *means* for such activities (Vinter, 1967). In the present chapter, we demonstrate the utility of selected behavior modification techniques for work with antisocial children in groups. It should be noted, however, that our focus is not solely upon a given population at risk, namely antisocial children, but also upon the *group level* application of behavior modification knowledge and, more importantly, upon the utilization of group contingencies for social work intervention.

The presentation begins with a theoretical framework for the application of behavior modification principles drawn extensively from the operant model. Where relevant, knowledge from the behavior modification theoretical frameworks of respondent and observational learning are utilized, as are empirical concepts from the field of social psychology—role, leadership, attitude change, and so forth. Next, we discuss the use of behavior modification techniques in order to establish relationships within groups of antisocial children. In subsequent sections, verbal communication and other behavioral techniques for increasing prosocial behavior will be discussed. Then the application of group contingencies in groups of antisocial children is reviewed. To date, discussion of the latter topic has appeared virtually nowhere in the social work literature. Finally, we discuss some theoretical issues that ought to be resolved if such techniques are to become more valid, powerful, and relevant for social group work practice.

Historical Development

The assumption that human beings are motivated to seek pleasure and to avoid pain—which is the central assumption of the operant model—can be traced as far back as the writings of the ancient Greek philosophers Epicurus and Aristippus (Gergen, 1969).* This assumption formed the historical basis for the philosophical doctrines of hedonism and utilitarianism, and became an integral part of Freud's psychoanalytic theory, as elaborated in terms of the pleasure-pain principle. Thorndike, early in the present century, engaged in a series of investigations which confirmed the validity of this assumption and which subsequently resulted in his postulation of the "law of effect" (Kimble, 1961). This law specified that responses that are followed by satisfying events are more likely than others to recur in the future; responses followed by unsatisfying events are less likely to recur.

---

* This section primarily provides the reader with basic details about the history of the operant model. For a detailed review of the historical development of other theoretical frameworks (respondent and modeling), see Ullmann and Krasner (1965, pp. 50–59); Yates (1970, pp. 3–23); Kimble, (1961, pp. 14–43); McLaughlin (1971, pp. 1–48).

A modern version of the foregoing principle is stated in Skinner's formulation of the law of the operant, which purports that the consequences that follow a behavior determine the probability of its recurrence. Hence behaviors followed by consequences that an individual evaluates positively are more likely to occur in the future than are other behaviors. Likewise, responses that are followed by negative events are less likely to recur (Skinner, 1953). Based upon these postulates, the operant model has been used successfully to modify the behaviors exhibited by a variety of children, including those who are autistic (Browning, 1971; Ferster, 1961; Gelfand and Hartman, 1968; Grossberg, 1965; Hamblin, Buckholdt, and others, 1971; Wolf, Risley, and Mees, 1964), hyperactive (Hamblin, Buckholdt, and others, 1971; Patterson, 1965; Patterson, Jones, and others, 1965; Doubros and Daniels, 1966; Twardosz and Sajwaj, 1972), and retarded (Berkowitz, Sherry, and Davis, 1971; Tate, 1972; O'Brien, Bugle, and Azrin, 1972; Foxx and Azrin, 1972; Vukelich and Hake, 1971; Whitman, Mercurio, and Caponigri, 1970). Related studies have focused on inner-city children with various behavior and learning problems, including deficient verbal, reading, and arithmetic performance (Hall, Panyan, and others, 1968; Hamblin, Buckholdt, and others, 1971; Hamblin, Hathaway, and Wodarski, 1971; Reynolds and Risley, 1968; Staats and Butterfield, 1965; Staats, Minke, and Butts, 1970; Wasik, Senn, and others, 1969; Wodarski, Hamblin, and others, 1972; Wodarski, Hamblin, and others, 1973; Wolf, Giles, and Hall, 1968). The coming years probably will witness the increasing application of Skinner's basic postulates to the alleviation of key societal problems.

Theoretical Framework

Behavior modification involves the application of specific techniques derived from social learning theory to produce behavioral changes in individuals (Ullmann and Krasner, 1965). Behavior modification theorists endeavor to determine the relationships between environmental variables and a person's behavior since, by definition, control over the former is likely to yield control over the latter (Reese, 1966). This is true whether the controlling agent is the worker or, as is the ultimate goal of all treatment, the client himself.

The basic concepts in the operant model are the probabilities of a behavior occurring and the events which control the rate of its occurrence (Skinner, 1969). The central focus is on changing rates of behavior or, in technical terms, the frequency of a given behavior per a given unit of time. Hence behavior modification theorists are concerned with gaining knowledge about, and control over, the events in a person's environment that immediately precede and follow the target behavior. These events control the rates of the target behaviors and, in large part, they can be modified in order to alter the client's own behaviors. To examine these, the worker must be capable of developing descriptive statements about events that affect rates of behavior. In turn, this requires that the relevant behaviors, including those to be changed, are quantifiable. Behavior modification does not concern itself with internal causes of behavior (such as unconscious hostilities, inadequate ego controls, and unresolved Oedipal conflicts), which are dealt with in terms of external interpersonal constructs, if at all. The focus is solely on observable behaviors, which are defined as the observable responses of human activity (Thomas, 1968). The proponents of the model believe that observable constructs lead to a more precise and reproducible account of causal behavioral change than do earlier models, which typically posit inner psychic phenomena as prerequisites for behavioral change.

Two basic procedures are central to behavior modification practice:

1. Analysis of the occurrence of target behaviors chosen for modification, especially in terms of observable events. This procedure necessitates that the target behaviors be defined in such a manner that two persons can agree consistently that they have, in fact, occurred.

2. Securing systematic data to determine if the isolated events (antecedents and consequents) differentially influence rates of the target behaviors chosen for modification (Baer, Wolf, and Risley, 1968; Bijou, Peterson, and others, 1969; Bijou, 1970).

✻ The basic goal of behavior modification treatment is the alteration of maladaptive behaviors through application of the same principles that governed the learning of those behaviors. Within such a framework, both the theorist and the therapist posit that a client's environment—including his peers—can shape, increase, decrease, or maintain his behaviors (Ullmann and Krasner, 1965). More generally, they posit that virtually any response of any individual can be conditioned (Reese, 1966; Logan, 1972). With particular reference to antisocial children, it is assumed that there exists a significant deficit of prosocial behaviors, primarily because such children's environments have not provided sufficient reinforcements for prosocial behavior or there exists a significant surfeit of antisocial behaviors, attributable also to corresponding environmental reinforcements. Interestingly, many early formulations concerning juvenile delinquency have been based upon similar premises. Among the foremost are the theories of differential association (Short, 1957; Sutherland and Cressey, 1966; Voss, 1969) and subcultural delinquency (Kvareceus and Miller, 1959; Miller, 1958; 1970). It is also noteworthy that some earlier versions of those formulations have been reconceptualized in terms of contemporary behavior modification theory (Hindelang, 1970; Jeffrey, 1965).

Social group workers who use a behavior modification approach with antisocial children should attempt to specify those behaviors that they wish to change, such as fighting, inability to concentrate on a given task, uncooperative behavior, verbal aggression, destruction of property, and so forth. They should then proceed to determine the antecedent and consequent events that determine the learning and retention of those behaviors. Utilizing the methods described below, they should endeavor to reduce the frequency of such behaviors over time by differentially influencing relevant antecedent and consequent events. Moreover, they may wish to specify new behaviors that are considered desirable and, concomitantly, to control additional social antecedents and consequences that will foster the emergence of such behavior.

Cognitive behavior modification. Until recently, behavior modification theorists have focused primarily on environmental factors and their functional consequences for controlling or changing a person's behavior. In recent years, however, behavior modification theorists also have shown increased interest in the cognitive components of behavior. Many investigators have posited that cognitive behaviors operate according to the same principles that govern overt human behaviors. Cognitive behaviors are defined as internal thought processes, such as the process of thinking, imagining events, forming concepts or ideas, and so forth. This has led to greater emphasis upon using behavior modification treatment to help clients gain cognitive control over their overt behaviors. The approach requires the client to learn how to control his behavior primarily through two techniques: by structuring consequences for appropriate behaviors and by eliminating or controlling antecedent conditions that cause those behaviors (Cautela, 1966; 1967; 1969 and 1970; Ascher and Cautela, 1972; Flannery, 1972). Thus, a child who has been erratic in school performance can be taught to use self-reinforcement when his behaviors are productive, and to avoid those events that cause him to do poorly in school, for example, arguments with parents, excessive fatigue, and so forth.

Analogous developments have been evident in social work as it has shifted to and fro between an emphasis upon the individual and upon his larger social environment. Half a century ago, Mary Richmond placed great emphasis on the social environment as a key diagnostic and treatment variable in her explication of social diagnosis. Her perspective might well have been considered an early forerunner of current operant models, wherein changes in environmental events are assumed to lead to alterations in clients' behavior. A more recent integration of social work's historical concern with individual personalities and their social environments has been achieved, in part, in Florence Hollis's *Casework: A Psycho-Social Therapy*. Hollis (1965) embraces a broad conceptualization of diagnosis and treatment, which emphasizes that a person must be evaluated within the context of his total stimulus environment. This, in turn, consists of environmental and cognitive phenomena. Her emphasis parallels current developments in behavior therapy, which not only stress assessment of the individual's external environment but also consider the individual's internal cognitive environment. Recent research indicates that this renewed focus may help to make the operant model much more productive than it has been heretofore.

Operant behavior. In order to present a theoretical framework for group-level behavior modification, a number of key concepts must be explicated. Among the most essential is *operant behavior.* Operant behavior may be defined as any behavior that is strengthened or weakened by the consequences that follow it

(Reese, 1966). Such behaviors constitute central diagnostic and interventive foci for both caseworkers and group workers. All verbal, cognitive, and physical behaviors have operant components. The basic factors that define an operant behavior are twofold: the behavioral events that occur just prior to its occurrence, and the behavioral consequences that occur immediately after its manifestation.

Social work practice focuses largely on verbal behavior. Verbal communication is deemed essential in order to accomplish changes in both cognitive and physical behaviors exhibited by a client. These include behaviors that may occur outside of the treatment context, such as meeting the demands of home and school environments, exerting more self-control, coping with adults, communicating more openly with authority figures, resisting negative peer influences, and so forth. Most of the relevant literature pertaining to the operant model focuses upon verbal conditioning (Salzinger, 1969; Matarazzo and Wiens, 1972). Essentially, this literature indicates that certain positive reinforcers, such as smiling, nodding, eye contact, and standard statements of a positive nature (such as "Please elaborate" and "Tell me more about that") which occur after a client's verbalizations, tend to increase desired verbalizations in the therapeutic context. Thus, for example, a group of children who have been consistently unable to carry out reasonable requests from authority figures might be encouraged to discuss their difficulties in conjunction with the worker's positive statements of praise. Discussion of possible solutions could be fostered by a worker through the use of positive reinforcing statements. However, a question still to be resolved in social work practice pertains to whether or not this type of verbal conditioning is beneficial over the long term. Available data do not clearly support the view that such learning necessarily, in fact, carries over into the verbal and physical behaviors that clients exhibit after they leave the therapeutic context (Bergin and Garfield, 1971).

Reinforcers. Data reported by a number of investigators readily support the view that maladaptive activities of antisocial children ought to be regarded as behaviors that can be either increased or decreased through the provision of appropriate consequences following their occurrence (Cohen, Filipczak, and Bis, 1967;

Burchard and Tyler, 1965; Schwitzgebel and Kolb, 1964; Shah, 1966; Tharp and Wetzel, 1969; Tyler and Brown, 1967; Wetzel, 1966; Cohen and Filipczak, 1971; Bailey, Timbers, and others, 1971; Boren and Colman, 1970; Bailey, Wolf, and Phillips, 1970; Phillips, Phillips, and others, 1971; Phillips, 1968; Fixsen, Phillips, and Wolf, 1972; Patterson, 1973; Fixsen, Phillips, and Wolf, 1973; Fixsen, Wolf, and Phillips, 1973; Phillips, Phillips, and others, 1973). Such consequences are commonly known as *reinforcers,* or as reinforcing stimuli. Specifically, reinforcers are defined as consequences that affect the future occurrence of operant behaviors (Morse, 1966).

A *positive reinforcer* is a consequence that follows a behavior and increases the probability of that behavior's occurrence in the future (Reese, 1966). Usually, three types of positive reinforcers are considered by investigators: primary, secondary, and generalized. Examples of *primary positive reinforcers* are food, water, and sexual release. Such factors tend to be reinforcing due to their inherent biological properties (Keller, 1954). The reinforcing power of these variables increases in proportion to the person's deprivation of them. Reinforcers such as candy (a primary positive reinforcer) frequently are offered to autistic children in order to help them establish eye contact, and to enlarge their repertoires of certain behaviors, such as social and linguistic skills (Hamblin, Buckholdt, and others, 1971). Primary reinforcers rarely are utilized intentionally in social group work practice. Nonetheless, their inadvertent use is frequent, and may result in many side benefits. This notion will be discussed later.

A stimulus with neutral reinforcing properties can acquire positive reinforcing properties through repeated association with another stimulus which has positive properties. Once acquired, this type of reinforcer becomes a *secondary positive reinforcer,* or a conditioned positive reinforcer (Kimble, 1961). Secondary reinforcement occurs, for example, when a teacher offers candy bars to children for working mathematics problems toward a certain level of performance, and then pairs distribution of the candy bars with a verbally reinforcing expression, such as "Good!" After a number of associations, the children will work for the expression "Good!" since, through its pairing with candy, it has gained reinforcing properties.

During the early phases of treatment, a group may be neither positively nor negatively valued by its members. In effect, it can possess neutral reinforcing properties. However, if subsequent participation in the group were to yield enhanced prestige (an important positive reinforcer), the group itself could become a secondary positive reinforcement through its pairing with the original reinforcer (prestige). Since the members might have acquired considerable reinforcement value for one another by that point, mere participation in the group could become highly reinforcing and satisfying, regardless of immediate prestige outcomes. Similarly, if group members can develop social adjustment skills which enable them to earn other positive reinforcers, such as money, the group itself is likely to assume the status of a secondary positive reinforcer. This mode of attraction to the group is characteristic of what Sarri and Galinsky have denoted as the "maturation phase" of group development (see Chapter Two). Various features of the group, such as the members, worker, situational context, or activities, may assume the properties of a secondary reinforcer (Staats, 1970).

The use of reinforcers is not new to social workers. Typically, practitioners endeavor to make themselves more attractive to clients through the careful dispensation of primary reinforcers. They may take children for a soft drink after a group meeting, assist a mother with a task, or help a client to overcome an operational difficulty in securing employment. It is through such actions, which provide reinforcement for clients, that therapists and others acquire secondary reinforcing properties.

Social workers utilize a variety of reinforcers in clinical practice. Typically, clients are more inclined to return for subsequent meetings if a social worker can proceed through a series of anxiety-reducing operations with them during the first meeting. Providing structure, defining a problem, and talking about means of remedying it can lead to the reduction of anxiety. Through this process, clients gain reinforcement and the social worker acquires reinforcing properties (Berscheid and Walster, 1969). Clients are reinforced for their participation when the therapist smiles, nods his head, and uses positive verbal statements. If skillfully applied, this approach provides incentives for clients' continued participation and it increases the attractiveness of the practice context which, in turn, strengthens the chances that clients will continue in treatment.

A stimulus that (1) follows a behavior and (2) enables the individual to secure other reinforcers is called a *generalized reinforcer*. In certain treatment milieus "tokens" have been used as generalized reinforcers (Ayllon and Azrin, 1968; Kazdin and Bootzin, 1972). These are exchangeable for valued items such as cigarettes, food, and home furloughs. In everyday life, resources such as money and prestige are common generalized reinforcers because they can be readily exchanged for other desired items. Skillful social work practice can enable clients to secure generalized reinforcers readily. For example, when a client is helped to gain employment, he not only gains self-worth but also secures other needed items such as food, housing, and so forth, through the money that he earns.

Intervention to Decrease Undesirable Behaviors

At least six types of behavior-modification interventions can be utilized in social group work practice in order to decrease undesired behaviors. These are punishment, avoidance conditioning, escape conditioning, time out, stimulus control, and extinction (Bandura, 1969). *Punishment* involves applying a stimulus after a behavior occurs which, in effect, decreases the probability of that behavior occurring in the future. When a client broaches an irrelevant topic, for example, one can punish him by changing the discussion to another topic, by probing another area before he is prepared for it, by suggesting that his behavior is inappropriate, or by exhibiting physical expressions of disinterest, such as frowns or grimaces, a disapproving physical posture, and so forth. It is important to note that there are a number of instances when one may wish to decrease certain behaviors, such as stealing, fighting, or truancy. However, if the worker wishes to increase participation, cohesiveness, and cooperative behaviors, the use of punishment may be inappropriate. Punishment simultaneously may increase the probability that the worker will lose reinforcing power, the client will quit the group, the group will lose reinforcement power, or the punished client will be stigmatized by other clients.

Avoidance conditioning occurs when an individual exhibits a behavior that prevents an aversive stimulus from occurring. During treatment, for example, clients may avoid certain topics of conversation, or resist the therapist's probing questions. If clients characteristically withhold information necessary for the resolution of difficulties, the worker may ask a series of catalyzing questions, such as, "Are you guys afraid of discussing your problems at school?" After a period of time, the clients may learn that the aversive stimulus (probing) can be avoided by providing the worker with the information that is desired. Avoidance behavior is also evidenced when a judge instructs an antisocial child that he will be incarcerated if he fails to attend group work meetings. The referred child may avoid the aversive stimulus (incarceration) by attending the group work sessions. Similarly, aversive contingencies are structured when a group worker says that members will *not* receive desired reinforcers if they exhibit certain behaviors such as hitting each other, damaging physical property, running away, jumping out of windows, making aggressive or threatening verbal statements, and so forth.

In *escape-conditioning,* the client terminates a noxious stimulus by exhibiting a certain type of behavior designed to escape from the situation. A child welfare worker threatens to remove children from an inadequate home if the parents do not improve their child-rearing practices. The parents may terminate the noxious stimulus (threat of removal of the child from the home) by improving their child-rearing practices. In many cases the therapist, by probing certain painful areas in order to secure information, may be considered a noxious stimulus to the client. The client may escape the therapist's probing questions by actually providing the information that the therapist wants *or* by avoiding him—even by discontinuing therapy. In a situation where group members fight frequently, the worker's restraining of a member may represent a noxious stimulus which is terminated by the reduction of the member's aggressive behavior. Moreover, the worker's verbal statements (such as "Don't do that!", "Be quiet!", "Sit in your place!", "That's wrong!", "Stop talking!", "Did I call on you?", "Are you wasting time?", "Don't laugh!", "You know what you are supposed to do!") indicate that a noxious stimulus may occur if the children do not modify their behavior. That is, they may be deprived of desirable reinforcers such as candy, free play time, and so forth. The difference between avoidance and escape conditioning involves the discriminative stimulus. In escape conditioning a definite discriminative stimulus occurs in the client's interaction context. For instance, the worker may verbally threaten to withdraw reinforcers after a client's exhibition of a problematic behavior. In avoidance conditioning a client may have previously experienced, in a similar behavioral context, an aversive stimulus that a particular behavior terminated. The client, therefore, learns not to exhibit certain behaviors in similar contexts in order to prevent the noxious stimulus from occurring.

Time out involves removing the client from a reinforcing situation for a limited period of time in order to decrease an undesired behavior. A worker employs this technique when he terminates a meeting prematurely because he feels the clients have not participated adequately, or when he indicates to the clients that a meeting will be rescheduled for a later date, at which time he hopes that the members will use the time more beneficially. Similarly, when clients do not return for interviews the worker is "timed out", and he probably would benefit from assessing and/or modifying his own practice behaviors. Time-out procedures are practiced by parents who withhold certain reinforcing experiences, such as borrowing the family car, when children exhibit antisocial behavior.

Stimulus control refers to the process of removing a stimulus that elicits certain undesirable behaviors. If one is working with a group of boys who have short attention spans, he might eliminate stimuli in the room that tend to decrease their attention spans, such as baseball bats, pianos, movie projectors, paints, and so forth. Interest in this technique has developed only recently. Preliminary research by Patterson (1973) has isolated various behaviors, or stimuli, which parents tend to exhibit just prior to their children's antisocial behavior. These include negative commands, disapproval, and teasing. If a group worker can isolate certain stimuli, such as teasing or negative commands from peers, that inhibit a child's capacity to successfully engage in certain sports, he may be able to eliminate them and, ultimately, to strengthen the possibility of adequate performance by the child. In addition, through other techniques, such as shaping, he can help the child to acquire behaviors necessary to participate more adequately.

Another important procedure entails withholding reinforcers from an individual when he exhibits a certain type of undesirable behavior. This is termed *extinction*. In social work practice, some types of behavioral responses are extinguished by withholding reinforcement when the client exhibits them. Thus, if the goal of a group meeting is to discuss employment possibilities, and if the clients spend a large amount of time talking about unrelated topics, one might choose to ignore those behaviors by breaks in eye contact, silence, and increasing the distance between himself and the clients. Eventually this will decrease the frequency of such irrelevant behaviors (Verplanck, 1955; Matarazzo and Wiens 1972; Matarazzo and Saslow, 1968). Likewise, if one wishes to reduce fighting, he might ignore it and reinforce prosocial behavior instead. This represents an extremely potent behavior modification procedure, namely, the use of extinction to decrease undesired behaviors, along with the concurrent application of positive reinforcement to increase desired, or prosocial behaviors (Bandura, 1969). The use of extinction to modify the behavior of certain group members will depend, essentially, on the extent to which the worker and members can exert control over the larger reinforcing environment. If, for example, the worker attempts to extinguish a given antisocial behavior while one or more of the other group members continue to reinforce it, his efforts will be to little avail. Therefore, other modification procedures, such as the introduction of group contingencies, may be used to exert greater control over the environment and to alter the target behaviors.

Stimulus Generalization and Stimulus Discrimination

When a response is learned in a given context, but proceeds to manifest itself in other contexts characterized by similar stimuli, the process is referred to as *stimulus generalization* (Staats and Staats, 1964). This process is invaluable since it enables individuals to engage in appropriate behavior in "new" situations. If stimulus generalization did not occur readily, it would be necessary to invent original behaviors for each and every new situation experienced in life. However, insofar as it does occur, people experience few truly "new" situations, that is, situations where previously learned behaviors are not at all applicable to features of the new environment. Social situations are totally unique only when all previously learned behavior is not appropriate. It is clear, then, that the development of effective coping skills by individuals, whether in or out of groups, may be partially viewed in terms of one's capacity to apply stimulus generalization skills to a large variety of life situations.

Stimulus discrimination is a counteractive process that controls and modulates the amount of stimulus generalization that can occur in any given situation. Individuals learn to expect reinforcements when they generalize certain behaviors in the presence of given stimuli. They also learn that some generalized behaviors are not reinforced in the presence of various stimuli. Stimuli that are present when reinforcement occurs are called *discriminative stimuli*. Presence or absence of the latter in any social situation indicates to an individual whether or not his generalized behavior will be reinforced. If discriminative stimuli were not to guide the generalization of behavior, confusion would be likely to reign since any behavior could be expected in any context, regardless of one's previous social experiences (Staats and Staats, 1964). Hence behavior is controlled not only by its consequences but, also, by antecedent discriminative stimuli.

Patterson (1965) demonstrated the function of a discriminative stimulus when he increased the frequency of appropriate classroom behaviors in a nine-year-old male child through the use of positive nonsocial reinforcement (pennies and candies) and positive social reinforcement (verbal praise). His conditioning procedure involved the use of a "teaching machine" that delivered a discriminative stimulus (light) to the child every time he engaged in an appropriate classroom behavior. Reinforcement followed the discriminative stimulus. After a number of therapy sessions, Patterson's entrance into the classroom actually became a discriminative stimulus for the subject, who then elicited certain prosocial behaviors learned in the former conditioning sessions.

In social group work practice the worker serves as a discriminative stimulus for the client, and vice versa. The client's presence, and certain behaviors such as discussing problems, acting aggressively, and exhibiting anxiety, serve as discriminative stimuli for the worker (Waters and McCallum, 1973). In turn, clients tend to react favorably to certain stimuli from workers, such as being attentive, warm, trusting, interested, and sympathetic toward the client's well-being. After a number of sessions, a therapist's behaviors may be viewed as signals, or discriminative stimuli, for certain client responses, such as talking about a problem area. Social and physical features of the therapeutic context also serve as discriminative stimuli for the worker and clients (Seabury, 1971; Dinges and Oetting, 1972; Lauver, Kelly, and Froehle, 1971; Widgery and Stackpole, 1972). Regardless of the social context in which a meeting takes place, the members usually look to the worker for reinforcement when their behaviors warrant it. Consequently, one objective of treatment entails decreasing the members' reliance upon the worker as a discriminative stimulus. As clients develop their respective capacities for autonomous social functioning, reinforcements from the worker should become relatively less important.

In large part, practice endeavors are likely to entail teaching clients to discriminate from among important stimuli. A variety of stimuli produce unnecessary fear and anxiety for clients. For example, if a client is fearful of animals, he must be helped to discriminate between those stimuli which should, and should not, be fear-producing. The procedure of discriminative training, it should be noted, is similar to the traditional social work activity of "clarification."

Intervention to Increase Desirable Behaviors

The development of new behaviors, including prosocial and adaptive behaviors, can be accomplished through the process of *shaping*. This process is predicated upon the reinforcement of ever-closer approximations of a desired behavior, until such time as that behavior is demonstrated by the client (Reese, 1966). Phobias, for example, have been treated by enabling clients to gradually move closer to a phobic object. Initial contacts may be with highly dissimilar objects, then with relatively similar objects and, finally, with the phobic object itself. In the case of animal phobias, such as an uncontrollable fear of dogs, the client may first become acquainted with inanimate furry objects, such as fur muffs, then with smaller and less harmless animals, such as puppies, and finally with the phobic object itself, a full-grown dog. If the goal is to shape problem-solving activities, the worker might first reinforce elementary attempts at problem-solving and gradually make reinforcement contingent upon more elaborate attempts until the terminal behavior is reached. The key to successful utilization of this procedure involves specifying an initial goal that is sufficiently easy to obtain. The notion of "response sequence" is analogous, that is, behavior rehearsals that entail helping clients to learn a *series* of behaviors required for completion of a complex task, such as securing employment. Completing such a task requires sequential skills in knowing where to go, how to present oneself physically and verbally, and being prepared to perform the job if it is obtained.

A behavioral contingency is an "if-then" statement that specifies the behaviors to be reinforced by an individual's social environment (Catania, 1968). Such contingencies may be structured as *individual contingencies* or as *group contingencies,* as explained below. Group contingencies exist if reinforcements for all or most of a group's members are dependent upon display of the given behavior(s) by all, or certain proportions of, the group's total membership.

Schedules of reinforcement delineate how, and with what frequency, clients' various behaviors will be reinforced. These schedules control both the acquisition and the maintenance of clients' behaviors. It is essential to reinforce a behavior continuously *while* it is being established but, conversely, not to reinforce it every time *after* it has been established. Otherwise, the behavior will be subject to rapid extinction. Operationally, schedules of reinforcement are somewhat akin to the program or activity sequences oftentimes denoted in traditional group work. Although group workers frequently exert great control over activity sequences, it is posited that maximum change potential can be effected when the members themselves exert such influence. Moreover, as implied earlier, one ultimate objective of all treatment programs is autonomous and adaptive self-programing by group members. This is the case regardless of whether "programing" is viewed in terms of traditional group work or contemporary behavior modification.

There are five basic schedules of reinforcement: continuous, fixed-ratio, fixed-interval, variable-ratio, and variable-interval. Only these basic schedules will be discussed here. An elaboration of more complex schedules for group work practice, such as multiple schedules, awaits further conceptual development. On a *continuous reinforcement* schedule, the appropriate responses of an individual are reinforced every time that they occur. This schedule keeps an individual responding at a high rate for certain periods of time, even when he has been minimally deprived of the reinforcer because he has secured large numbers of them previously. However, by reinforcing each response *satiation* may occur. When this takes place the reinforcer loses its reinforcing value to the organism. With such a schedule the target individual learns to expect a reinforcer every time that he exhibits the desired behavior. But once the behavior is established, if reinforcement does not follow display of the desired behavior, its rate of occurrence will decrease rapidly.

Fixed-interval reinforcement schedules make the reinforcement of an appropriate response contingent on the passage of a fixed interval of time since occurrence of the preceding reinforced response. An individual on this schedule will temporarily pause after the reinforcement. His response rate will only increase as the next reinforcement interval approaches (Bachrach, 1962). Through use of such a schedule with normal children, Long and his associates (1958) were unable to maintain the stability of learned responses. Data indicate that this schedule is the least stable for the sustained control of human behavior. Moreover, behaviors that are produced by the first such reinforcement tend to decrease in frequency through time (Reese, 1966), even when they are reinforced at fixed intervals. Variables that account for this instability are undue deprivation of reinforcement, that is, length of time that the subjects have gone without reinforcement; reinforcement quantity, that is, the size or quantity of the reinforcer to be used; and novel stimuli, that is, characteristics of the environmental context that may deter effective response patterns.

An individual who is reinforced each time that he emits a

certain *number* of responses is on a *fixed-ratio reinforcement* schedule. Individuals on this schedule consistently perform at a high rate. However, certain problems, such as a reduction in the frequency of the desired behavior, can occur when the ratio size is increased too quickly. Likewise, an individual can accumulate an extremely large number of reinforcements, thus decreasing the size of the response ratio and, ultimately, decreasing his response rate.

On a *variable-ratio reinforcement* schedule, the number of responses that must be emitted for an individual to secure a reinforcer tend to vary around a certain mean. Theoretically, this schedule should generate the highest rates of responding. Orlando and Bijou (1960), who used this schedule with retarded children, found that their subjects responded at an exceedingly high rate. On a *variable-interval reinforcement* schedule, the interval of time during which reinforcers are available to an individual varies around a certain mean. When this schedule is correctly constructed it eliminates the cyclical variations characteristic of the fixed-interval schedule. Data collected by Long and others (1958) indicate that this schedule is effective in producing stable behavioral rates among normal children. As a rule, behaviors that are conditioned on variable-ratio or variable-interval schedules are maintained longer than are behaviors conditioned on continuous, fixed-interval, or fixed-ratio schedules (Ullmann and Krasner, 1965).

Available data suggest that continuous reinforcement schedules should be used for the acquisition of behaviors in group work practice. However, once such behaviors are acquired, reinforcements should be provided on an intermittent basis in order to insure the maintenance of those behaviors. This is particularly important since continuous schedules are highly susceptible to extinction. *Variable-ratio* and *variable-interval* schedules should maintain prosocial behavior learned in group work treatment for a longer period of time than continuous, fixed-interval, or fixed-ratio schedules.

It should be noted that Schwitzgebel and Kolb (1964) used variable-ratio and variable-interval schedules to sustain stable patterns of prosocial behavior among delinquents with whom they worked. A fixed-ratio schedule maintained a given behavior for a shorter period of time than did a variable-ratio or variable-interval schedule. In applying this finding to the stabilization of certain verbal skills among delinquents, such as the proper use of verb tenses, one should vary the number of responses that are reinforced. Similarly, one should vary the amount and number of primary reinforcers used to reinforce prosocial academic behaviors. If one decides to use an interval schedule, the period of time that elapses between reinforcement and nonreinforcement of a particular emitted response should be varied. A word of caution is in order, however, about the relationships posited, especially those concerning how different reinforcement schedules influence the behavior exhibited by antisocial children. Many of these postulates, like those for other formulations, await extensive empirical verification. Nonetheless, unlike many other formulations, most of the postulates have been derived from a logically consistent theoretical framework supported by an increasing body of experimental studies.

To recapitulate, then, a fundamental acquaintance with certain social learning concepts is essential for the subsequent elaboration of group-oriented diagnostic and interventive strategies. Included in these concepts are *operant behavior, positive reinforcer, positive secondary reinforcer, generalized reinforcer, stimulus generalization, stimulus discrimination, discriminative stimulus, shaping, reinforcement schedule, behavioral contingency* and, most important for the present discussion, *group behavioral contingency.*

The three basic interrelated elements of the operant model are discriminative stimuli, the operant (or behavior), and the consequences that follow the operant. Each one of these elements may be dealt with individually, but they usually constitute a unit called the "unit of analysis." If the operant model is to be applicable to social group work practice, these are the essential elements that each worker will wish to delineate and to control, after an adequate diagnostic period, in order to bring about changes in client behaviors.

Behavioral Diagnosis

To modify behaviors in a group context, a worker must be able to assess, or diagnose, problematic and/or target behaviors in terms of observable events, and antecedent and consequent conditions that attend these behaviors. Basically, problematic behaviors of antisocial children can be classified into two broad categories: *be-*

havioral deficits that children exhibit, such as a significant lack of participatory skills, verbal ability, self-confidence, or initiative, and *behavioral excesses,* such as excessive frequencies of disruptive behavior, fighting, school truancy, and so forth. These are key behaviors upon which workers may wish to focus in the group context. Similar types of diagnostic data may be required in order to deal with problematic behaviors outside of the group context. The group worker must ascertain how the child's peers and relevant others reinforce the problem behavior. He must also ascertain which behaviors *they* exhibit prior to manifestation of the target child's problematic behaviors, what resources are available for change in terms of modification techniques (for example, group versus individual contingencies, stimulus control versus positive reinforcement, and so forth), who can best apply the techniques (the worker, parents, or peers), what reinforcers (or incentives) are available, how much reinforcement the current behaviors provide for the client, and whether changing the client's behavior will lead to any new difficulties. Additional questions include how effective, or reinforcing, will be the reinforcers chosen for the client and what prosocial behavioral assets of the client can be increased. Beyond the treatment group context, the examination of antecedent conditions and consequences must include considerably larger units of analysis, such as family members' reinforcement patterns, the behaviors of significant peers, and so forth (Kanfer and Saslow, 1969).

Establishing Relationship

Proponents of different therapeutic approaches disagree on many points. However, there is general consensus that one potent treatment variable is the relationship formed between worker and client and, in group work, among the clients themselves (Goldstein, Heller, and Sechrest, 1966). Many theorists have conceptualized this crucial treatment variable at a high level of abstraction but few have been able to define *relationship* in an operational and discrete manner. From a behavior modification perspective, however, Rosen (1972) has viewed the relationship between two or more individuals as an interactional situation that consists of a series of behavioral exchanges or, more specifically, of stimulus-response exchanges. At any point during ongoing social interaction, a person can draw upon a large pool of potential behaviors. Every behavior enacted by a worker or client is considered to have certain cost and reward values for each participant and, consequently, the interaction between any two behaviors results in its own unique cost and reward outcomes for the respective participants (Thibaut and Kelley, 1959). Therefore any prolonged series of behavioral exchanges produces differing net cost and reward balances for the worker and/or client(s). Although these outcomes, or differential results of social interaction, may vary for each individual, they influence crucial facets of treatment such as relationship formation, continuance, and involvement in the therapeutic process. With particular reference to group work, it should be apparent that the above formulation represents a considerably refined version of the traditional group dynamics definition of group cohesiveness as "the resultant of all the forces acting upon all the members to remain in the group" (Cartwright and Zander, 1968).

A basic assumption underlies the foregoing conceptualization, to wit, that individuals strive to maximize the outcomes of their social interaction or, in other words, to engage in behaviors that yield the greatest rewards at the least costs. This variant of hedonic calculus need not be conscious or well-articulated. And to be sure, it is rarely simple. Nonetheless, when two or more individuals assess the outcome of their social interaction, at least two relatively clear criteria can be posited. First, the *comparison level*, refers to the client's subjective evaluation of his outcomes when viewed solely within the context of his current interactional, or group, situation; in other words, how satisfying is that particular social situation for the client? The second criterion for outcome evaluation is the *comparison level for alternative situations*. This refers to the client's subjective evaluation of his outcomes as he compares them to those available in alternative social situations.

A number of key insights are derived if therapists accept the simple assumption that group members' satisfactions are related not only to events *within* the group but, also, to members' perceptions of *extra-group* alternatives. Thus, for instance, it becomes obvious that the worker's diagnostic and interventive activities must not be restricted to the treatment group per se. The group's social environment necessarily becomes an additional focus for such endeavors. This is the case simply because alternative outcomes considered available within the environment significantly influence members' interactions within the treatment group itself. The foregoing distinction also lends a new perspective to the heretofore disappointing relationship noted between initial treatment successes, especially in closed correctional institutions, and ensuing high rates of recidivism. Success frequently occurs not only because inmates truly value or benefit from treatment programs, but because no other alternatives are available for them! Upon their release to the open community, where countless other social alternatives, including deviant ones, may become available, the benefits gained from earlier treatment may be insufficient to sustain therapeutic change. Indeed, some social work researchers have noted that one undesired phenomenon, that is, disengagement from treatment, is more likely to occur in communities with many treatment agencies than in communities with few treatment resources (Rosenblatt and Mayer, 1966). As external alternatives become more available the client is less constrained to remain in a given social situation unless it is highly satisfying.

The above distinctions also are of value when considering the formation of relationships with, and among, antisocial children. It becomes evident, for instance, that a worker can sustain attraction to the group only if members engage in behaviors that maintain their net positive evaluations of the group at a higher level than those considered available for alternative interactional situations. Such evaluations may depend upon the worker's capacity to make satisfactions visible to the members and, moreover, upon the members' capacities to realistically assess the satisfactions available in alternative social situations. In addition to codifying and expanding the knowledge base of group work, the foregoing conceptualization also reaffirms certain principles basic to most group work practice with antisocial children. Thus, for example, in order to assure positive behavior exchanges during initial interactions among the members and himself, it is apparent that the worker ought to structure program activities which are relatively high in reinforcement value, but low in terms of aversive costs. As treatment progresses, the worker should try to diminish artificial discrepancies between rewards and costs, and should prepare members to tolerate sustained periods of negative outcomes pending future periods of satisfactory outcomes.

Similarly, it is clear that workers can enhance initial behavioral exchanges by concurrently presenting members with primary reinforcers. Schwitzgebel and Kolb (1964), for example, were able to successfully engage delinquents in subsequent behavioral exchanges by presenting food as a primary reinforcer. Additionally, they established their workers' capacities for reinforcement by paying delinquents a one-dollar bonus following exploratory visits to the site of their experiments. Workers also can establish themselves as positive reinforcers by helping children to perform various tasks outside of the group (Goldstein, Heller, and Sechrest, 1966). A worker can increase members' attraction to one another, and to himself, through the judicious use of verbal approval for appropriate behaviors and, also, by reducing members' anxieties concerning problematic tasks or discussions (Berscheid and Walster, 1969). As a result of continued association with positive reinforcers, group members' behavioral exchanges are likely to be accorded increasingly favorable evaluations. Consequently, members' attraction to the group may be enhanced and there will be a greater likelihood of continued participation in the group. In the initial stages of group formation the worker should take an active role in planning programs, reinforcing the children, and structuring group contingencies. He then should gradually decrease his active role, letting the group assume more responsibilities in relevant areas (Goldstein, Heller, and Sechrest, 1966). This procedure appears to be highly reinforcing for group members. It also enhances the likelihood of continued participation by the group members (Goldstein, Heller, and Sechrest, 1966).

Although the foregoing techniques may not appear particularly novel to the experienced group worker, a behavior modification perspective serves to redefine traditional practice concepts and techniques in a cogent and clear-cut manner. Concepts such as *group cohesiveness* and *attraction to the group* may be viewed in terms of workers' and members' capacities to maximize rewards (or reinforcements) and to minimize costs for one another and, moreover, to do so more ably than the members of other groups in the immediate environment. The unique contribution of this formulation inheres, then, in the ease with which it can be joined to second-order concepts to facilitate the development of a relatively comprehensive and systematic theoretical framework for the elaboration of group work practice principles.

Verbal Communication

Verbal communication is one form of behavior that represents both a consequence of preceding contingencies and a determinant of future social interaction within a group. As a discrete behavioral category it, too, is subject to examination in terms of the theoretical framework set forth above. Such an analysis can lead to more accurate specification of the relationships between verbal communication and the emergence of prosocial behavior in groups of antisocial children. Rosen (1972) and Rosen and Lieberman (1972), for example, have conceptualized two communication variables—verbal congruence and content relevance—and have indicated how outcome values associated with each can influence the probabilities of children remaining in a given interactional situation.

Verbal congruence is defined as the extent to which two or more persons' verbal exchanges are related to one another. The more congruence in verbal exchanges, such as between worker and children (or among children themselves), the more positively will those parties evaluate their social interaction. Similarly, as verbal exchanges become more congruent the probability of members' continuation in a treatment group is likely to increase. The foregoing postulates, although referring only to a single communication variable, would suggest the efficacy of relatively homogeneous grouping for members and workers, especially as to language capacity and corresponding antecedents such as age and social class.

Content relevance refers to the extent to which the content of an interactive response is perceived by a participant as relevant and admissible to his definition of the interactional situation. It can be postulated that the presentation of expected content in an interactional situation is likely to be highly reinforcing to all concerned and, consequently, that the situation itself will be evaluated positively by the participants. This postulate has been supported by much social work literature concerning the compatibility between role expectations held by clients and therapists (Mechanic, 1961; Aronson and Overall, 1966; Oxley, 1966; Rosenfeld, 1964; Sapolsky, 1965; Thomas, Kounin, and Polansky, 1967).

By keeping characteristics other than antisocial behavior highly similar, a worker can enhance the probability that the group's members, including himself, will use one another as role models. This is an important consideration, since a voluminous literature indicates exposure to prosocial models will facilitate the enactment of prosocial behavior by children (Goldstein, Heller, and Sechrest, 1966). In addition, by keeping characteristics between the worker and the children similar, greater identification with the worker's value system may occur (Kelman, 1961), attraction between the children and himself will be advanced (Byrne, 1969), and communication difficulties will be minimized. Likewise, the therapist will serve as a model for verbal behaviors that the children will exhibit in the future.

A substantial body of research indicates that a worker can influence children's future verbal behavior, such as the number of utterances, pauses between verbal exchanges, rates of speech, number of interruptions, length of silence between verbal exchanges, and length of verbal statements. Hence, if a therapist wishes to increase any of these behaviors he should model them (Matarazzo and Wiens, 1972; Matarazzo and Saslow, 1968; Salzinger, 1969) and engage in other behavior-increasing activities, such as shaping and selective reinforcement, that is, reinforcing others who exhibit the requisite behaviors. For example, if a relevant treatment goal is to increase the leadership behavior exhibited by a certain member, the worker can reinforce that member's verbal output to achieve this objective. Considerable research suggests that enhanced quantity and quality of verbal output is associated with an individual's ascendancy to leadership positions (Shapiro, 1963; Hayes and Meltzer, 1972). Another important environmental variable for influencing verbal behavior is the group's seating arrangement. Data from various studies indicate that when individuals are placed at right angles to one another they are likely to converse more than individuals who are parallel to each other (Seabury, 1971). In addition, seating highly verbal persons across from individuals with low verbal output enhances the probability that the latter will increase their verbal activity (Steinzor, 1950).

Reward and Punishment

In working with antisocial children it is clearly desirable to focus on the positive, or prosocial, behaviors exhibited by group members. This principle contrasts with certain other therapeutic approaches which primarily rely on punishment and confrontation in order to achieve behavioral change. Research conducted on lower organisms, as well as on children, indicates that punishment is an ineffective means of modifying long-term behavior. Punishment frequently eliminates undesirable behavior, but it also tends to generalize to desired behaviors, eliminating them as well. Moreover, the worker who punishes often becomes an aversive stimulus to his clients, thus hindering development of a positive therapeutic relationship. Finally, punishment may result in the emergence of new aggressive responses in the person being punished (Reese, 1966). Instead, the worker should emphasize positive reinforcement of any behaviors that contribute to the enhancement of clients' prosocial repertoires. In this manner he can augment his referent power, demonstrate his ability to serve as a change agent, and increase the members' attraction to the group itself.

It is important to note that this stance should not be equated with traditional notions of permissiveness. Lack of punishment should not be construed as approval nor should it connote a lack of structure. Punishment is frowned upon not because of any given ideological or philosophical stance, but because it is considerably less effective and predictable in producing behavioral change than are other techniques.

Techniques for Prosocial Behavioral Change

Just as behavior modification can be used to suggest guidelines for relationship formation, it can be utilized to formulate specific suggestions for the development of prosocial behavior among antisocial children. Workers can engage in a variety of interventive procedures in order to promote such behavior. These can include systematic efforts to provide positive reinforcements for members, to create time-out procedures, to shape members' behaviors, to develop members' stimulus generalization and stimulus discrimination skills, and to structure group contingencies.

The worker's expectations regarding the direction and extent of clients' changes usually represent a potent influencing factor. Recent empirical investigations indicate that if a worker believes a client can change positively, there will be a greater probability that the client's behavior actually will change in the expected direction. This research also indicates that if a therapist believes little behavior change can take place, there will be a greater probability that the client's behavior will not change. The available literature tends to support the general proposition that behavior change techniques should be applied by workers who hold the distinct expectation that behavioral changes will, in fact, occur, thus increasing the probability of success as a result of interventive attempts (Goldstein, 1962; Rosenthal and Rosnow, 1969; Rosenthal and Jacobson, 1966). Moreover, the communication of change expectations should be directed toward the client. This procedure is likely to increase the client's susceptibility to behavioral influence (Goldstein, Heller, and Sechrest, 1966; Goldstein and Simonson, 1971). Relevant expectations also can be communicated to clients in pretherapy contexts, such as diagnostic interviews, diagnostic testing, tours of group meeting sites, and, even, at trial attendance sessions.

Contracting is an especially important technique with antisocial children. At the initial and, even, at subsequent meetings, the worker should clearly state the contingencies that are operative and the specific goals of the group, including how members are expected to participate and what the leader's duties are. This process in itself is highly reinforcing for group members, since it adds structure to the group situation (Reid and Epstein, 1972; Goldstein, Heller, and Sechrest, 1966). In addition, a situation in which all or a majority of the members agree on a contract provides a context where the members' influence over one another is greater than in low-agreement contexts (Goldstein and Simonson, 1971).

Positive reinforcement—praise, attention, money, food, television privileges, and countless other behaviors and material resources—can be used to promote prosocial behaviors in both antisocial and prosocial children if the worker makes them directly contingent upon the display of such behaviors. For example, praise can be made contingent upon improvement in peer relationships, family functioning, or classroom performance. Movies, hockey games, field trips, and other valued activities can be made contingent upon the development of various criterion behaviors, such as extended impulse control. Moreover, systems of generalized reinforcers can be negotiated with antisocial children and their families. These systems may involve the presentation of monetary reinforcers that are contingent upon improved behavior.

Although humans have provided monetary reinforcements to one another for centuries, the actual applications of such reinforcement have been rather haphazard and, therefore, the resultant behaviors have been correspondingly unpredictable. Parents, for example, tend to provide allowances to children at fixed intervals. Consequently, parental reinforcement schedules are relatively independent of the child's behavior, except as allowance time approaches. Parents also tend to withdraw allowances or monetary rewards following negative behavior, unwittingly fostering the liabilities associated with punishment. The contributions of behavior modification theory do not rest in the delineation of particular reinforcers, such as money, but in the *systematic* application of such reinforcers in order to produce behavioral changes, including enhanced client functioning. The group worker's knowledge concerning reinforcements desired by his clients, his control over the client's environment, and his creative ability to formulate reinforcement contingencies are among the few factors that enhance his capacity to develop prosocial behaviors among previously antisocial children.

p 109 * *Token systems* are used in some group situations to modify various behaviors. Tokens may include items such as money, plastic discs, or point scores that children receive for exhibiting various behaviors. In utilizing a token system, the group worker should explicitly state what behaviors will be rewarded with a token, and constantly monitor the system to determine whether or not the children are receiving too many tokens, thus becoming satiated. In such cases he can modify the system by increasing the prices paid for various items, consequently assuring that the children will not become satiated. Conversely, he can decrease the amount of tokens received for a given behavior, but should bear in mind that this might prove relatively ineffective since tokens may acquire secondary reinforcing properties. Reducing the number of tokens might reduce the available incentives for children to exhibit desired rates and types of behavior. Finally, if poor monitoring enables the children to steal tokens, the system will not operate effectively!

In using a token system, the worker and/or members typically structure a point goal to be earned, such as the attainment of 250 points. Attainment of this goal can be rewarded by allowing the group members to choose an activity that they enjoy, such as attending a professional sports event or skating. A point system can then be structured that is built on both individual and group efforts. Each child, for example, may receive five points for coming to a meeting; if all the children attend, an additional five points can be awarded to each member. Ten points can be given to a child if he does not fight during a meeting; similarly, each child can receive an additional ten points if no one engages in a fight for an entire meeting. Each child also can receive ten points for staying with the group for an entire session; if all the members remain throughout they each can receive an additional ten points. Token systems can be structured with either individual or group contingencies. The more a token system uses group contingencies, the more likely it is to help the group become a potent vehicle for change. Pressures for group members to exhibit desired behaviors will increase because each person's reinforcers will be dependent not only on his own performance but, also, on the performance of his peers.

Shaping is another procedure that has been useful in fostering behavioral change among children. Academic skills have been shaped, for example, by reinforcing a child's initial efforts at studying for a short period of time. Once the initial periods are stabilized, reinforcements can be made contingent upon longer periods of study and upon the display of related behaviors, such as asking questions in class and seeking help with school problems from parents, classmates, group members, the worker, or relevant others.

Efforts to modify maladaptive behaviors may be particularly problematic during the early phases of group treatment. To shape a group's endeavors, the worker may use positive reinforcements such as smiling, listening, moving closer, or offering desired resources when the members engage in appropriate behaviors. If the members wish to become proficient in baseball, for example, the worker could reinforce each attempt at catching a ball by making remarks such as "Good try!" or, if appropriate, "Good catch!" As such skills are developed, the worker might shape the behavior further by making subsequent reinforcements contingent upon actually catching the ball. As noted earlier, Schwitzgebel and Kolb (1964) shaped attendance among antisocial children who would not visit a meeting site by actually leaving their offices and meeting clients at locations successively closer to the site. They also shaped punctuality by awarding bonuses each time subjects arrived closer to the scheduled participation time.

Guided group interaction, one treatment approach believed to be particularly effective with antisocial children, has been premised in part upon the foregoing technique. This approach utilizes shaping procedures concurrently with worker efforts to develop socially acceptable norms within the group. After such norms are established, additional antisocial children are brought into the group. Through the distribution of appropriate reinforcers, the group then proceeds to shape prosocial behaviors among the new members (Pilnick, Elias, and Clapp, 1966; Empey and Rabow, 1961).

For certain behaviors with low frequencies of occurrence, shaping may be a very time-consuming process. In such cases the worker can model the desired behaviors or he can provide systematic reinforcement for those children who do model them, thus increasing the probability that targeted children will emulate the behavior (Bandura, 1969). Children will model behaviors more readily when they are exhibited by high status models or by models who are similar to them in essential characteristics, that is, race, age, sex, and social history, or by models who are reinforced for such behaviors while in their presence (Bandura, 1971).

Stimulus generalization and stimulus discrimination, effectively used, can alleviate one of the major problems associated with most treatment programs, namely, the low transferability of ingroup behavioral change to the open community. It is axiomatic that behaviors learned in children's groups are controlled not only by the worker but also by peers. Since such behaviors are learned in group contexts they can be associated with a wide range of individuals. Consequently there is a greater likelihood that they will generalize to other settings and, therefore, that they will be stabilized within the open community.

Generalization of behaviors learned in the group can be enhanced by conducting meetings in a variety of contexts, regardless of how mundane they might appear to be. Drugstores, auto repair shops, and athletic fields may be as important as the school or the worker's office. If behavior is learned and repeated solely in one context, the stimuli unique to that context may acquire discriminative properties that will prevent generalization to other settings. Generalization is likely to increase if members are exposed to differing tasks and individuals, especially during the later phases of group treatment. Along with conducting sessions in different settings, the use of several group workers for any one group may have merit with reference to the likelihood of generalizing newly learned behaviors (Holmes, 1971).

Once the learned behavior is exhibited in differing contexts, reinforcement schedules should be designed to inhibit extinction. For example, the members of a group may have unduly short attention spans. The worker should begin to increase their attention spans by gradually introducing various reinforcements in the group setting. Next, he should help the members to increase their attention spans in other contexts, such as the school setting. He can meet with teachers and structure procedures that will result in reinforcement when the child exhibits the desired behaviors. Once the behaviors are established in this context, a program of reducing the required number of reinforcements can be initiated. Reduction of reinforcements should be based on those schedules that are most resistant to extinction.

All procedures mentioned thus far have focused on increasing prosocial behaviors. However, in some instances an aversive contingency may be desirable, especially for behaviors that disrupt a group so extensively that effective treatment is precluded. Time-out procedures represent one technique for decreasing maladaptive behaviors exhibited by antisocial children. Time out entails removal of a child from a reinforcing situation, such as the treatment group, for a limited period of time. Although this technique can be used in both open and closed settings, it has been especially successful in residential institutions (Burchard and Tyler, 1965). The worker may utilize time-out procedures each time a child engages in a serious maladaptive behavior, such as fighting. However, it is probable that this procedure's efficacy is inversely related to the frequency with which it is used. Moreover, its effectiveness is highly dependent on the child's attraction to the group. Time-out procedures tend to be most successful when attraction is high or when the group has high reinforcing value for the child. Considerable empirical research remains to be done in order to ascertain the optimum lengths of time-out periods for varying types of antisocial behaviors and group contexts. To maximize the efficacy of time-out procedures, the worker should be sure that the time-out context provides minimum reinforcement potential, the time out occurs immediately after the maladaptive behavior, and the worker does not exhibit any reinforcing behaviors while executing the time-out procedure, such as arguing with the child, laughing, and so forth.

Structuring Group Contingencies

Although we have endeavored to cite the particular utility of the foregoing procedures for group work practice, it is apparent that virtually all of them can be utilized at the individual level, that is, in social casework treatment as well as in group work. In order to elaborate treatment formulations that are uniquely suitable for social group work, it is necessary to derive particularized second-order concepts that will take cognizance of individual members' capacities to provide reinforcements for one another. Such a task is an extraordinarily complex one but, nonetheless, it can be predicated upon social learning principles. Ultimately, such formulations are likely to be based upon complex multivariate matrices. These, in turn, may be based on probability estimates that will account for the interaction among a variety of behaviors, behavioral contingencies, and reinforcement schedules for group populations. However, simpler formulations will have to suffice for the present since such matrices are unlikely to be developed in the immediate future. In the meantime, it is possible to conceive of more immediate group contingencies that can influence the behavior of group members.

Group contingencies are reinforcements awarded to all or most group members following the accomplishment of certain objectives by the whole group (such as building a club house or successfully resolving a problem) or by selected members (such as more frequent prosocial or cooperative behavior). In either case, a significant portion of the membership obtains reinforcement following manifestation of the desired behavior. Although such contingencies are difficult to apply in a prolonged sequence of behavioral exchanges, they nonetheless may be characterized by relatively high predictive potency when certain focal behaviors are clearly prescribed by the worker or members (Hamblin, Hathaway, and Wodarski, 1971; Wodarski, Hamblin, and others, 1972; Wodarski, Hamblin, and others, 1973). This technique is a good example of the advantages that group treatment may have over individual behavior modification therapy.

When group contingencies are conceptualized in terms of proportionate group membership, they can vary along at least two major dimensions. These dimensions are represented by the proportion of members who must enact a given behavior in order to receive reinforcement, and the proportion of members who are to receive reinforcement for the enacted behavior. If viewed as ratios, these dimensions, respectively, may be denoted as the *enactor ratio* and the *recipient ratio*. It is posited that varying group contingencies will result in differential conformity pressures exerted upon those group members who are expected to enact a given behavioral response. Such members may be denoted as *enactors*. The conformity pressures emanating from different group contingencies will result in differing degrees of "conformity proneness" for the enactors in a group. Conformity proneness is considered to be a function of the relationship between a group's enactor ratio and recipient ratio. The appropriate formula for determination of an enactor's conformity proneness is $C_E = [(E) - (N-E)^2/N] - (R/N)$, where $N =$ number of members in the group, $E =$ number of enactors in the group (that is, those members who must enact the given behavior in order for reinforcement to occur), $R =$ number of recipients in the group (that is, those members who will receive reinforcement once the given behavior is enacted), $C_E =$ conformity proneness for each enactor.

No effort is made here to set forth a discrete unit of analysis for conformity proneness. Rather, C_E denotes an estimated probability, varying in range from 0.00 to 1.00, that represents each enactor's likelihood of yielding to conformity pressures that can result from the interaction between enactor ratios and recipient ratios. More specifically, C_E is considered to be a function of both the extent to which conformity expectations are shared among peers (enactor ratio) and the extent to which reinforcements for the enacted behavior are distributed among group members (recipient ratio). The resultant probabilities should be interpreted more as heuristic aids rather than as actual statistical estimates. Their predictive utility is likely to be greatest when values for a given set of group contingencies, such as those set forth in Table 1, are analyzed in rank-order form.

The rationales underlying the above formula are derived from the juxtaposition of two major empirical generalizations plus one hypothetical relationship that should be subjected to empirical investigation. One of the empirical generalizations applies to the relationship between conformity behavior and the proportion of group members upon whom conformity pressures are exerted. The first portion of the equation, that is $[(E) - (N - E)^2]/N$, suggests that such a relationship is an inverse curvilinear one. This assumption is supported by a substantial literature. On the one hand, many experimental studies suggest that a single group member is highly susceptible to conformity pressures from his peers when he is cast as a minority of one, that is, when all of his peers exert pressures upon him alone to conform to their expectations (Asch, 1952; Backman, Secord, and Pierce, 1966; Feldman, 1967). However, as the size of the minority is enlarged, those members who are subjected to peer group conformity pressures become correspondingly less susceptible to them. On the other hand, the available literature also suggests that when conformity pressures are exerted upon *all* group members, there is a high degree of norm consensus (Biddle and Thomas, 1966), expectation consensus (Feldman, 1970), or goal interdependence (Thomas, 1957) within the group and, consequently, a high incidence of conformity behavior among the members. It would appear plausible, then, that the least conformity should take

TABLE 1. HYPOTHETICAL CONFORMITY PRONENESS PROBABILITIES FOR INDIVIDUAL ENACTORS
(BASED UPON TWO GROUP CONTINGENCY DIMENSIONS)

Enactor Ratio	N	Recipient Ratio									
		1.00 / 10	0.90 / 9	0.80 / 8	0.70 / 7	0.60 / 6	0.50 / 5	0.40 / 4	0.30 / 3	0.20 / 2	0.10 / 1
1.00	10	1.000	.900	.800	.700	.600	.500	.400	.300	.200	.100
0.90	9	.640	.576	.512	.448	.384	.320	.256	.192	.128	.064
0.80	8	.360	.324	.288	.252	.216	.180	.144	.108	.072	.036
0.70	7	.160	.144	.128	.112	.096	.080	.064	.048	.032	.016
0.60	6	.040	.036	.032	.028	.024	.020	.016	.012	.008	.004
0.50	5	.000	.000	.000	.000	.000	.000	.000	.000	.000	.000
0.40	4	.040	.036	.032	.028	.024	.020	.016	.012	.008	.004
0.30	3	.160	.144	.128	.112	.096	.080	.064	.048	.032	.016
0.20	2	.360	.324	.288	.252	.216	.180	.144	.108	.072	.036
0.10	1	.640	.576	.512	.448	.384	.320	.256	.192	.128	.064

Note: **Range** = 0.00 to 1.00; predictions are based upon a hypothetical group of $N = 10$.

place somewhere between those two extremes and, presumably, at that point where approximately half of the group's members are expected to enact a given behavior while the other half are not expected to do so. This situation is expressed in Table 1 where, in a hypothetical ten-member group, conformity proneness would appear to be least ($C_E = .000$) for enactors when five members are expected to display a certain behavior while the remaining five members are not expected to do so.

Likewise, a review of the first column of Table 1 suggests that high conformity proneness can be expected for an enactor who is the only one subjected to his peers' expectations ($C_E = .640$). However, as another enactor joins him in the minority position, the corresponding conformity pressures for each are significantly diminished and conformity proneness is reduced ($C_E = .360$). In comparison, conformity proneness is greatest when group contingencies are applied to all members of the group ($C_E = 1.000$). Group contingencies also are likely to be highly effective when unanimously directed toward a single antisocial child. However, when such contingencies are applied to intermediate proportions of the group's membership they can be expected to be relatively less effective (see Table 1).

The second empirical generalization focuses upon the relationship between conformity behavior and the proportion of group members who receive reinforcement for the enacted behavior. This relationship is assumed to be a direct and positive one, that is, $C_E = R/N$. At this juncture, it is important to reemphasize that the above model assumes a possibility for certain group members to obtain reinforcement when members *other than themselves* are the enactors within the group. Thus, for example, it is possible to structure a group contingency wherein *all* the group members will receive reinforcement, such as a ten dollar bonus, if just one antisocial member substantially improves his behavior during a given time period. Such a contingency is a very potent one for the lone enactor since all the other group members will direct strong conformity pressures toward him in order to assure their own reinforcements. This situation is illustrated hypothetically by the last figure in Column 1 of Table 1 ($C_E = .640$). In contrast, if fewer members are promised reinforcement for progress made by the single antisocial child, the corresponding conformity pressures are likely to be much weaker. This situation can be expressed graphically by reviewing the last row of Table 1. Conformity pressures directed toward a single member are likely to be strongest when *all* members are promised reinforcement ($C_E = .640$), much weaker when only half the members are promised reinforcement ($C_E = .320$), and even weaker when only one member is promised reinforcement ($C_E = .064$). This supposition has been confirmed by recent, albeit preliminary, empirical research regarding behavior modification and group contingencies (Hamblin, Hathaway, and Wodarski, 1971). It also has been supported in part by earlier group dynamics research concerning varying group reward structures (Deutsch, 1949; Thomas, 1957).

The hypothetical relationship mentioned above pertains to the posited interaction effects among the foregoing variables. The extent of conformity proneness for any given enactor(s) is presumed to be a function of the overall interaction between proportion of enactors (an inverse curvilinear one) and proportion of recipients (a direct positive one) within the group. The squaring of proportions set forth in the first part of the conformity proneness equation suggests that the extent to which reinforcements are distributed to group members (the recipient ratio) is considered to be a more potent factor than the extent to which conformity pressures are shared among group members (the enactor ratio). Consequently, the former factor is weighted more heavily. Although the posited relationships are hypothetical, Table 1 provides a logical basis for the elaboration of testable hypotheses.

Group Contingencies versus Individual Contingencies

It is important to stress that prosocial behavioral exchanges can be promoted through peer group experiences where *either* individual reinforcement contingencies *or* varying group reinforcement contingencies are structured by the worker and/or members. This distinction is analogous to the worker's differentiation between direct and indirect modes of intervention, as posited by Vinter, and to his view of the group as a context for treatment rather than as a means for treatment (Vinter, 1967). By employing only individual reinforcement contingencies, however, group workers necessarily employ suboptimal procedures for the development of prosocial behavior. First, the reinforcements that can be provided by a worker are relatively limited in comparison to those available from the group as a whole. Second, individual contingencies make reinforcement dependent upon individual performances which, when viewed in the aggregate, may be at variance with the particular treatment needs of given members or, indeed, of the group as a whole. Since such contingencies place special emphasis upon discrete individual performances, overall group integration may be diminished, especially if varying individual performances tend to countervail one another or if they lead to the monopolization of available reinforcements by certain group members. In contrast, through the systematic application of group reinforcement contingencies, the worker can structure exchanges that will lead to increased group integration and to more frequent interpersonal helping. In large part, this is likely to occur because each member's reinforcements are contingent upon the entire group's performance rather than upon isolated and uncoordinated individual performances (Staats and Staats, 1964).

The preceding discussion, along with research evidence accumulated over the years by a number of investigators (see, for example, Bachrach, Candland, and Gibson, 1961; Dinoff, Horner, and others, 1960; Hastorf, 1967; Shapiro, 1963; and Sherif, 1956), indicates that a variety of behaviors, including prosocial and antisocial behaviors, can be produced in group contexts by structuring differential reinforcement contingencies. Another series of experiments, based primarily on Skinner's conceptualizations of cooperation and competition, and of operant behaviors, has been conducted in order to investigate the development of cooperative behaviors in children (Azrin and Lindsley, 1965; Cohen, 1962; Hart, Reynolds, and others, 1968; Hinztger, Sanders, and DeMeyer, 1965; Lindsley, 1966). These studies provide further confirmation that differing group reinforcement contingencies can lead to the development of prosocial behaviors among members. Additional support also is available from a series of group dynamics experiments concerning varying group reward structures (Deutsch and Gerard, 1967).

Indirectly, group contingencies can contribute to the attainment of another group work objective, namely, enabling members to acquire prosocial reinforcement value for one another. If an entire group is offered reinforcement for improved behavior by certain of its antisocial members, two obvious consequences can be posited: greater peer group pressures toward the enactment of prosocial behavior and greater interpersonal attraction among the members as they share in the reward. These outcomes are mutually reinforcing. Greater attraction leads to stronger conformity pressures, increased susceptibility to such pressures, more effective goal attainment, more frequent reward sharing and, in turn, to greater interpersonal attraction (Cartwright and Zander, 1968).

In contrast, individual contingencies frequently lead to dysfunctional or unanticipated outcomes. For instance, structuring of competitive activities among group members may result in failure or rejection for some members, exclusion from power positions in the group, lower goal attainment for the group as a whole and, perhaps, in increased antisocial behavior. Likewise, by reinforcing only selected members in the presence of others, the worker actually may withdraw available reinforcements from those who are not rewarded. The latter members may perceive such relative deprivation as a form of punishment, resulting in all the dysfunctions thereof. Hence, the utilization of individual reinforcement contingencies within the group (a common practice, incidentally, in social group work) may produce a number of undesired outcomes. It not only may entail adverse consequences for the unreinforced members but, in addition, may decrease the members' attraction to one another, obstruct group sharing and goal attainment and, in sum, diminish the group's overall effectiveness as a treatment vehicle. Moreover, the few children who receive individual reinforcements may acquire aversive stimulus and discriminative properties for the others, who might conclude that further interpersonal exchanges with the "successful" members will result in continued failure to receive desired reinforcements. Consequently, as the number of nonreinforcing exchanges increases, the tendency for children to interact with their peers and to remain in the group may decrease.

By employing group reinforcement contingencies with antisocial children the worker also can eliminate the likelihood that only a limited number of children will receive reinforcement within the group. Hence it becomes unnecessary to induce competition for available reinforcers. Instead, members can be encouraged to exhibit prosocial behaviors that will contribute to the procurement of reinforcers for all. Moreover, they may be likely to exert strong pressures upon their peers to exhibit such behaviors. These behaviors can lead to the acquisition of additional reinforcers after a number of pairings with the original one and, therefore, to the acquisition of secondary reinforcing properties (Staats and Staats, 1964). As the group develops valuable reinforcing properties its effectiveness as a treatment vehicle is likely to be enhanced. Consequently, the group no longer will serve solely as a context for behavioral change. It also will constitute an active agent for behavioral change.

Relevant Issues

The foregoing model requires that practitioners delineate and specify variables concretely. When the model is employed in the animal laboratory it is relatively easy to define relevant discriminative stimuli, behaviors, and their consequences. However, when the same concepts are applied in social work practice, ambiguities often exist regarding the definition of discriminative stimuli, target behaviors, and reinforcing consequences. Specifically, what are the dimensions of a discriminative stimulus? How does it differ from behavior per se, if at all? How does behavior differ from reinforcement? In group work practice it is especially necessary to isolate discriminative stimuli and the consequences that influence antisocial behaviors within the group.

It is generally agreed that certain reinforcers have properties that are very potent for most individuals. These include praise, food, and money. However, even this assumption depends on other functional variables, such as absolute and relative levels of deprivation. The extent of time that an individual has forgone a reinforcer, the quantities of it that he has received in the past, and the quantities available to others with whom he compares himself, serve to determine the potency of a given reinforcer for an individual. Since there is little systematic knowledge regarding which reinforcers are effective for specific client groups, further research concerning this topic is essential. It would be useful, for example, to develop an inventory of reinforcers that can be utilized, particularly with antisocial children of one kind or another. Needless to say, the classification of reinforcers will represent an enormous task since there will be many individual differences among various populations.

Additionally, one cannot overlook the many value questions associated with the determination of which behaviors are to be increased or decreased. This does not appear to be a critical problem for adults who are capable of living in the open community. Many therapists plan treatment programs for such clients in full cooperation with them. However, there may be problems for clients within closed or semiclosed institutions, such as mental hospitals, prisons, and schools. In most instances, it appears that therapists have addressed such issues by regarding the targeted behaviors as necessary attributes of effectively functioning individuals or environments, for example, teaching mathematics so that children will be able to tell time and make change, helping hospitalized patients to learn self-care, helping children to acquire behaviors necessary for effective learning, and helping adults and juvenile offenders to learn vocational skills essential for successful reintegration into society (Bandura, 1969; O'Leary, Poulous, and Devine, 1972; Winett and Winkler, 1972; O'Leary, 1972). Safeguards against the misuse of behavior modification frequently are provided through the careful preparation of professionals who will apply its principles within the framework of a well-elaborated code of professional ethics. Professional associations that reinforce such values should further develop standards against which practice activities can be evaluated. In addition, they should endeavor to impose sanctions when professional ethics are violated. It should be noted, however, that the same concerns can be voiced for all powerful and effective treatment technologies.

It is evident also, as noted previously, that most interventions utilized by behavior modifiers have been applied on a one-to-one basis, with a specific focus on modifying a single individual's behavior (Wahler, 1969; Walker and Buckley, 1972; Hartman and Atkinson, 1973). This may result in relatively few transfer effects to the open community because behaviors learned on a one-to-one basis tend to be associated with the single therapist or the lone context in which therapy took place. In other words, the general characteristics of the therapist and the therapeutic context may acquire a discriminative function over the new behavior learned by the client. This situation can be altered if one further analyzes how social systems can be modified in order to maintain the behaviors produced in therapy. It is interesting to note that any social system can be conceptualized as a series of interconnected reinforcers utilized to maintain prosocial behaviors. In addition, it is evident that many social systems, such as psychiatric hospitals, prisons, and institutions for the retarded, often maintain the behaviors that they are structured to modify and, furthermore, sometimes teach additional maladaptive behaviors to clients. Hence, the basic question may be: How can one modify social systems effectively after the client has changed his own behavior? And how can one help individuals to learn to modify those systems that originally induced maladaptive behavior?

Another issue pertains to the applicability of this method in an open setting. Open settings do not readily provide the controls necessary for implementation of such a technology, especially in terms of capabilities for securing adequate baselines and reliable data. Particular difficulties are encountered in monitoring a client's behavior and in enabling him to carry out treatment plans without supervision. These concerns, however, are characteristic of most treatment modalities. Procedures employed to alleviate such problems might include teaching clients to keep daily charts of their behavior, and to record events which occur before and after their problematic behaviors.

Successful application of behavior modification to open environments will require greater ability to develop adequate monitoring systems implemented by significant persons in the client's environment. Similarly, the practitioner may need to learn how to gain greater control over a client's natural environment. If treatment is to take place in a closed environment, education of staff members involved in the basic treatment plan is essential in order for them to coordinate and participate in the structuring of proper reinforcement contingencies. This principle is also applicable to the open environment. Moreover, involvement of significant others in treatment, such as family members, will increase the probability of success. Another organizational variable which must be assured is channels of feedback which indicate whether or not the behavior modifier is, in fact, effectively implementing the method. Sufficient incentives must be required to assure the successful implementation of such techniques.

Aside from the value issues noted above, it is relevant to question whether or not paraprofessionals can implement such a methodology effectively. It would seem that behavior modification technology lends itself nicely to the execution of tasks by paraprofessionals, especially with social workers or other professionals as supervisors. However, a note of caution is advised. Research in other fields indicates that certain characteristics, such as motivation, self-adjustment, verbal ability, and so forth, are essential for paraprofessionals to execute treatment effectively (Gruver, 1971; Berkowitz and Graziano, 1972). It is imperative that such characteristics be identified in order to select paraprofessionals who can successfully implement the treatment technology. Likewise, once defined, it is necessary to structure appropriate work environments in order to create conditions conducive to maintenance of the foregoing attributes.

The role of expectations in the operant model also must be noted. There is substantial research to indicate that a most crucial variable in the achievement of therapeutic change is the type of communication from therapist to client, especially communications which indicate that the therapist believes the client will improve (Goldstein, 1962; Rosenthal and Rosnow, 1969). Future research should clarify the role of expectations, how they are communicated, and how they can be appropriately controlled.

Similar questions will pertain to the future use of modeling in behavior therapy. Practitioners most likely will learn how to use high status, powerful models more effectively in order to help antisocial children to acquire prosocial behaviors. However, further research should be applied to questions such as, for example, when to use modeling, for what problems, for what types of clients, and in what contexts. Such questions obviously are relevant, also, for most of the other techniques mentioned in this chapter (Paul, 1969).

Training and Supervision

It is recommended that students first acquire a general knowledge of behavior modification principles through the careful examination of references, such as those cited in this work. Next, professional group workers who are knowledgable in the method should role-play various aspects of group treatment meetings, especially where they serve as therapist models for the students. Such sessions should include demonstrations of techniques and illustrations of how behavioral diagnoses are made. After students have had occasion to observe the professionals in action, they should be afforded an opportunity to lead the group. Immediate feedback from practitioners and other students should enhance their learning.

Another mechanism for providing feedback entails the use of videotapes, which enable various facets of practice to be replayed and examined immediately and repetitively. Students should review tapes, make a behavioral diagnosis, and design a corresponding intervention plan. Their performance on such tasks should meet the two basic criteria cited earlier: behaviors to be modified must be clearly specified, especially in terms of observable referents, and treatment interventions must be clearly specified in order to achieve the requisite modifications. Moreover, students should be trained to collect systematic data regarding the behaviors to be changed. Preferably, these should be graphed. This requirement necessitates that students become skilled in systematic observational techniques.

Systematic behavioral observation entails delineation of a specific time period during which the target behaviors are to be counted. Such behaviors may be counted at previously determined, fixed time intervals (such as at ten-second intervals) or continuously throughout an observational period. The unit of time depends on the type of behavior chosen for modification, the availability of technical equipment, the anticipated frequency of the behavior, and similar desiderata.

Once students have been introduced to observational techniques they can be provided with information concerning the use of experimental designs. This will help them to evaluate whether or not their interventions are having the desired effects on target behaviors. The classical design in behavior modification is the A,B,A,B design. Data in Figure 2 provide an example of the typical A,B,A,B design. In this figure, percentage frequencies of prosocial, nonsocial, and antisocial behavior are graphed for a group of ten children meeting for two-hour sessions over a period of fourteen weeks. In the first phase, the children are exposed to a *baseline period,* during which the group worker does not purposely plan interventions that are likely to influence the display of prosocial, nonsocial, or antisocial behaviors within the group. This is analogous to a traditional diagnostic technique postulated by Sallie Churchill (1965), where the group worker refrains from intervention during the early stages of diagnosis so that he can more accurately assess the treatment needs

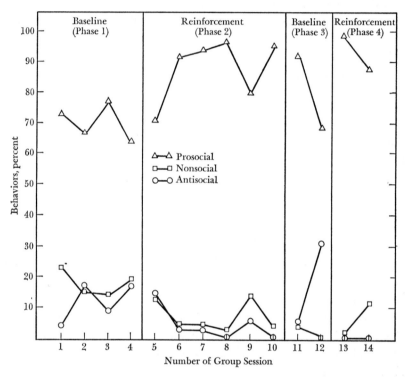

FIGURE 2. Average percentage of prosocial, nonsocial, and antisocial behaviors exhibited by ten children, according to number of group session.

of the clients without undue contamination from his own interventive efforts. As indicated in Figure 2, after the children's observed incidence of antisocial behavior reaches a stabilized, or "natural," level, treatment is introduced and members' behaviors are monitored (phase two) until they stabilize once again. After the behaviors are stabilized, a baseline condition is reintroduced (phase three). This condition is termed the "reversal" period. The procedure enables the therapist and others who evaluate the treatment program to determine whether the treatment itself was responsible for the various changes in behavior. Immediately after it is evident that the treatment has been effective in reducing antisocial behavior, the reinforcement procedures are applied once again (phase four).

In some situations the A,B,A,B design may not be feasible because of the types of behaviors being modified and, possibly, for ethical reasons. On some occasions the behavior to be modified will not be reversible. On others, reversals might be unduly damaging to the client or to significant others. For example, once fighting is brought under control it hardly seems therapeutic to revive it.

An alternative is the multiple baseline design, where the worker focuses on a *series* of modifiable behaviors. Predictions are made regarding the various techniques that will affect different behaviors. Then each behavior is modified according to a given time schedule. Usually, one set of incompatible behaviors is modified at a time. For example, a worker might wish to decrease behaviors such as yelling, fighting, hoarding, and running away from the group. Concurrently, he may wish to increase calm discourse, cooperation, sharing, and attendance. First, he might choose to ignore yelling and to use positive reinforcement to increase countervailing appropriate behaviors. Once yelling decreases, he can proceed to reduce the second, third, and fourth undesired behaviors while reinforcing more positive ones. Each time that the requisite behaviors change in the predicted direction the procedure becomes correspondingly more powerful.

Finally, it is useful for students to have their groups videotaped periodically. Students should view the tapes alone at first, then with their supervisors and, finally, with peers. This review procedure provides increasing feedback concerning implementation of the method.

Following an adequate diagnostic period, implementation can be attempted through the use of schematic aids, such as an evaluation form to be completed by the worker after each meeting. This form can help the worker to bear in mind key treatment objectives. An adequate evaluation form can consist of a series of columns with the following headings, respectively: client's name; problematic behavior; preceding events; following events; duration; frequency; type of individual or group contingency structured; reward. Under the heading of "problematic behavior," the worker should describe in detail the key behaviors exhibited by each child in the group, especially those which interfere with the group's functioning. Examples of such behaviors are hitting, slapping, whistling loudly, and so forth. One should list only those behaviors which are observable and quantifiable. Under "preceding events" (discriminative stimuli), the worker should list those behaviors which the children or the worker exhibited immediately before the child displayed the problematic behaviors. For instance, "William and George teased Johnny before he fought." Under "following events" (consequences), the worker should list those behaviors which the children or worker exhibited immediately after the client displayed the problematic behaviors cited. Under "duration," he should estimate how long the child exhibited the requisite behaviors, in terms of minutes and seconds for each time that they occurred. He also should describe the frequency of those behaviors at each meeting. Next, he should note the type of individual or group contingency to be structured in order to increase targeted prosocial behaviors and/or to decrease antisocial or nonsocial behaviors. It is important to remember that a group contingency can be used to increase or to decrease the behavior of one child, of several children, or of the group as a whole. Finally, under "reward" the worker should indicate what type of reinforcement is to be provided for the child, or children, for responding to the contingency.

A similar group evaluation form also can be prepared. Under "problematic behavior," one should list the behaviors which two or more individuals exhibit simultaneously, especially if they disrupt the group. The worker should indicate how many children exhibited the behavior, and their names. Preceding events, following events, duration, frequency, the type of group contingency, and reward are completed in the same fashion as specified in the instructions for the individual evaluation. It should be noted that the individual and group evaluation forms may be completed after each group meeting, thus resulting in the accumulation of schematic process recordings throughout the duration of treatment.

Interventive Methods: Case Illustrations

In order to exemplify some of the many points that have been discussed, especially regarding the formulation of behavior modification plans, two illustrative cases will be discussed briefly.

Fred, a sixteen-year-old boy, was referred by a residential treatment center for antisocial children. He exhibited the following problematic behaviors: not staying with the treatment group, not participating in group activities, distracting other members from planning activities by bird calls or whistling, and physically threatening the majority of the group members if they did not go along with the things he wanted to do. The worker decided to work on all four of these behaviors by structuring the following contingencies. In order to help Fred stay with the group, it was concluded that stimulus control would be employed. The worker would meet with the children away from the agency in a context which would not enable the child to leave the group meeting readily. Most of the meetings were held at a member's house or at the leader's house. At the same time, it was agreed that the group members would try to structure activities that would appeal to Fred in order to help make the group more attractive to him and to exert a more potent influence on his behavior. To deal with his fighting it was decided to structure a group contingency. If no fights occurred during the meeting, all the members could buy ice cream, go bowling, or go out for a pizza. Finally, as treatment progressed, and as Fred could stay with the group for increasingly longer sessions, meetings were returned to the agency. At the same time, the worker reinforced Fred's participation in planning activities through using physical reinforcement, such as pats on the back, praise, and attention.

Stan is a nine-year-old boy in the fourth grade of a school system which is one of the most progressive in the metropolitan area. His parents are rather affluent. Stan appears to be of normal height, weight, intelligence, and health for his age. Stan's behaviors during the baseline period included pushing and throwing furniture at people, running in the halls, disrupting other groups by name-calling, making loud noises, and withdrawing from group activities. Diagnosis suggested that his key antisocial behaviors were maintained by positive reinforcement through peer attention, particularly from his buddy Tom, who laughed, joined with him, and physically reinforced him for such behaviors by pats on the back and smiling. Additionally, it was apparent that the group worker's reprimands to Stan tended to reinforce such behavior, rather than diminish it, particularly by reaffirming Stan's behavioral problems among his peers.

Contingencies of behavioral change were implemented after baseline. The worker began by engaging the group in an activity that interested the members. As in previous instances, Stan and Tom attempted to disrupt the activity. Because the majority of members wished to engage in the activity, the group worker reinforced them for their participation with smiling and praise. At the same time, he ignored the behaviors of Stan and Tom. In a short time disruptions by Stan and Tom ceased. They began to participate increasingly in the group's activities. As they did so, the worker reinforced their behavior with smiles and verbal praise. In order to enhance the members' efforts to build cooperative relationships, and to plan and complete increasingly demanding tasks, the group worker paired the children with one another in subsequent sessions and structured further contingencies. Specifically, the members were told that each person would earn twenty cents if the group could plan an activity in which everyone could participate. Likewise, the members were informed that each person would receive an additional twenty cents if *everyone* participated in the chosen activity. These contingencies helped Stan and Tom to plan, and to participate more effectively and consistently in group activities. Additionally, as they earned social reinforcements from the worker and their peers, they were more readily accepted by the members and felt more comfortable in the group. In order to avoid satiation with monetary reinforcements, other group contingencies and other reinforcers were introduced at periodic intervals. Thus, for example, the group was asked to engage in an activity without anyone disrupting the others, after which the members would have a party, go swimming, or have refreshments.

Toward termination of the group, the monetary contingency was structured on a less frequent basis to insure some maintenance of the behavior. If everyone participated in planning and performing an activity without disruptive behaviors such as fighting, throwing objects, and so forth, each member would receive thirty cents. However, for each individual disruption the entire group was penalized five cents per person. Throughout, the leader used reinforcers such as praise, smiling, nodding of the head, eye contact, and physical contact, in order to foster prosocial behavior by Stan and Tom.

Summary

Behavior modification principles provide social group work with additional techniques for altering the behavior of antisocial children. Through the use of such principles, many group-work concepts can be redefined, operationalized, and analyzed in order to establish their predictive potency. Following a review of behavior modification concepts applicable to both casework and group work, efforts were made here to explicate and illustrate group behavioral contingencies that are uniquely suitable for group work theory and practice. Preliminary evidence suggests that group contingencies can change certain behaviors more rapidly than individual contingencies. Previous research also supports the assumption that given behaviors can be maintained more readily when reinforcement is based upon group, rather than individual, contingencies. Since group contingencies avoid many of the unanticipated and dysfunctional outcomes associated with individual contingencies, they are especially valuable for social group work. Group contingencies may be of particular relevance in helping social work to reduce the competitive nature of many therapies and to enhance members' concern for one another.

The discussion set forth in this chapter should be viewed primarily as an initial statement regarding the application of group-level behavior modification to social work practice. It is evident that features of the model will change in forthcoming years. Within the foreseeable future, it seems apparent that the formulations set forth will be elaborated and synthesized in such a way as to make them even more suitable for group-work application. These additions may include the elaboration of complex group contingencies and member-member and worker-member reinforcement matrices.

Group-Centered
(No-Treatment) Method

◆◆◆
◆◆◆

The usefulness of any given treatment method can be ascertained, in part, without necessarily contrasting its effects with those of other treatment methods. Utilization of the typical A_1-B_1-A_2-B_2 experimental paradigm, for example, will enable an investigator to contrast the effects of no treatment (A_1) with the implementation of treatment (B_1), with temporary withdrawal of the treatment (A_2), and with subsequent reinstatement of the treatment (B_2). Should a subject improve markedly during period B_1, temporarily retrogress during period A_2, and improve again during period B_2, it can be assumed that the treatment provided during periods B_1 and B_2 did, in fact, result in behavioral changes not obtained during the no-treatment periods A_1 and A_2. Moreover, usually it is possible to gauge the actual extent to which behavioral frequencies noted during periods B_1 and B_2 vary from those observed during A_1 and A_2. Nonetheless, certain relevant questions cannot be answered satisfactorily unless a given treatment method also is contrasted over time with one or more other treatment methods. The latter may include a "no-treatment" modality. By "no-treatment" we refer to a method in which the group *leader* makes *no* systematic or purposive efforts to diagnose, evaluate, treat, or change members' behaviors. This is not meant to con-

150

Control member

note that no treatment at all is likely to occur in the group context since, in fact, the group members may "treat" one another or themselves, or the leader may inadvertently engage in therapeutic activities.

The purposeful employment of no-treatment methods may be advisable for several reasons, discussed below.

Reasons for Use

Cost effectiveness comparisons. Most centrally, one cannot conduct effective cost-benefit comparisons between treatment methods unless they are subjected to comparable test conditions. Utilizing the two previously cited group treatment methods as examples, it may be possible to prove that such methods do, indeed, result in measurable behavioral changes for subjects exposed to them. Requisite data could be obtained from typical A_1-B_1-A_2-B_2 experimental paradigms. They could not, however, answer the question of whether or not such methods are likely to work more effectively, over a given period of time, than one or more other treatment methods, including a *no*-treatment method. To answer that question, the no-treatment method must be applied to similar groups operating within similar situational contexts over similar periods of time. Likewise, standardized measures of "effectiveness" must be utilized, whether they refer to units of behavioral change, frequency variations in certain types of behavior, or per capita dollars and cents expenditures.

In order to evaluate the efficacy of the traditional group work and group level behavior modification methods during the St. Louis Experiment, it was deemed advisable to ascertain not only whether each of the methods results in discernible changes for subjects but, also, whether or not each results in greater behavioral change than the provision of no treatment at all. For, contrary to much popular supposition, there is a significant body of research which indicates that subjects who are not exposed to treatment will manifest behavioral changes which are similar in type and extent to subjects who have, in fact, undergone various modes of treatment (Bergin and Garfield, 1971). The withholding of treatment for subjects, be they regarded as mentally ill, antisocial, or behaviorally maladapted by any other designation, does not necessarily suggest that those persons will be arrested in their behavioral development. On the contrary, some subjects may show significant behavioral improvements for one reason or another, including normal maturational processes which may occur within their social environments or themselves.

By the same token, it is possible that the provision of treatment for subjects will result neither in improvement nor, even, in the absence of any observable behavioral changes. Indeed, a substantial literature suggests that treatment may even result in retrogression, or in heightened probabilities for subsequent behavioral maladaptations. This is especially apparent from a review of recent studies concerning treatment programs for antisocial boys (for example, Berleman and others, 1972; Warren, 1970; Wolfgang and others, 1972).

Similarly, a number of investigators have reported that rudimentary treatment interventions applied by untrained practitioners, including college students (Poser, 1966) and placebo-equipped experimenters (Frank, 1961; Fish, 1973), may result in desired behavioral changes that equal or surpass those obtained by highly trained professionals. No-treatment experiments, at the very least, raise a central question with reference to the critical assessment of any given treatment method, namely: To what extent, if any, is that method more effective than either no treatment at all or treatment administered by relatively untrained practitioners?

Maturation effects. From a research perspective, the application of a no-treatment method is invaluable in order to test differentially for two basic phenomena. The first is *differential cost effectiveness* between two or more methods, as discussed above; the second is *maturation*. Variations of the latter include "historical effects," "placebo effects," "Hawthorne effects," and "Rosenthal effects."

Maturation refers to behavioral alterations that may take place among subjects due to normal developmental processes. More specifically, maturation refers to processes which occur within or among respondents, and which primarily are a function of the passage of time per se (Campbell and Stanley, 1963, p. 175). Illustrative processes include growing older, hungrier, or more tired.

Frequently, effects that are attributed to treatment interventions are, in fact, due solely to such developmental processes and not at all to the interventions themselves. However, it is absolutely impossible to differentiate treatment changes from those due to maturation unless one concurrently compares subjects who receive no treatment with those who do receive a particular treatment. In brief, if one studies both types of subjects under identical circumstances, any behavioral changes noted for the former must be attributed to maturation, whereas those observed for the latter can be attributed to the dual effects of maturation and the treatment itself. The extent to which there are behavioral variations between the two groups of subjects can be attributed to the effects of intervention, that is, to the treatment method. Such effects conceivably can be of either a positive or a negative nature.

Similarly, certain contextual or historical factors can stimulate changes among subjects. These may be independent of, or above and beyond, those produced by a treatment itself. Specifically, such factors refer to particular events, in addition to the experimental variable, which occur between a first and a second measurement. Thus, for example, if one studies the differential effects of two types of wheat-sowing procedures, it is important to contrast the procedures in adjacent plats of land. Otherwise it will be difficult, if not impossible, to control for the effects of factors that may vary in accord with the differing locations of the two study sites, such as amount of sunshine, rain, temperature variations, and so forth. By the same token, the social environment of a given treatment institution may exert certain common influences upon subjects who obtain treatment within it. In effect, these may be significantly different from the influences to be found in other agencies offering similar treatment programs. Consequently, in order to test adequately for the differences between a given treatment modality and a no-treatment method, it is essential to conduct the tests within the same social milieu. In particular, such an approach will control, in large part, for the differential effects of social history and social context, as well as for maturation effects.

A rigorous test of two different methods will control not only for those effects that may vary due to differing social environments, but also for effects that may be attributable to variations in timing or sequencing of relevant interventions. Thus, in contrasting the effects of two or more treatment methods, it is essential to assure that treatment (or no treatment) will be applied to all subjects for simultaneous time periods of identical duration. For instance, although two groups might be subjected to different treatment methods for comparable twenty-week periods, an investigator could reasonably anticipate differing absence rates if one twenty-week period primarily took place during the winter while the other occurred primarily during the summer. Likewise, institutional climates and resources may vary with certain seasons or holiday periods. As a result, they may indirectly influence the treatment methods applied by staff.

In order to provide an adequate test for two or more treatments, it also is important to assume that the methods will be applied to highly similar groups of subjects. This may be assured by *matching* subjects along key dimensions or through the *random assignment* of subjects who are entered into a control pool due to one or more common factors relevant for the experimental investigation. Since subjects rarely can be matched identically in terms of all major sociobehavioral criteria, it is usually more desirable to assign subjects randomly to differing treatment methods. In essence, then, adequate comparisons between treatment and no-treatment groups depend upon proper controls for variations in subjects' sociobehavioral attributes and social environments.

Finally, it is important to note that certain pretreatment variables also should be comparable for treatment and no-treatment groups. This is most essential in the case of no-treatment baseline periods, which precede the actual implementation of treatment itself. These should be identical in duration and content so that subjects from one group or another will not encounter undue differences in pretest social experiences.

Hawthorne effects and Rosenthal effects. In addition to those forms of social maturation that may be regarded as features of the normal development of individuals or groups, similar processes often arise as by-products of an experimental procedure. To

the extent that these result in behavioral changes that are independent from those directly induced by the experimental treatment,
they may be viewed as a type of maturation process. Moreover,
without the contrasting data provided by a no-treatment group,
their effects cannot be delineated clearly from the particular effects
of the treatment.

The first series of studies to demonstrate such effects were the
classic Hawthorne Western Electric studies conducted by Roethlisberger and Dickson (1939). In conjunction with an experiment
performed by the Harvard Business School, the investigators were
asked to determine the effects of variations in lighting upon the
performance of work teams engaged in the assembly of intricate
telephone wiring units. As expected, a significant increment in the
number of lumens available for lighting the work area resulted in a
greater rate of employee productivity. To the investigators' astonish-
ment, however, a significant reduction in the number of lumens *also*
led to greater productivity, thus establishing one conclusion as a
result of their empirical studies, to wit, that workers' productivity
was not directly correlated with the extent of work area lighting!
Instead, the investigators concluded that, regardless of the available
lighting, the workers under both conditions responded positively to
the knowledge that they were participants in an experimental study,
thus increasing their productivity. This phenomenon has become
widely known as the "Hawthorne effect."

In order to differentiate between the Hawthorne effect and
the additional changes that may be attributed to treatment interventions, it is necessary, first of all, to expose a given category of subjects
to all facets of an experimental situation, except for the particular
treatment interventions to be studied. It is assumed that both the
treatment and no-treatment subjects will face an equal likelihood of
experiencing the Hawthorne effect, but that only the former will
have occasion to experience any additional effects attributable to the
treatment interventions themselves.

More recent research by Rosenthal (1966) and his associates
has illustrated a phenomenon denoted, appropriately, as the "Rosenthal effect." In these studies, categories of presumably identical
subjects were differentially labelled by an experimenter in order to
ascertain the differential responses of other persons to those subjects

and, ultimately, to define any significant variations that might occur in the subjects' behavior. In one study, for example, students who obtained similar scores on cognitive tests were divided into two categories by the experimenter. He informed the classroom instructor that one group of students had obtained high scores on the test while the other group had obtained low scores. Both groups of students, in fact, had obtained very similar scores. A subsequent follow-up study indicated that the students who had been falsely labeled as "high scorers" showed better performance on the retest, whereas the students who had been falsely labeled as "low scorers" did not perform as well. This variation of the Hawthorne effect was one in which the experimenter created differential expectations for the two sets of subjects, namely, that one group would respond well to teaching and that the other would respond poorly. This expectation effect, or experimenter effect, apparently was communicated to the teacher who, in turn, may have devoted extra time or attention to the "high scoring" students, thus enhancing their performance capacities. Likewise, it is conceivable that the teacher may have communicated corresponding expectations to the respective student groups, thus influencing their self-conceptions and/or learning performances accordingly (Rosenthal, 1966; Rosenthal and Rosnow, 1969).

The Rosenthal effect, also, can be best examined by contrasting no-treatment subjects with treatment subjects. It is essential, however, that all communications to members of the no-treatment and treatment groups, as well as communications to their respective leaders or experimenters, be identical in nature and content. Otherwise, varying sets of experimenter effects, or expectation effects, will be communicated to each group and it will be impossible to control for either. It is interesting to note, also, that the Rosenthal effect has been found to occur in a study of albino rats who were bred systematically in order to assure virtually identical genetic constitutions and learning capabilities. As with the foregoing study, the rats were divided into two categories and the trainer was told that one group of rats consisted of rapid learners whereas the other consisted of slow learners. Following a series of maze-learning experiments, those rats which had been labelled as fast learners traversed the maze much more rapidly than those labelled as slow learners (Rosenthal and Fode, 1963).

Placebo effects. A related series of experimental phenomena have been classified as placebo effects. One of the most interesting discussions of these effects in biological experimentation has been reported by Frank (1961). As Frank notes, a placebo is a pharmacologically inert substance that a physician administers to a patient in order to relieve his distress when, for one reason or another, he does not wish to use an active medication. Since a placebo is inert, its effectiveness rests solely in its ability to mobilize the patient's expectancy of help. On occasion, Frank states, a patient's expectations have been shown to affect his physiological responses so powerfully as even to reverse the pharmacological action of a drug. In a dramatic example, he reports that "evidence that placebos can have marked physiological effects has been afforded by demonstrations of their ability to heal certain kinds of tissue damage. The placebo treatment of warts, for example, by painting them with a brightly colored but inert dye, and telling the patient that the wart will be gone when the color wears off, is as effective as any other form of treatment, and works just as well on patients who have been unsuccessfully treated by other means as on untreated ones. Apparently the emotional reaction to a placebo can change the physiology of the skin so that the virus which causes warts can no longer survive" (1961, pp. 67–68).

In a further illustration, Frank reports (1961, p. 68):

> Placebo treatment can also activate healing of more severely damaged tissues, especially when the damage seems related to physiological changes connected with unfavorable emotional states. In one study of patients hospitalized with bleeding peptic ulcer, for example, 70% showed 'excellent results lasting over a period of one year,' when the doctor gave them an injection of distilled water and assured them that it was a new medicine that would cure them. A control group who received the same injection from a nurse with the information that it was an experimental medication of undetermined effectiveness showed a remission rate of only 25%.

In both instances it is clear that the mere expectation that the treatment would produce a positive effect did, in fact, contribute significantly to results in the anticipated direction. This occurred even when such an effect was manifestly impossible upon the basis of the chemical composition of the "treatment" agents. Frank has extended his analysis to the social realm by suggesting that various forms of religious healing, mystical cures, and, even, psychotherapeutic results can be attributed to analogues of the so-called placebo effect. Likewise, Halmos (1966) and Fish (1973) have set forth a similar interpretation for therapeutic cures. Recently, Back (1972) has viewed certain of the purported benefits of sensitivity group and encounter group experiences as representative of the placebo effect. As with the foregoing examples, to the extent that subjects' expectations regarding the presumed benefits of treatment do, in fact, account for requisite changes, the latter cannot be gauged accurately unless no-treatment control groups are studied simultaneously for purposes of comparison. Identical instructions, communications, and expectations must be conveyed to both types of groups.

In summary, then, no-treatment control groups can be extremely useful in experimental research into the differential effects of one or more group treatment methods. Aside from research efficacy, however, the available literature regarding behavioral change among subjects participating in no-treatment groups points to the possible therapeutic advantages, also, of a no-treatment method. However, the theoretical rationales for such an approach rarely have been delineated in the small group literature.

Group-Centered Method as Treatment Modality

Virtually all group treatment methods posit purposive, preplanned, and systematic treatment interventions by the group worker. This is certainly the case for the two formulations set forth in the preceding chapters. A number of more recent books written by social group workers also express the same theme, although in a less systematic and consistent form than set forth here. Hartford (1972), for example, has explicitly pointed to the necessity for group workers to set well-defined treatment objectives in therapeutic work with groups (1972, pp. 139–158). Similarly, Northen (1969) has cited in great detail a number of essential characteristics of social work practice. These are presumed to apply to work with small groups as well as with individuals. Moreover, they explicitly denote the purposive and preplanned nature of the social worker's interventions. Among the cited characteristics are the following (pp. 6–7): (1) The social worker's practice is purposeful. (2) The social worker develops a professional relationship as an instrumentality for helping individuals and groups. (3) The social worker engages in the interrelated processes of social diagnosis, formulation of plans for action, implementation of the plans, and evaluation of outcomes, as these are adapted to particular purposes. (4) The social worker individualizes his work with persons and groups. (5) The social worker clarifies his role and works for congruence between the client's and his own perceptions of role expectations. (6) The social worker participates collaboratively with a person or a group in decision-making processes which enable the client to use the social environment toward improving his life situation. (7) The social worker facilitates the participation of clients in all aspects of the service. (8) The social worker makes use of agency and community resources, contributes his knowledge toward the development of new or improved services, collaborates with others who are serving his clients, and participates in efforts to influence desirable changes in policies and procedures in behalf of his clientele.

In another recent work, Trecker (1972) has set forth a listing of essential skills for group workers. These also point to the purposive nature of worker interventions. They include skills in establishing purposeful relationships, analyzing the group situation, participation with the group, dealing with group feelings, group development, evaluation, and using agency and community resources (pp. 86–87). Similar skills are cited, typically in the form of case illustrations, in a recent work by group workers Schwartz and Zalba (1972). Without question, then, the bulk of contemporary group-work literature, as well as the literature regarding treatment for individual clients, points to the desirability or necessity for purposive, preplanned, and systematic interventions by the therapist.

Nonetheless, some investigators have posited that therapeutic advantages accrue from approaches that are predicated upon few, if any, systematic interventions by the therapist.

Rogerian therapy. Perhaps the best known advocate of such an approach is Carl Rogers. Rogers has posited that a highly non-directive treatment modality, denoted as "client-centered therapy," yields a number of significant and unique therapeutic benefits. Presumably, the most important of these are the client's opportunities for individual expression and inner freedom. The worker's overt interventions take place minimally, if at all, in this method. Consequently, the client is permitted to display his natural behavioral dispositions in a manner that is relatively uncontaminated by the therapist's prior interventions, thus facilitating accurate diagnosis by the therapist and by himself.

The touchstone of client-centered therapy, according to Rogers, is its capacity to facilitate the client's *inner* freedom. This is "something which exists in the living person, quite aside from any of the outward choices of alternatives which we so often think of as constituting freedom" (Rogers and Stevens, 1967, p. 52). In Rogers's view, a growth-facilitating, or freedom-promoting, relationship contains at least three significant qualities. The foremost is that the therapist "is what he *is*" (p. 53), and that he comports himself in a genuine manner when in relationship with the client. The therapist should avoid any "fronts" or facades, and should be open about the feelings and attitudes which are within him at any given moment. Rogers has denoted this quality as *congruence.*

The second important quality is *unconditional positive regard* for the client. Presumably, positive change is effected when the therapist experiences a warm, positive, and accepting attitude toward what is in the client. Rogers notes (1951, p. 54):

> [This quality] involves the therapist's genuine willingness for the client to be whatever feeling is going on in him at that moment—fear, confusion, pain, pride, anger, hatred, love, courage, or awe. It means that the therapist cares for the client, in a non-possessive way. It means that he prizes the client in a total rather than a conditional way. . . . He does not simply accept the client when he is behaving in certain ways, and disapprove

of him when he behaves in other ways. It means an outgoing positive feeling without reservations, without evaluations.

The third essential quality denoted by Rogers is *empathic understanding.* "When the therapist is sensing the feelings and personal meanings which the client is experiencing in each moment, when he can perceive these from 'inside', as they seem to the client, and when he can successfully communicate something of that understanding to his client, then this third condition is fulfilled" (p. 55). Presumably, as the therapist exemplifies these three qualities the client becomes better able "to listen to himself" or to recognize his own inner feelings, becomes both more accepting and respecting of himself, and becomes more responsible for his own behavior. As he becomes correspondingly less evaluative and more accepting toward himself, the client also "moves toward being more real." In effect, this means that the client will be less defensive and more self-aware, self-accepting, self-expressive, and open, thus enabling himself to better experience human growth.

Obviously, therapists who use either of the treatment methods cited in the previous chapters would point to a basic inconsistency in the above exposition, namely, one's incapacity to engage in responsible or more adaptive behavior so long as he avoids systematic self-evaluation. Without continuous and accurate self-evaluations, it would appear to be exceedingly difficult, if not impossible, to gradually shape one's behavior in an adaptive manner. Nonetheless, in voluminous writings Rogers has stated the case for this approach to treatment. Moreover, he cites prior work conducted along similar lines. August Aichorn, for instance, conducted an experiment in the reeducation of delinquents in which the subjects were permitted freedom, within the institutional setting, to conduct themselves as they desired in the group led by himself. After a period of chaos, the subjects gradually chose a social, disciplined, and cooperative life as something that they preferred. As reported by Rogers, they "learned, through experience in an accepting relationship, that they desired responsible freedom and self-imposed limits rather than the chaos of license and aggression" (p. 57).

Similarly, A. S. Neill's Summerhill experiment has focused

on the provision of a learning milieu very similar to that espoused by Rogers and Aichorn. As a result, students at Summerhill have been reported to "develop a zest for living, a spontaneous courtesy, as well as initiative, responsibility, and integrity" (p. 57). Likewise, Rogers cites the progressive education movement and recent efforts at student-centered teaching as exemplars of his approach.

In further elaboration of the client-centered method, Rogers has suggested that clients benefit from the therapeutic relationship only if they are faced with a real problem, or problems, during the course of therapy. Requisite learning and human growth can result only as one confronts, and successfully deals with, meaningful problems in living. The therapist must hold a deep trust in the human organism in order to sustain himself through the arduous process of client growth which, at least in the beginning phases, may be chaotic. Moreover the therapist's functioning must be characterized by sincerity, realness, and absence of a facade. He also must demonstrate an attitude which accepts and prizes the client's feelings, opinions, and learning efforts. If the therapist can accept the client's occasional apathy, his desire to explore by-roads of knowledge, and his disciplined efforts to achieve major goals, he will promote the requisite learning. This prizing, or acceptance, of the client can be regarded as an operational expression of the therapist's essential confidence in the capacity of the human organism and, to some extent, might be likened to the "Rosenthal effect" discussed earlier. In addition to empathy, the effective therapist also facilitates the client's learning to be free by the provision of needed resources. These may refer to human resources as well as physical ones.

Rogers has also indicated those steps that the therapist or teacher should avoid in order to assure the effectiveness of this method. Although he concentrates on creating a facilitative climate, providing resources, and enabling clients to confront meaningful problems, the therapist does *not* set lessons or therapeutic tasks. "He does not assign readings. He does not lecture or expound (unless requested to). He does not evaluate and criticize unless the student wishes his judgment on a product. He does not give examinations. He does not set grades. . . . Such a teacher is not simply giving lip service to a different approach to learning. He is actually, operationally, giving his students the opportunity to learn to be responsibly free" (p. 61).

In summary, it is readily apparent why the Rogerian approach has been designated as "client-centered" therapy. The focus throughout is upon the *client's* own feelings, attitudes, and behaviors directed toward subsequent human growth. At the *overt* level, the therapist's behaviors are minimally interventive. Indeed, systematic overt interventions are virtually precluded to the extent that the therapist, in truth, can avoid evaluation of the client's behavior and, accordingly, any purposive efforts to overcome "maladaptive" client behaviors. However, the paucity of overt interventions in the Rogerian schema should not be equated with the absence of treatment interventions. To the contrary, it should be emphasized that the Rogerian approach represents one effort to derive a viable means of helping disabled individuals, albeit one which calls for a minimum of overt interventions by the therapist. To this extent, the treatment relationship is purposefully developed as one designed to advance client growth.

Analogues. Although a substantial literature has been produced by Rogers and his colleagues, it is important to note that the great bulk of that literature focuses on one-to-one relationships between therapists or teachers and their clients or students. This tends to be the case even when the learning encounter is situated primarily in a group context, such as a classroom. Most probably, such a focus has been manifested because therapists can assume an accepting, empathic, and nonevaluative stance more readily on their own behalf than they can for others in the group, such as the clients and their peers. Consequently, it is much easier to maintain the proper climate for such a therapeutic approach in a one-to-one situation than in a large peer group context. Paradoxically, the therapist can control more of the relevant treatment variables in a dyadic encounter, even if such variables pertain to the elaboration of a "noncontrolling" environment. Nonetheless, in the literature of group psychotherapy and social group work there have been a few beginning efforts to elaborate learning contexts similar to those postulated by Rogers.

Perhaps the best known are efforts by immediate colleagues

of Rogers. These include the early essays of Elaine Dorfman, Nicholas Hobbs, and Thomas Gordon. Drawing primarily from case illustrations, Dorfman has described a basic approach to play therapy that utilizes the Rogerian framework. As with client-centered therapy, this mode of treatment assumes that "the child's decision to do or not to do a particular thing is more beneficial than the actual performance of it. The child's opportunities for responsible self-direction are maximized, on the theory that the therapy session is a good place to begin to practice it. As in adult therapy a basic hypothesis is that a relationship of acceptance, as contrasted with positive or negative evaluation, reduces the need for defensiveness, and thus allows the child to dare to explore new ways of feeling and behaving. Because of this hypothesis, the therapist does not try to affect the pace or the direction of therapy; he follows rather than leads the child. . . . There is no attempt to alter the child, but only to make possible his self-alteration, when and if he wishes it" (Rogers, 1951, pp. 275–276).

In a seminal essay concerning group-level application of the Rogerian method, Hobbs was the first to introduce the term "group-centered therapy" (Rogers, 1951). For the most part, however, his discussion refers merely to certain similarities or differences between individual and group-level applications of the method, and to a discussion of case examples of the latter. Perhaps the best explication of a group-level application of Rogerian principles has been set forth in Gordon's essay concerning group-centered leadership and administration. Gordon asserts that the "most effective leader is one who can create the conditions by which he will actually lose the leadership" (Rogers, 1951, p. 334). In terms of his approach, the leader places value on two goals: the ultimate development of the group's independence and self-responsibility, and the release of the group's potential capacities. Accordingly, Gordon states (Rogers, 1951, p. 338):

> The group-centered leader believes in the worth of the members of the group and respects them as individuals different from himself. They are not persons to be used, influenced, or directed in order to accomplish the leader's aims. They are not people to be "led" by

someone who has "superior" qualities or more important values. The group-centered leader sees the group or organization as existing for the individuals who compose it. It is the vehicle for the expression of their personalities and for the satisfaction of their needs. He believes that the group as a whole can provide for itself better than can any single member of the group. He believes in the group's fundamental right to self-direction and to self-actualization on its own terms.

To facilitate achievement of the central objectives of the method within the above-cited assumptive framework, it is necessary for the group-centered leader to create certain supportive conditions. These include the creation of opportunities for member participation, freedom of communication, and a nonthreatening psychological climate. In order to foster such conditions, Gordon further posits that group leaders must perform a number of distinctive functions, such as conveying warmth and empathy, attending to others, understanding the meaning and intent of members' communications, conveying acceptance and permissiveness, and "linking" members' interactions with one another. These functions clearly suggest that the therapist in the group-centered situation necessarily will be somewhat more directive and, therefore, relatively less spontaneous, than in the individual-centered context, at least during the early phases of treatment. Ultimately, as with virtually all therapies, the therapist's role is meant to be eliminated, on the assumption that the members themselves subsequently will be capable of total self-direction.

Unlike most writers on either individual-centered or group-centered therapy, Gordon posits explicitly the outcomes of such a method for clients who participate in it. In particular, he attempts to discern the meaning of a group-centered experience for the individual members. More importantly, he endeavors to derive such meanings from the basic principles underlying the approach. He concludes, for instance, that such an approach helps group members to feel that they are understood, to feel that responsibility for evaluation lies within themselves, to gain understanding of themselves, to internalize functions of the group-centered leader, and to alter group functioning from ego-centered to group-centered participation. Correspondingly, there will occur an increase in spontaneous expression of feeling and meaning, a decrease in dependence upon the leader, and an acceptance of group standards. Although little empirical research has been performed to test the validity of these propositions, it is noteworthy that they are, in fact, stated in testable form.

Among social group workers who have adopted facets of the Rogerian approach, Tropp (1965, 1969, 1971) has tended to view members' social growth as the primary concern of group work. Tropp asserts that group workers need have no particularized or differentiated knowledge of each individual in the group. Likewise, he decries the use of diagnosis in group work and deprecates the study-diagnosis-treatment approach that has been so typical of group work, in particular, and of social work in general. Nevertheless, although he devalues the importance of individual diagnosis and treatment, Tropp points to the desirability of assessing, planning, and evaluating developments and interventions at the group level.

To a lesser extent, Klein (1970) has pointed to the many benefits of a group therapeutic environment that is relatively unstructured and that promotes clients' testing, freedom-seeking, and growth behaviors. He suggests (1970, p. 79):

> [It] is true that by allowing considerable structure, anxiety can be relieved. . . . If the purpose is to facilitate achieving a group task, such structuring may be desirable, but if the purpose is enhancing social functioning, perhaps the members need to learn to deal with each other as people and not escape as role carriers. The less structure a group provides, especially at its inception, the more the members will enact their usual modes of behavior, adaptation, defenses, and games because they will be reacting to stress, anxiety, fear, conflicts, and human contact. Bereft of structure they must be themselves, unprotected by a script. Such a living situation may afford maximum social learning.

Although Klein points to the possible dysfunctions of overly structured groups, he also suggests that certain types of group structure are conducive to effective treatment. Even more important, he delineates the relevance of purposeful interventions by the group worker, whether intended to enhance or diminish any particular type of group structure. Hence, regardless of the type of group structure that is desired, the group worker conducts himself as a purposeful change agent within the group. To that extent, his approach to therapy is much less nondirective than that espoused by Rogers. For these, and other reasons noted earlier, the client-centered group worker is obliged to engage more actively in interventions than would be occasioned by the typical one-to-one therapeutic encounter.

Possible Approaches

In order to evaluate the efficacy of the previously described traditional and behavior modification approaches to group work, it was deemed necessary to operationalize a valid and consistent no-treatment method—at least with reference to the leaders' activities—that could be applied to similar groups. In many respects it is possible to envision such an approach as highly similar to Rogers's "client-centered" therapy. Consequently, this method of group treatment was denoted as the "group-centered" method. Its focus is upon group members *other than* the therapist as the key actors and originators of social behavior within the group context. As with client-centered therapy, the group worker functions essentially as a natural, spontaneous, accepting, and nonevaluative member. To the extent that the group itself functions "naturally," it can be regarded as a no-treatment comparison group, or baseline group, available for comparison with other treatment modalities. Likewise, to the extent that members' behaviors change discernibly and significantly as a result of applying this method, it can be viewed as a viable form of group treatment. As with the two other group treatment methods, however, this determination essentially represents an empirical question which constituted a central concern of the St. Louis Experiment.

The elaboration of a "group-centered" method entails considerably greater thought than may first meet the eye. Such an approach should not necessarily be construed as suggesting that a group worker does little, or nothing at all, within the group context.

This would be quite dissimilar from the "natural" behavior of most individuals, including group leaders. Hence, a critical question is raised when such a method is applied at the group level rather than the individual level. That is, to what extent should the group worker assume that *other* group members, as well as himself, will behave in a "nondirective" or "natural" manner in order to facilitate effective treatment? Moreover, if he does proceed to structure the group accordingly, will he, in effect, be compromising the naturalness and nondirectiveness of his own behavior? These concerns and others point to several possible variations of a group-centered method, most of which must be dismissed since they are relatively incompatible with an approach that is truly group-centered.

Total nonintervention. Regardless of the operational definition of a no-treatment group, all such entities are predicated upon a common assumption, namely, that the group leader must not "treat" the members in any preplanned, purposive, or systematic way. All treatment interventions must be avoided, except for those required due to the most extenuating of circumstances, e.g., to preclude significant physical, psychological, or social harm to members. A literal, and highly conservative, interpretation of such a charge might suggest that the group worker should avoid *all* interaction with members of the group. In effect, he ought to conduct himself as a nonparticipant observer and should try to avoid either initiating social behaviors or responding to other members' social overtures.

The sole justifications for a leader's presence in such a group would be two-fold. The first would be to provide a physical occupant for the leader's position, thus making the group structurally, but not functionally, comparable to other groups that might be studied concurrently. In essence, although the formal leadership position in such a group would be occupied, the leader would be an inert or inactive one. This would provide structurally similar stimuli for initial member expectations that might be mobilized regarding effects of the leader's presence or regarding his anticipated interventions. In large part, this would control for possible Hawthorne or placebo effects. Second, the leader's presence might be regarded as an ultimate safeguard, especially if it should be necessary to intervene within the group in order to avert any imminent dangers that might beset one or more of the members.

In some modes of nondirective treatment the therapist has been reported to behave in such a manner. That is, he interacts minimally, if at all, with the client, thus enabling the client to verbalize his thoughts and feelings with virtually no interference or contamination from the therapist. This approach is typical of many free association techniques. It should be noted, however, that these are not particularly comparable with the usual Rogerian approach. In the latter, the therapist endeavors to behave primarily in a natural, rather than in an inert, inactive or dispassionate manner. It is questionable, moreover, whether a leader can, indeed, remain in a group without interacting with the members in one way or another.

Even more important is the question of what, in fact, might be the consequences for a group's development if a leader actually could perform a totally inactive role credibly? It is plausible, for instance, that the sustained presence of a noninteracting member could serve to stultify social interaction within a group, to deter natural developmental processes, or to extinguish desired member behaviors. In truth, few normal groups are characterized by the presence of a member who *never* interacts with his peers. To the contrary, groups with such members may manifest relatively deviant social patterns, such as serious scapegoating behavior.

In experiments concerning the delivery of individual treatment modalities such as social casework, no-treatment subjects frequently are placed on a waiting list, or are never enrolled in the study at all. Consequently, such subjects never come into contact with a treatment agent, even one who may be instructed to act in a totally nondirective or inactive manner. Typically, however, such a procedure cannot control for some of the methodological artifacts noted previously, such as differential placebo or expectation effects that may skew the treated clients' behaviors. Likewise, in order to control for such effects in the study of group treatment modalities, it is necessary to constitute a group *per se* but, nonetheless, to preclude interventive behaviors by the group leader. Although a formulation based upon the leader's total nonintervention effectively meets such a criterion, it is clear, nonetheless, that such an approach cannot be regarded as illustrative of "normal" group behavior.

Random intervention. In order to deal with some of the

deficiencies of the previously cited approach toward the elaboration of a no-treatment method, it is essential, first of all, to enable the group leader to interact with the group's members. Yet, such interactions must in no way contribute, either purposely or inadvertently, to a systematic pattern of treatment interventions. One possible strategy for the implementation of such an approach might entail leader interactions that are relatively frequent, but random, in their direction or content. For instance, a leader might be instructed to interact with varying group members either at fixed time intervals or at intervals previously determined upon the basis of random selection. Similarly, those members with whom he would interact might be predetermined upon the basis of a randomly selected sequence of numbers identical with numerical designations for the respective group members.

Although such an approach would be consistent with a formulation that calls for leader-member interaction, albeit of a noninterventive nature, it is obvious that several major problems are associated with it. A random intervention approach necessarily would be rather complex to administer and, in that regard, expensive in terms of staff-training, implementation, and monitoring. Most important, again, would be the probability that such an approach could foster a distinct likelihood of artificial or detrimental social interactions between the leader and the members and, subsequently, among the members themselves. Hence it could not be considered consistent with a conceptualization that enables normal or natural group developmental processes to take place.

Focused intervention. A third approach to the creation of no-treatment groups might vary considerably from the former two. Rather than avoiding all interactions with group members or, on the other hand, engaging in purely randomized interactions, a group leader might wish to engage in deliberate interventions with a unique purpose, namely, to assure that all of the other members interact with one another in a manner that facilitates natural group developmental processes. In contrast with the two foregoing methods, which entail no systematic interventions by the leader, the group worker in the present instance presumably would attempt to structure group interactions in order to assure normal development. The facilitative components of Rogers's client-centered therapy are somewhat akin to this perspective. In fact, they represent a main feature of his approach that draws the therapist away from a totally non-directive role.

Such an approach betokens two serious deficiencies, however, which preclude its effective utilization as a no-treatment method. First, it assumes an a priori model of normal group development which will serve as the criterion for the leader's interventive efforts. Yet, to date, investigators have reached no consensus regarding such a model or, even, regarding its basic parameters. To the contrary, a number of models for group development can be set forth.

Even more important, "normal" group developmental processes cannot necessarily be equated with "natural" ones. Natural behavior within one group, or one particular category of groups, may be highly abnormal when considered within the context of most other groups of similar size or constituency. The natural behavior of any given number of groups may be highly variable and, by itself, may be regarded essentially as an empirical question.

In addition, even if such a formulation actually could assure that members would conduct themselves within the parameters of natural group development, this observation would not apply for one essential group member, namely, the leader himself. His behaviors would be far from spontaneous since they would, in point of fact, be continuously and systematically oriented toward shaping the group in a predetermined manner.

Natural interaction. In essence, in any naturally developing group the leader can be the arbiter only of his own social behavior and interventions. To provide the basic prerequisites for natural behavior by a group's members, a leader cannot be permitted to interact consistently or systematically with any predetermined objectives, even if they pertain solely to the presumed goal of assuring natural or normal developmental processes.

It is likely, therefore, that the only procedure capable of addressing the above considerations is one which will enable the worker to behave in a natural manner while minimizing the probability of his learning or applying any knowledge that can be construed as treatment-related. Consequently, in line with certain facets of the Rogerian approach, the group leader in a no-treatment method should be permitted, even encouraged, to behave in whatever manner is natural and normal *for himself,* even if his behavior should not be congruent with that of other group leaders. At the same time, leaders in a no-treatment method should have *no* prior exposure to learning or training which prepares them to diagnose member behaviors and to intervene accordingly. Likewise, during the course of a study they should be excluded from any such training programs that might be offered for leaders of other treatment methods.

Of the several possible approaches toward the elaboration of a no-treatment method, the latter is viewed as the one most capable of effective functioning. Moreover, it is considered to be the one most consistent with the prerequisites for natural group development. In such an approach the group leader does not serve as an unnatural and noninteracting entity within the group. Nor does he conduct himself as a randomly interacting group member. Neither is he an individual who purposely and systematically intervenes within the group, even with the avowed intention of facilitating natural developmental processes.

Instead, he behaves naturally as an untrained group leader who interacts with the other members in a way that is usual and normal for himself. If he intervenes on occasion, it is at the level of an untrained, albeit involved, individual who relies in part upon intuition and in part upon partial and fragmented past learning experiences which, most probably, never before have been directed toward a treatment encounter. This would appear to be the most faithful and appropriate approach toward the establishment of a truly group-centered method.

Finally, it is relevant to reemphasize that the label "no-treatment" is presented here in a restrictive and narrow sense. It is meant to denote a method which strives to maximally reduce worker interventions which might be purposive, preplanned, or otherwise manipulative. In a broader conceptual sense, however, even such an approach as this necessarily must be acknowledged as representing one approach toward the worker's interaction with clients and, therefore, toward group "treatment."

Implementation

Implementation of the group-centered method bears many similarities to the formulations cited earlier by Rogers, Gordon, and others. In the St. Louis Experiment, group leaders were informed that the prime objective of the method was to enable group members to interact in a natural manner and, accordingly, to permit the group to undergo natural developmental processes. There were to be no systematic applications of rewards or punishments by the leader in order to influence any particular member behaviors. Instead, with reference to the leader's activities, each and every member behavior was to be accorded equally great potential for positive or negative reinforcement as any other behavior. To facilitate these objectives, the group leaders were instructed to observe two cardinal principles. First, they were to avoid all evaluations of behavior and to make no conscious, purposive, preplanned, or systematic attempts to alter behavior. Exceptions to the foregoing principle were permitted only if group members directly requested the leader to intervene. In such instances, leaders were instructed to restrict their responses to the explicit member request. It was not permissible, for example, to generalize one's responses or answers beyond the parameters of the original request. Nor was it permissible to encourage members to extend their requests by querying them, in turn, or by asking if they desired further elaboration. In brief, all deliberate behavioral interventions of group leaders were solely in response to the direct requests of members, were behaviorally specific, and did not extend, in time or substance, beyond demands posed by the explicit requests of group members.

Such guidelines were deemed to be relatively compatible with the second cardinal principle for leaders' behavior, namely, that they must behave in a *natural manner* in all of their interactive relationships with group members. This dictum was set forth with the full knowledge that natural behavior for some group leaders was likely to result in wide variations of behavior at different times. Unlike those therapists who may have been trained to behave in a neutral or dispassionately objective manner throughout the therapeutic encounter, it is conceivable that a given group leader using this method might be subdued or somber at one point in time, yet ebullient or enthusiastic at another. Similarly, the principle was set forth with the full understanding that there might be substantial behavioral variations *among* group leaders, depending upon their respective backgrounds and behavioral dispositions.

It is relevant to note that the two guidelines set forth above pose one major inconsistency. That is, if a leader's natural behavioral tendency is to act in a directive, evaluative, or highly preplanned manner, how can he resolve the seeming paradox with reference to nonintervention? To deal with this problem, leaders were instructed to regard the first-cited principle as their top priority. Except for immediate and direct requests by members, they were asked to honor their commitment to avoid all preplanned evaluations or interventions, especially those that might be construed in any way as treatment-oriented. This is not to suggest that leaders could never provide direction for members, ask for information, or engage in similar behaviors. Such actions were considered acceptable so long as they were required for the leader's natural social functioning. However, they were not permitted if the leader entertained the least suggestion of shaping a member's behavior toward a preconceived treatment objective. It was considered acceptable, for example, for a leader to show a child how to catch a baseball, but *not* permissible if the leader intended to do so in order to progress toward the attainment of a series of behavioral objectives designed to result in the acquisition of an integrated set of athletic skills by the child.

A number of additional guidelines were devised for the group leaders. They were instructed never to set goals or objectives for the group or for its individual members, either short-term or long-term. They also were cautioned against evaluating or sanctioning any member's behavior at any time and especially against doing so in the presence of others. Further, leaders were instructed to avoid posing unnecessary questions for group members or directing them to perform given activities or behaviors.

At the group's first meeting the leader was instructed to inform members that they were to design the group's programs and activities throughout the year, and that the leader would not participate actively in such plans. Yet members also were told that the leader would be available to provide needed resources and to be present should his assistance be required for any special reasons. When confronted with questions by group members, leaders were instructed to respond only with factual answers and never with opinions. For instance, if members asked, "Do you think we would have fun at a party?", or "Should we plan a party?", the appropriate type of answer would be "That's up to you" or "You guys can decide that." In contrast, if members were to ask "Is room 305 available tonight?", a straightforward response would be appropriate, such as "Yes" or "No, another group is meeting there." To some extent, therefore, the leader who utilizes such a method is posed with substantially more behavioral constraints than is the typical Rogerian therapist.

Controlling variables. Although the possible merits of the group-centered approach as a bona fide treatment method have been discussed, it must be remembered that this approach has been set forth primarily as a research tool. To promote effective application of the method, it is essential to emphasize that virtually all conditions, other than application of the method itself, must be relatively consistent and comparable with those that are operative for other methods to be studied concurrently. It is crucial, for example, for all group leaders to be selected according to the same general criteria, placed into a common pool of candidates, and then to be randomly assigned to one group method or the other. Were leaders permitted to choose their own treatment methods, there would be a heightened probability of selective biases which, in turn, might differentially influence the actual delivery of one method or the other.

Similarly, leaders for all methods, including the group-centered method, should undergo the same general training program. They should receive the same orientation to the treatment agency and should be informed of general agency rules and guidelines that may constrain their behavior. For instance, in the agency where the St. Louis Experiment was conducted, it was standard procedure for group leaders to telephone members who had been absent for two consecutive meetings in order to establish the reason for such absences and to offer assistance, if necessary. This procedure was followed by group-centered leaders as well as by leaders utilizing the other methods. Likewise, since agency rules prohibited fighting on the grounds, leaders for all methods were instructed to stop fights when they were encountered. In such instances, however, procedural variations tended to occur in conjunction with the respective methods. Typically, leaders using the two more directive methods would impose sanctions upon members, establish behavioral contracts, or counsel members regarding the antecedents, concomitants, or consequences of such behavior. In contrast, group-centered leaders merely would stop the fighting with the factual and comparatively nonevaluative comment that "fighting is against agency rules."

Group-centered leaders also were asked to complete report forms and to attend supervisory conferences at time intervals equal to those for other group leaders. However, the content of such forms and meetings varied greatly from those of the other leaders. In order to minimize the systematic evaluation of members' behavior, their report forms solicited primarily a listing of activities in which the group participated at a given meeting.

Safeguards. It is relatively easy to implement a nondirective treatment modality with a single client and within the confines of a therapist's office. It is much more difficult, however, to implement such a modality with a substantial number of interacting group members and within the context of a community agency, particularly one with a prior history of extensive direct service programs for its clientele. During the St. Louis Experiment, agency staff members were concerned about four major potential problems: (1) whether or not substantial damage might occur to the physical plant, (2) whether or not significant physical, or other, harm could occur for group members, or for other clientele at the agency, (3) whether or not sustained deterioration could take place within groups and, if so, what to do about it, and (4) whether or not prolonged stagnation could take place within groups and, if so, how to cope with it. These concerns were paramount, naturally, because the experiment called for the presence of large numbers of antisocial or delinquent boys in the groups under study at the agency. Such concerns had to be dealt with satisfactorily in order to assure requisite agency support for implementation of such a program.

In the St. Louis Experiment, the first two concerns were dealt with by assuring staff that subjects participating in the group-centered method would be constrained by the same agency rules and directives that applied to all other members. Typically, the leaders of such groups would respond to flagrant violations of agency rules in a highly delimited, explicit, and straightforward manner. This procedure was observed diligently not only in order to provide agency staff with necessary assurances but also in order to assure consistency among all groups with reference to common realities such as agency rules.

Staff concerns regarding absences and withdrawals were addressed through reiteration and routine observance of the general agency procedures regarding telephone contact of members who were absent for two consecutive meetings. To deal with staff anxieties regarding sustained patterns of antisocial behavior, a slightly more complex procedure was evolved. It was agreed to arrange a staff conference following any period of three consecutive weeks characterized by a continuous and significant increase in members' antisocial behavior. Such a conference could be requested upon the basis of data compiled by the group leader, his supervisor, or other staff, such as trained nonparticipant observers. Following staff consensus that significant deterioration had occurred, it would be permissible to consider implementation of a more directive treatment modality.

Agreement regarding such a procedure was deemed necessary primarily in order to secure staff approval and support for a treatment program that was highly foreign to the agency's prior experience. In fact, however, over a three-year experience it never proved necessary to initiate the first step of the above-cited procedure, that is, to request a staff conference for any particular group. In isolated cases of seriously antisocial behavior, leaders assigned to the group-centered method did use the approach cited previously, that is, members were notified that the given behavior violated agency rules or posed a strong likelihood of serious physical danger for someone and, therefore, that it was necessary to cease and desist immediately. No other evaluations were made of antisocial behavior. Moreover, antisocial behavior that neither violated agency rules nor posed serious physical danger was not heeded by the leader. Consonant with the general principles of the group-centered method, it was the members' prerogative to deal, or not to deal, with such behavior in accord with their own predilections.

Finally, it is relevant to note that some staff had been concerned lest a given group "stagnate" for a prolonged period of time. More particularly, they feared that some groups might be consistently unable to agree upon programs or future directions or, conversely, that others would reiterate the same activity pattern for the entire program year—choosing, for instance, to play basketball at each and every group meeting. Actually, such concerns should not be relevant for implementation of a group-centered method since rigorous adherence to the method would suggest that it is within the members' own purview to select such activity patterns should they wish to do so. Again, however, in order to provide requisite assurances for staff, a backup procedure was devised which, in fact, was utilized only rarely as a matter of necessity. Leaders were provided with a list of twenty activities commonly enjoyed by children within the age ranges studied. Prior to each group meeting they were instructed to randomly select five activities from the list. The leaders were permitted to inform members that all of the five activities were available for member participation only if members directly asked for assistance in selecting programs or if there had been sustained evidence of members' incapacity to decide upon program activities over a period of several weeks. In order to minimize the possibility of systematic influence over the group's decision-making processes, leaders were instructed to *randomly* select activities from the list and to refrain from participating in members' discussions following presentation of the listed activities. In large part, the above safeguards not only assured staff that anticipated problems could be dealt with satisfactorily but, more importantly, also addressed latent concerns regarding the ethical implications of providing a "no-treatment" method for children who had been deemed much in need of social work help.

Summary

This chapter discussed the implementation of no-treatment methods in a small group context. Relevant differences between the demands of dyadic and small-group situations were noted. Rationales for application of a no-treatment group method also were discussed. These included the need to control for maturation, history, Hawthorne, and placebo effects, and to provide the bases for adequate cost-effectiveness comparisons with other treatment methods.

A variety of possible no-treatment approaches were discussed, including total nonintervention, random intervention, focused intervention to assure natural development, and natural interaction.

Guidelines for implementation of the latter approach were delineated. Finally, requirements for controlling extraneous variables were discussed, as were possible safeguards for averting potential liabilities associated with the group-centered method.

Emerging Trends

Without question, the coming years will witness a number of important changes in both the focus and the substance of social group work. External factors that are likely to influence the social work profession are myriad, and changing constantly. These include broad-range social, political, and economic variations within the larger American society (Briar, 1971; Kahn, 1973; Kidneigh, 1965; Lubove, 1965; Meyer, 1971; Pumphrey and Pumphrey, 1961; Wilensky and Lebeaux, 1958). To a considerable extent, the practice objectives of social work and of social group work have been shaped by the prevalent social problems in American society. Thus, for example, when immigration to the United States was at its peak, group workers directed much of their attention to the rapid socialization of newcomers to American society and to training in "democratic" decision-making processes. When the larger society was beset by an economic depression, social workers primarily attended to problems such as economic dependency, skill training, and employability. During the height of the civil rights movement, group workers accordingly shifted much of their attention to the arenas of community and racial integration. Concomitant with these changes the profession's direction has been influenced by shifts in federal funding priorities, many of which represent responses to the same societal problems that affect the profession more directly.

Obviously, the particular types of knowledge utilized by the social work profession are likely to be determined, in large part, by its own overarching priorities in practice. However, the profession's knowledge base necessarily will be influenced, also, by substantive developments in allied professions and fields. As knowledge proliferates within disciplines such as sociology and psychology, new resources will be made available for social work (Pratt, 1969). Thus, for example, it is relevant to note that traditional social casework methods have been dependent upon antecedent developments within psychiatry. More recently, conceptual developments within social casework have been dependent upon prior work done by experimental psychologists. And community organization programs in social work were slow to evolve until the requisite knowledge base concerning community level phenomena had been elaborated by sociologists.

The mere proliferation of relevant knowledge within allied disciplines is not sufficient, however, for application to social work. Organizational linkages and diffusion mechanisms must be developed among the relevant entities. Consequently, social work, like other professions, is subject to the principles and mechanisms that tend to govern the diffusion of knowledge within the larger society (Rogers, 1962). Yet it is probable that developments within allied fields are even more important for social work than for other professions, since social work has adopted an especially broad practice focus and an unusually strong interdisciplinary thrust. Moreover, since its knowledge base has been relatively sparse—due, in large part, to structural deficiencies within the profession—social work has been highly reliant upon knowledge generated elsewhere. This has tended to produce an additional set of problems which have affected the course of the social work profession, namely, problems of professional domain (Feldman and Specht, 1968).

A large number of internal factors also have influenced progress within the social work profession. Problems pertaining to the nature of, and interrelationships among, professional associations, professional schools, and formal accreditation bodies have been especially significant (Meyer, 1971). These have been integrally associated with ambiguities and uncertainties regarding legitimation of the profession by the larger society. In turn, legitimate auspices and organizational settings tend to influence practice knowledge. With particular reference to group work, Feldman and Specht (1968, p. 83) note:

> The efforts of group work practitioners have been legitimated, in large part, by the agency structures within which group work has been practiced. Vast numbers of psychiatric and correctional institutions provide ready employment, promising career opportunities, and legitimation through their functional interdependencies with related professions and community agents who are vested with both legal and moral authority. Such legitimation has presented obvious benefits for professionals but, conversely, has also proved costly in a number of ways.
>
> Among the major liabilities of this type of legitimation has been retardation of the development of a unique group work knowledge base, at least in settings where legitimation is granted in measure with emulation of the legitimating profession's goals and practice methods. In addition, the ready availability of supervisory and training personnel within treatment agencies has only served to perpetuate the entrenchment of traditional modalities of group work practice via educational channels. Correspondingly, the practice focus of group work has been unduly limited to clinical or pseudo-clinical settings to the neglect of other possible areas for legitimate practice.

An historical overview of the profession also reveals that internally generated research within social work has been minimal (Silverman, 1966; Briar, 1971; Briar and Miller, 1971). Within the past decade, however, a large number of research-oriented training programs have been initiated by the profession, particularly at the doctoral level. These have resulted in a substantial proliferation of needed research. However, only a small portion of this research has been directed toward social group work. In the absence of a validated and well-developed knowledge base, group work may be inordinately susceptible to two critical tendencies. First, it is likely to be further dependent upon substantive knowledge developed elsewhere, with the attendant problems of knowledge diffusion, knowledge assimilation, and professional domain. Second, it may be readily susceptible to diverse pressures that will urge changes in its central focus, particularly with reference to the types of populations served and social problems addressed. This could entail movement away from the traditional practice orientation of group work.

Multiple Practice Foci

Despite the pervasiveness and unpredictability of the above forces, it is probable that social group work will proceed toward further development and validation of its knowledge base, thus retaining its primary orientation toward clinical practice. And, for reasons discussed elsewhere (Feldman and Specht, 1968), it is possible that the clinical orientation of social group work will be retained even in the absence of adequate validation of its knowledge base. So long as countervailing data are not forthcoming regarding the efficacy of pertinent treatment methods, reified institutional patterns may continue to sustain questionable service-delivery mechanisms.

Even if group workers should maintain a predominant interest in clinical practice, however, it is obvious that their future efforts will address a number of varying practice foci. To some extent, for example, it is likely that they will continue to provide services oriented toward the *socialization* of newcomers to American society, in general, and to certain sectors of that society, in particular, such as urban areas. This can be anticipated in view of continuing high rates of population mobility, both horizontally and vertically.

A second traditional focus is integrally related to the foregoing one, that is, group work's emphasis upon *democratic decentralization*. This conception of group work is one which emphasizes the crucial importance of small groups in maintaining a democratic society and in preparing individuals for active social participation in such a society. As Vinter (1965) has noted, "Small groups, within or linked to larger social units, [are] viewed as providing significant opportunities for collective decision-making, for facilitating individual participation in important social movements, and for articulating the otherwise isolated citizen with broader social processes. From such foundations, . . . a conception of group work developed that served the requirements of a democratic society for citizen participation, decentralized but shared decision-making, and active pursuit of social goals" (p. 716). Groups such as the Boy Scouts and Girl Scouts have oriented their programs toward such objectives for many years. Recently, their efforts have been directed increasingly toward inner-city youth and the residents of urban ghettos.

A third traditional focus which is likely to be retained by future group workers pertains to a practice emphasis upon the achievement of *developmental goals*. Although related to the earlier-mentioned concern with socialization, this approach tends to be somewhat more inclusive. It can be applied to clients of any age, including small children. The contemporary social work bases for this approach can be found primarily in the work of Tropp (1969, 1971) and Klein (1970). In large part, the developmental approach focuses upon the common concerns of other group work modalities, such as improved social functioning, greater self-actualization, and the realization of each individual's full potential. Unlike such approaches, however, group workers with a developmental perspective rarely focus upon phenomena such as pathology, abnormality, illness, social malfunctioning, treatment, or cures. Instead, their knowledge base is derived largely from phenomenological, humanistic, and existential views of man. Accordingly, practice guidelines for workers with this orientation tend to be relatively limited. Even so, the developmental approach has been received with great interest by many social workers. Despite the few practice principles thus far generated, it has constituted a central focus for group work activity.

Although less integrally associated with the mainstream of group work tradition, a number of other orientations bear similarities to the developmental approach. These include various offshoots of the so-called growth movement and related small-group experiences such as sensitivity groups, encounter groups and, to a lesser extent, T-group (or "training" group) experiences. As with the developmental approach, the practice guidelines and requisite empirical validation for these modalities tend to be rather sparse. The lone exception, perhaps, is the relatively systematic research concerning training groups that has been performed by colleagues of Kurt Lewin, primarily at The University of Michigan Center for the Study of Group Dynamics, and at The Tavistock Institute in London, England. Yet, in accord with broader societal trends, research and practice contributions by each of these groups have proceeded along highly divergent paths. In effect, the English cohort has adopted a research-oriented approach that focuses primarily upon the industrial and applied uses of training groups. Their American colleagues, in contrast, have embarked upon a broad variety of activities. These include, on the one hand, formation of the National Training Laboratories, the creation of scholarly journals, and the performance of rigorous social psychological experimentation on small groups and, on the other hand, extensive contributions to more entrepreneurial activities, such as the creation of "human growth" centers (Back, 1972).

Within social group work, a somewhat related model, known as the *interactionist approach* (Schwartz, 1971), or the *mediating model* (Shulman, 1968), has been set forth by a number of investigators. This approach views the social work function "as one of mediating the often troubled transactions between people and the various systems through which they carry on their relationships with society—the family, peer group, social agency, neighborhood, school, job, and others" (Schwartz, 1971, p. 1258). Hence it is relatively different from developmental models and from more treatment-oriented approaches. In essence, the group worker serves as an important mediator or, on occasion, as a social broker who helps individuals to overcome obstacles to effective social growth.

Somewhat similar are those models which call upon group workers to engage in *social action* activities. Such models tend to focus primarily upon macro-problems rather than micro-problems. That is, they emphasize social problems that adversely affect vast numbers of present or potential social work clients, have a determinate etiological relationship to major secondary problems for clients, and, most important, afford multiple foci for effective group work intervention *other than* the client population itself (Feldman and Specht, 1968). Prime examples of such problems are poverty, unemployment, and inadequate housing. The social action approach presents a number of relevant modifications for group work practice. Thus, for instance, conceptions of client systems (those who are to benefit from proposed interventions) and target systems (those who are to be subjected to practice interventions) are likely to be more variable than in traditional clinical practice. Not only are client groups less likely to constitute direct target groups, but they may sometimes serve as action systems, that is, as the persons who actually bring about change. In those situations where the group worker serves as an activist and as an advocate for the client, traditional notions regarding worker-client relationships are likely to be altered significantly. Requisite worker activities also will vary accordingly.

Despite the foregoing variations, social group work most probably will retain its basic concern with *social rehabilitation*. Consequently, it will continue to direct the greatest part of its efforts toward client populations who have been judged in need of clinical service due to particular problems of social dysfunctioning or social maladaptation. For the most part, practitioners with such concerns will draw upon knowledge bases such as those presented in the preceding chapters. However, so long as group work retains a clinical focus, essential questions will persist concerning future developments within those modalities. Some of these will be discussed shortly.

Finally, it is relevant to note that substantial numbers of group workers can be expected to perform clinical activities primarily by drawing upon group knowledge from auxiliary *practice modalities*. Thus, for example, separate practice developments will be based upon formulations such as guided group interaction (Empey and Rabow, 1961; Empey and Erickson, 1972), transactional analysis (Berne, 1961, 1964, 1966, 1972; Harris, 1967), and activity group therapy (Scheidlinger, 1952). Regardless of the validity of such formulations, their acceptance by social group workers is likely to contribute to a further fragmentation of social work knowledge and group work practice foci. This may serve to further deter the rate at which group work will develop a distinctive, yet coherent and well-integrated, conceptual basis and practice framework.

In brief, then, it is probable that future group workers will pursue a number of directions simultaneously. As with the larger social work profession, group workers unquestionably will retain their central concern with social rehabilitation and social treatment. Moreover, to varying degrees, their corresponding knowledge bases are likely to flow, in large part, from treatment methods such as those described in the preceding chapters. It is germane, then, to inquire about potential knowledge developments with reference to those methods.

Convergent Theoretical Frameworks

No doubt coming years will witness an even greater concentration upon group-level approaches to social treatment than has been the case heretofore. Even those formulations which have been identified primarily with individual treatment are being reconceptualized in terms of multiple relationships. Requisite higher order concepts are being formulated which tend to link both individual and group-level constructs. In a prototypical endeavor, Homans (1958, 1961) has attempted to link psychological and sociological constructs through the use of social exchange theory. More recently, Burgess and Bushell (1969) have reframed a number of sociological constructs within the parameters of social learning theory. Jeffrey (1971) and Burgess and Akers (1966), in more focused discussions, have redefined Sutherland's sociological notions concerning differential association within the purview of social learning theory. And, to bring matters full circle, Skinner's (1966, 1971) recent works, which proceed from a distinctly psychological perspective, have been regarded as singular theses concerning multiple-person social interaction. Even broad level economic patterns have been reformulated within the context of social learning theory (Kunkel, 1966, 1970). Hence the foundation has been constructed for a conceptual integration of frameworks which encompass broad ranges of human behavior. Although the relevant units of analysis tend to vary from the "individual" through "society" itself, it is apparent that linkages among such social units can, in fact, be achieved through the further elaboration of related theoretical frames of reference and through a synthesis of their basic constructs.

It seems probable that the more directive treatment approaches espoused by social group work will build upon both the traditional and behavior modification perspectives cited earlier. However, as conceptual formulations become even more sophisticated, those approaches may very well blend into a single, unified practice orientation that might proceed substantially beyond the separate modalities set forth here. Such a formulation is likely to be predicated upon conceptual inputs from at least three frames of reference, namely, social exchange theory, social role theory, and social learning theory. To some extent, each of those frameworks has endeavored to address issues pertaining to individuals' interrelationships with their social environment, including peers.

Social exchange theory. Perhaps the most important contribution to social exchange theory has been the classic discussion set forth by Thibaut and Kelley (1959). Utilizing a framework which draws heavily upon an economic perspective, they have viewed social behavior as a result of individuals' particular "rewards," "costs," and corresponding "outcomes" of social interaction with others. They posit that group members' behavioral outcomes tend to be mutually interdependent. Furthermore, Thibaut and Kelley suggest that an individual's outcomes from a given social relationship will depend largely upon the standard against which he evaluates the attractiveness of the relationship, or how satisfactory it is and, also, upon the standard that he uses in deciding whether to preserve or abandon the relationship. Respectively, these standards have been labeled as one's "comparison level" and "comparison level for alternatives."

Within this basic framework, Thibaut and Kelley have been able to generate prototypical matrices which can predict broadly the likelihood of various behavioral acts by members of a dyadic relationship. Although such matrices have been limited to a small number of relevant variables, and to dyadic social relationships, it should not be difficult to extend them considerably beyond their present limits. Such matrices, it ought to be noted, are not substantially unlike the one set forth in Chapter Five. However, the latter focuses upon larger groups of individuals and upon sociobehavioral contingencies. Conceivably, future work will produce a conceptual and practical synthesis derived from such rudimentary endeavors.

Following the seminal work of Thibaut and Kelley, relevant elaborations and extensions of social exchange theory were generated by a large number of other investigators, including Blau (1964), Turk and Simpson (1971), and Emerson (1969). Emerson, in particular, has endeavored to link social exchange theory with operant psychology concepts. More recent applications of social exchange theory have stressed its utility for the critical analysis of certain small groups, including family units (Edwards, 1969; Richer, 1968). Similarly, some analyses of delinquent behavior in small groups have been based essentially upon social exchange formulations (Briar and Piliavin, 1965; Strodtbeck and Short, 1964).

Through a systematic extension of the basic concepts of social exchange theory, Thibaut and Kelley have been able to discuss substantive concerns that are particularly relevant for group treatment, such as social power, member interdependencies, group goals and tasks, conformity to norms, and social roles. The latter topic is of special interest because it clearly exemplifies the possibilities for conceptual linkages between social exchange theory and social role theory and, ultimately, with group-work practice theory.

Social role theory. Many facets of the traditional social group work method have been based upon concepts of social role. Social role theory has represented one of the major linkages between two key social science disciplines—sociology and psychology. In large part, it also has provided the conceptual basis for the elaboration of a separate social science discipline, namely, social psychology. From its inception, role theory has focused upon the social determinants of individuals' *role behaviors.* Hence, like social exchange theory and social learning theory, this formulation decidedly emphasizes the observable behaviors of human beings. Consequently, the major methodological and analytical concerns of role theorists are likely to be congruent with those of social exchange and social learning theorists.

In brief, role theorists are concerned primarily with the social *positions* which individuals occupy within given social structures, including small groups. Some relevant sociological positions of interest to group workers are the "leader" (Blum and Polansky, 1961), "parent" (Fanshel, 1961, 1966; McCoy, 1962), "client" (Glasser, 1962; Perlman, 1968; Deasy, 1969; Wolken and Haldeman, 1969), "delinquent" (Lentz, 1966), and "scapegoat" (Feldman, 1969d).

As noted in our case illustration concerning scapegoating behavior (Chapter Four), role theorists posit that the occupants of certain positions in groups, such as the scapegoat position, have certain characteristics in common. These may be common attributes, behaviors, or reactions of others toward them. Considerable research has indicated, for example, that occupants of the scapegoat position tend to express relatively weak commitment to group norms, contribute negligibly to the performance of basic group functions, express low liking for peers, and are attributed extremely low social power. Their peers within the group tend to express intense disliking for them.

From a role-theory perspective, the role behaviors of position occupants are shaped, in large part, by the *role expectations* that relevant other persons, including peers, hold for them (see, for example, Freeman and Simmons, 1959; Goldstein, 1966; Heine and Trosman, 1960; Olsen and Olsen, 1967; Entwisle and Webster, 1972). Additionally, position occupants' role behaviors are determined by role expectations which they themselves hold for their own position. Role expectations, in turn, depend substantially upon members' prior role performances, functional interdependencies, shared norms, reward and sanctioning systems, and liking for one another.

Utilizing such a theoretical framework, it is possible to conceptualize a large variety of sociobehavioral problems, including those experienced by members of treatment groups. Relevant examples include problems pertaining to individuals' *role conflicts* (Bell, 1966; DeLange, 1963; Simmons, 1968; Wolfe and Snoek, 1962; Hall, 1972; Miller and Podell, 1971; Olson, 1972; Soyit, 1971), *role ambiguities* (Dibner, 1958; Erikson, 1957; Heller, 1968), *role discontinuities* (Cutler and Dyer, 1965; Garabedian, 1963; Burr, 1972; Hobbs, 1968; Richards, 1966), and *role asynchronies* (Garvin, 1969; Luckey, 1960; Thomas, 1966; Thomas and Feldman, 1967). In addition, it has been possible to delineate the manner in which certain group dysfunctions, such as inadequate functional or normative integration, contribute to the social problems of selected group members, such as scapegoats (Feldman, 1969b). Likewise, it has been possible to conceptually define particular group deficiencies, such as various types of position nonintegration and position malintegration (Feldman, 1970), and to suggest their implications for member functioning.

Most important, perhaps, role-theory concepts have demonstrated a capacity to lend themselves readily to advanced conceptual development, to empirical research, and to a variety of link-ages with both social exchange and social learning concepts. Thus, for example, Biddle and Thomas (1966) have extended role-theory formulations through the elaboration of partitioning concepts for persons and their behaviors and through the delineation of relevant linkages with reinforcement concepts.

Role theory has constituted one of the major foundations for the traditional social group work method. It has also provided the basic framework for a comprehensive integration of sociological, psychological, and social psychological principles which, in turn, have been applied toward a further elaboration of the traditional group work method. To the extent that these principles, and their underlying conceptual frameworks, can be joined with other potent formulations, they are likely to form the framework for a significant extension of social group work theory and practice.

Social learning theory. The basic components of social learn-ing theory have been described in Chapter Five, especially as they pertain to treatment in small groups. In that discussion it was noted that only a very small portion of the literature concerning social learning theory has focused upon small group treatment. Moreover, most of the relevant literature has described highly delimited treat-ment procedures, such as group desensitization (Lazarus, 1961). Typically, such procedures have taken little cognizance of the in-terpersonal dynamics that operate within small groups, that is, of the members' patterned social interactions with one another. Instead, their focus has been primarily, if not entirely, upon group members' interactions with the leader, and vice versa. The group has been viewed essentially as the context for the leader's treatment efforts, rather than as an integral means for facilitating treatment.

From another perspective, under the rubric of social learn-ing theory, initial work has begun concerning the specification and evaluation of group contingencies. However, virtually all of the experimental work regarding such contingencies has been performed in highly structured settings, such as school classrooms (Bushell and others, 1968; Wodarski and others, 1972). Nevertheless, as indi-cated in Chapter Five, it appears that group contingencies will be readily amenable to more advanced conceptualization and to ex-perimental investigation in relatively open settings. Important as group contingencies may be, however, it is obvious that they cannot constitute the sole social learning focus of group work. Instead, it will be necessary to draw upon the complete armamentarium of social learning theory and to redirect its attention to persons' behavior within small groups.

Perhaps the best beginning step in this direction is represented by the work of Rose and certain of his colleagues. Rose (1972) has drawn heavily upon social learning theory in order to diagnose maladaptive behavior in children's groups and to delineate appropriate treatment strategies. More importantly, he also has examined relevant group dynamics and has indicated their relationship to basic social learning principles. Thus, for example, he has discussed group norms, group goals, group cohesiveness, and similar phenomena which are of relevance for group workers. Related work, based largely upon the utilization of token economies, also has been done within the context of social learning theory (see Phillips, 1968; Wolf and others, 1968; Cohen and Filipczak, 1971; Ayllon and Azrin, 1968). Despite the significance of such contributions, however, it is clear that they do not draw sufficiently upon available small-group theory in order to extend and refine their basic formulations. Since the essential concepts of social learning theory have been explicated previously they will not be reviewed further at this juncture. Instead, we shall proceed to a discussion of the manner in which the three foregoing orientations may contribute to a more sophisticated understanding of human behavior, with particular reference to social group work.

Toward a Synthesis for Social Group Work

Without question, the basic concepts and principles of social learning theory can be further integrated with those of social exchange theory and social role theory in order to extend all three perspectives toward the study of human behavior. Ultimately, it is conceivable that such a synthesis will result in the articulation of a more systematic and comprehensive approach toward social group work practice. A number of relevant converging trends can be suggested.

Perhaps the most promising concatenation of theoretical

trends can be noted with reference to the recent work concerning token economies. Although token economies have proven to be potent treatment vehicles, they have been conceptualized rarely in terms of group dynamics constructs or even in terms of higher order mathematical matrices. Instead, they have tended to focus solely upon the reward and cost components of individual behavior without adequately exploring the reciprocal effects of members' behaviors upon requisite outcomes. Perhaps these deficiencies can be corrected by further delineation of the relationships among token systems, group contingencies, matrices such as those suggested by social exchange theory, and role expectation sets such as those posited by social role theory. Initial work along these lines has focused upon the interrelationships between group cooperation and various social reinforcement patterns (Mithaug and Burgess, 1968; Azrin and Lindsley, 1965). Similarly, longitudinal trends within small groups may be better understood through the long-term study of phenomena such as group development and activity programing, role emergence and role differentiation, functional interdependencies among group members, and extended patterns of behavioral chaining. Respectively, contributions regarding these mutually related developmental phenomena can be anticipated from traditional group work theory, social role theory, social exchange theory, and social learning theory.

In a similar manner, the latter three formulations, respectively, can supplement available practice knowledge through a mutual synthesis of information regarding group norms and sanctions for norm-violating behaviors, reward-cost matrices for members' behavior, and positive and negative behavioral reinforcements. Schedules of reinforcement, additionally, can be related to knowledge concerning developmental trends in small groups. It is possible, even, that certain features of the group-centered method can be interpreted in terms of formulations such as those posited by social learning theory and social role theory. For instance, the nondirective nature of this treatment modality may bear certain similarities to the process of behavioral extinction and, in fact, may be particularly effective for the treatment of certain client problems, such as depression (Stuart, 1967). Similarly, the mere presence of the therapist, even though he may be relatively inactive, may exert relevant placebo and expectational effects, such as those associated with role-theory formulations (Shapiro, 1971).

With reference to more specific concepts, it is clear that both social role theory and social learning theory have shown a continuing concern with modeling behavior in small groups (Baer, 1964; Bandura and McDonald, 1963; Bandura and Kupers, 1964; Bandura, Ross, and Ross, 1961; Strean, 1967). It is likely that the specificity and rigor of the social learning approach will enhance current researchers' emphases upon modelers' social attributes and interpersonal behaviors, which tend to be formulated primarily in terms of social role theory. Similarly, the latter's concern with various positions in social structures is likely to benefit from the former's contributions concerning behavioral repertoires and reinforcement contingencies. Both perspectives are likely to further the current interest of social group workers in position structuring in therapeutic groups (Glasser and Garvin, 1971).

Finally, a number of more general trends in social group work can be inferred from various facets of the above formulations. Unquestionably, group workers will become increasingly concerned with the observable behaviors of group members. Little, if any, attention will be paid to internal constructs, or to the inference of social phenomena such as clients' attitudes and feelings. Correspondingly, interventive and evaluative data will become increasingly quantifiable, especially in terms of rates, or incidences, of observable member behaviors.

It is probable, also, that members' varying influences upon one another will be conceptualized in more sophisticated ways. Complex reward-cost matrices, behavioral grids, and group contingency tables are likely to be elaborated. These will refer to a large number of social variables. Most importantly, they will endeavor to systematically delineate group members' present and potential influences upon each other's behavior, thus taking cognizance of each member's relevant social environment, especially his peers. Interestingly, as theorists become more aware of relevant social influences upon target members' behaviors, there may be a heightened awareness of the importance of larger social units, such as the community, in shaping members' social behavior. Consequently, group workers may express renewed interest in the community as a locus of behavioral diagnosis and intervention.

Such a focus is likely to be further enhanced by a stronger and more systematic emphasis on relevant antecedent and consequent behaviors exhibited by other persons in the client's environment. In accord with such a focus, group workers are bound to express greater interest in monitoring clients' behaviors in their natural environments, such as the family and the peer group, rather than in relatively artificial environments, such as the treatment group. Similarly, group work interventions are more likely to be directed toward natural environments. Finally, without the closed structure, and associated technological aids, of the experimental laboratory or the treatment agency, it is likely that there also will be a strengthened emphasis upon the development of new approaches to data collection, behavioral monitoring, and the measurement of client change.

Summary

This chapter has discussed a number of variables that are likely to influence the future direction of social group work. Both external and internal factors are bound to affect knowledge development, the dissemination of knowledge, and the practical applications of knowledge within the social work profession. It seems probable that various features of the traditional group work method and of group level behavior modification will undergo a further synthesis in coming years. To a lesser extent, it is possible that elements of the group-centered method also will be incorporated into such a synthesis. At least three theoretical frames of reference can be expected to contribute significantly to future developments within group work, especially since each shares many common conceptual referents and practice foci with the others. These are social exchange theory, social role theory, and social learning theory. Although social group work is likely to be directed toward a broad range of practice concerns, it is apparent that recent trends presage the development of a more systematic, comprehensive, and unified theoretical base than has been the case heretofore. Consequently, there is strong reason to believe that the practice base of social group work will become increasingly potent, even as its practice concerns may become correspondingly more diffuse.

Bibliography

Selected references are annotated to indicate their relevance for readers who wish to explore a given topic beyond the scope of presentation in *Contemporary Approaches to Group Treatment*. Particular emphasis is placed upon books or articles that pertain to group treatment.

AKERS, R. L. "Problems in the Sociology of Deviance: Social Definitions and Behavior." *Social Forces,* 1968, *46*(4), 455–465.

ARONOWITZ, E., AND WEINBERG, D. "The Utilization of Reinforcement Theory in Social Group Work Practice." *Social Service Review,* 1966, *60*(4), 390–396. One of the first articles in the social work literature to discuss the use of reinforcement theory for group-work treatment.

ARONSON, H., AND OVERALL, B. "Treatment Expectations of Patients in Two Social Classes." *Social Work,* 1966, *11*(1), 35–41.

ASCH, S. *Social Psychology.* Englewood Cliffs, N.J.: Prentice-Hall, 1952.

ASCHER, L. M., AND CAUTELA, J. R. "Covert Negative Reinforcement: An Experimental Test." *Journal of Behavior Therapy and Experimental Psychiatry,* 1972, *3*, 1–5.

ATKINSON, J. W., AND FEATHER, N. T. (Eds.) *A Theory of Achievement Motivation.* New York: Wiley, 1966.

AUSTIN, D. "Goals for Gang Workers." *Social Work,* 1957, *2*, 43–50.

AYLLON, T., AND AZRIN, N. *The Token Economy: A Motivational System for Therapy and Rehabilitation.* New York: Appleton-

Century-Crofts, 1968. Describes the implementation and monitoring of ongoing token reinforcement systems. Discusses relevant topics for behavior therapy, such as reinforcer sampling and priming for reinforcers.

AZRIN, N. H., AND LINDSLEY, O. R. "The Reinforcement of Cooperation Between Children." In L. P. Ullmann and L. Krasner (Eds.), *Case Studies in Behavior Modification.* New York: Holt, Rinehart, and Winston, 1965.

BACHRACH, A. J. *Experimental Foundations of Clinical Psychology.* New York: Basic Books, 1962.

BACHRACH, A. J., CANDLAND, D. K., AND GIBSON, J. T. "Group Reinforcement of Individual Response Experiments in Verbal Behavior." In I. A. Berg and B. N. Bass (Eds.), *Conformity and Deviation.* New York: Harper and Row, 1961. One of the first discussions of group reinforcement for individual behavior change.

BACK, K. *Beyond Words: The Story of Sensitivity Training and the Encounter Movement.* New York: Russell Sage Foundation, 1972. Describes the historical growth of sensitivity and encounter training, viewing both as a social movement; extensively reviews relevant deficiencies in conceptualization and experimental support.

BACKMAN, C. W., SECORD, P. F., AND PIERCE, J. R. "Resistance to Change in the Self-Concept as a Function of Consensus Among Significant Others." In C. W. Backman and P. F. Secord (Eds.), *Problems in Social Psychology.* New York: McGraw-Hill, 1966. An experimental study that illustrates the relationship between one's self-concept and the social expectations of significant others.

BAER, D. M. "The Development of Imitation by Reinforcing Behavioral Similarity to a Model." *Journal of Abnormal and Social Psychology,* 1964, *69,* 1–9.

BAER, D. M., WOLF, M. M., AND RISLEY, T. R. "Some Current Dimensions of Applied Behavior Analysis." *Journal of Applied Behavior Analysis,* 1968, *1,* 91–97. A description of the basic tenets of behavior-modification theory.

BAILEY, J. W., TIMBERS, G. D., PHILLIPS, E. L., AND WOLF, M. M. "Modification of Articulation Efforts of Pre-Delinquents by Their Peers." *Journal of Applied Behavior Analysis,* 1971, *4,* 265–281.

BAILEY, J. W., WOLF, M. M., AND PHILLIPS, E. L. "Home-Based Reinforcement and the Modification of Pre-Delinquents' Classroom Behavior." *Journal of Applied Behavior Analysis,* 1970, *3,* 223–233.

BALES, R. F. *Interaction Process Analysis: A Method for the Study of Small Groups.* Reading, Mass.: Addison-Wesley, 1950a. A detailed description of the classic technique for interaction-process analysis devised by the author; has been used extensively in studies of group development, decision making, and leadership behavior.

BALES, R. F. "A Set of Categories for the Analysis of Small Group Interaction." *American Sociological Review,* 1950b, *15,* 257–263.

BALES, R. F., AND SLATER, P. "Role Differentiation in Small Decision-Making Groups." In T. Parsons and R. F. Bales (Eds.), *Family, Socialization, and Interaction Process.* New York: Free Press, 1955.

BALES, R. F., AND STRODTBECK, F. L. "Phases in Group Problem-Solving." *Journal of Abnormal and Social Psychology,* 1951, *46,* 485–495. A detailed report of a series of studies of small-group development in which groups were found to progress sequentially through phases characterized primarily by orientation, evaluation, and control behaviors.

BANDURA, A. *Principles of Behavior Modification.* New York: Holt, Rinehart, and Winston, 1969, 293–348 and 501–563. A classic text that covers all aspects of behavior modification.

BANDURA, A. (Ed.) *Psychological Modelling.* Chicago and New York: Aldine-Atherton, 1971. A textbook presentation of the basic aspects of modeling theory; also discusses relevant future research issues.

BANDURA, A., AND KUPERS, C. J. "Transmission of Patterns of Self-Reinforcement Through Modelling." *Journal of Abnormal and Social Psychology,* 1964, *69,* 1–9.

BANDURA, A., AND MC DONALD, F. J. "Influence of Social Reinforcement and the Behavior of Models in Shaping Children's Moral Judgments." *Journal of Abnormal and Social Psychology,* 1963, *67*(3), 274–281.

BANDURA, A., ROSS, D., AND ROSS, S. A. "Transmission of Aggression Through Imitation of Aggressive Models." *Journal of Abnormal and Social Psychology,* 1961, *63,* 575–582.

BARKER, G. H., AND ADAMS, W. T. "The Social Structure of a Correctional Institution." *Journal of Criminal Law, Criminology, and Police Science,* 1959, *49,* 417–427.

BECKER, H. S. *Outsiders: Studies in the Sociology of Deviance.* New York: Free Press, 1963.

BELL, R. R. "Parent-Child Conflict in Sexual Values." *Journal of Social Issues,* 1966, *22,* 34–44.

BERGER, E. M. "The Relation Between Expressed Acceptance of Self and Expressed Acceptance of Others." *Journal of Abnormal and Social Psychology,* 1952, *47,* 778–782.

BERGIN, A. E., AND GARFIELD, S. L. *Handbook of Psychotherapy and Behavior Change: An Empirical Analysis.* New York: Wiley, 1971. One of the most comprehensive and informative collections of edited articles on psychotherapy and behavior change; based primarily on reviews of empirical studies.

BERKOWITZ, B. P., AND GRAZIANO, A. N. "Training Parents as Behavior Therapists: A Review." *Behavior Research and Therapy,* 1972, *10,* 297–317. Review of the literature; excellent resource for those who plan to train parents in behavioral techniques.

BERKOWITZ, S., SHERRY, P. J., AND DAVIS, A. "Teaching Self-Feeding Skills to Profound Retardates Using Reinforcement Fading Procedures." *Behavior Therapy,* 1971, *2,* 62–67.

BERLEMAN, W. C., SEABERG, J. R., AND STEINBURN, T. W. "The Delinquency Prevention Experiment of the Seattle Atlantic Street Center: A Final Evaluation." *Social Service Review,* 1972, *46* (3), 323–346. Reports the findings of an unsuccessful community-based program oriented toward the prevention of delinquency.

BERNE, E. *Transactional Analysis in Psychotherapy.* New York: Grove Press, 1961.

BERNE, E. *Games People Play.* New York: Grove Press, 1964. Popularized discussion of principles of transactional analysis; focuses primarily on the analysis of clients' behavioral "games."

BERNE, E. *Principles of Group Treatment.* New York: Oxford University Press, 1966. Discusses the use of transactional analysis for group treatment.

BERNE, E. *What Do You Say After You Say Hello?* New York: Grove Press, 1972.

BERNSTEIN, S. "Conflict and Group Work." In S. Bernstein (Ed.), *Explorations in Group Work: Essays in Theory and Practice.* Boston: Boston University Bookstores, 1965.

BERNSTEIN, S. (Ed.) *Further Explorations in Group Work.* Boston: Milford House, 1970. Sets forth and explains group-work treatment concepts developed by present and former faculty members of the Boston University School of Social Work.

BERSCHEID, A., AND WALSTER, E. H. *Interpersonal Attractions.* Reading,

Mass.: Addison-Wesley, 1969, 29–42. A theoretical presentation, derived from empirical research, that explains how individual change agents can enhance their reinforcement value for relevant others.

BETTINGHAUS, E. P. *Persuasive Communication.* New York: Holt, Rinehart, and Winston, 1968.

BIDDLE, B. J., AND THOMAS, E. J. (Eds.) *Role Theory: Concepts and Research.* New York: Wiley, 1966. Collected readings about social-role theory. Early chapters present an original and sophisticated extension of role-theory concepts.

BIERI, J., ATKINS, A. L., BRIAR, S., LEAMAN, R. L., MILLER, H., AND TRIPODI, T. *Clinical and Social Judgment: The Discrimination of Behavioral Information.* New York: Wiley, 1966.

BIJOU, S. W. "What Psychology Has to Offer Education—Now." *Journal of Applied Behavior Analysis,* 1970, *3,* 65–71. Discusses application of behavior-modification theory to problems in education.

BIJOU, S. W., PETERSON, R. F., HARRIS, F. R., ALLEN, K. E., AND JOHNSTON, M. S. "Methodology for Experimental Studies of Young Children in Natural Settings." *Psychological Record,* 1969, *19,* 177–210. Describes the use of measurement, experimental design, and other features of behavior modification in natural settings.

BLAU, P. M. *Exchange and Power in Social Life.* New York: Wiley, 1964. A broad-ranging discussion that uses social-exchange concepts to explain common modes of social behavior.

BLUM, A. "Peer-Group Structure and a Child's Verbal Accessibility in a Treatment Institution." *Social Service Review,* 1962, *36*(4), 385–395.

BLUM, A., AND POLANSKY, N. "Effect of Staff Role on Children's Verbal Accessibility." *Social Work,* 1961, *6,* 29–33.

BOEHM, W. "The Nature of Social Work." *Social Work,* 1958, *3,* 10–18.

BOEHM, W. *Objectives of the Social Work Curriculum of the Future.* Social Work Curriculum Study. Vol. 1. New York: Council on Social Work Education, 1959.

BOREN, J. J., AND COLMAN, A. D. "Some Experiments on Reinforcement Principles Within A Psychiatric Ward for Delinquent Soldiers." *Journal of Applied Behavior Analysis,* 1970, *3,* 29–37.

BRETSCH, H. S. "Social Skills and Activities of Socially Accepted and Unaccepted Adolescents." *Journal of Educational Psychology,* 1952, *43,* 449–458.

BRIAR, S. "Social Casework and Social Group Work: Historical and Social Science Foundations." In R. Morris (Ed.), *Encyclopedia of Social Work.* Vol. 2. 16th issue. New York: National Association of Social Workers, 1971. A comparison of social casework and social group work, focusing on their historical backgrounds and foundations in social science.

BRIAR, S., AND MILLER, H. *Problems and Issues in Social Casework.* New York: Columbia University Press, 1971.

BRIAR, S., AND PILIAVIN, I. "Delinquency, Situational Inducements, and Commitment to Conformity." *Social Problems,* 1965, *13*(1), 35–44.

BROWN, J. S. *The Motivation of Behavior.* New York: McGraw-Hill, 1961.

BROWNING, R. M. "Treatment Effects of a Total Behavior Modification Program with Five Autistic Children." *Behavior Research and Therapy,* 1971, *9*(4), 319–327.

BURCHARD, J., AND TYLER, V., JR. "The Modification of Delinquent Behavior Through Operant Conditioning." *Behavior Research and Therapy,* 1965, *2*(4), 245–250.

BURGESS, R. L., AND AKERS, R. L. "A Differential Association-Reinforcement Theory of Criminal Behavior." *Social Problems,* 1966, *14*(2), 128–147. Uses sociobehavioral concepts to reinterpret Sutherland's theory of differential association, particularly with reference to criminal behavior; a unique effort to link psychological and sociological perspectives.

BURGESS, R. L., AND BUSHELL, D., JR. "A Behavioral View of Some Sociological Concepts." In R. L. Burgess and D. Bushell, Jr. (Eds.), *Behavioral Sociology: The Experimental Analysis of Social Process.* New York: Columbia University Press, 1969. An early effort to link sociological and behavior-modification concepts.

BURKE, P. J. "Authority Relations and Disruptive Behavior in Small Discussion Groups." *Sociometry,* 1966, *29*(3), 237–250.

BURKE, P. J. "Scapegoating: An Alternative to Role Differentiation." *Sociometry,* 1969, *32*(2), 159–168. A study of scapegoating from a role theory perspective.

BURNS, M. E., AND GLASSER, P. H. "Similarities and Differences in Casework and Group Work Practice." *Social Service Review,* 1963, *37*(4), 416–428.

BURR, W. R. "Role Transitions: A Reformulation of Theory." *Journal of Marriage and the Family,* 1972, *34*(3), 407–417.

BUSHELL, D., JR., WROBEL, P. A., AND MICHAELIS, M. L. "Applying 'Group' Contingencies to the Classroom Study of Behavior of

Preschool Children." *Journal of Applied Behavior Analysis,* 1968, *1,* 55–61. One of the first studies to investigate the effects of group contingencies.

BYRNE, C. "Attitudes and Attraction." In L. Berkowitz (Ed.), *Advances in Experimental Social Psychology.* Vol. 4. New York: Academic Press, 1969.

CAMPBELL, D. T., AND STANLEY, J. C. "Experimental and Quasi-Experimental Designs for Research on Teaching." In N. L. Gage (Ed.), *Handbook of Research on Teaching.* Chicago: Rand McNally, 1963.

CARTWRIGHT, D. "The Nature of Group Cohesiveness." In D. Cartwright and A. Zander (Eds.), *Group Dynamics: Research and Theory.* 3rd ed. New York: Harper and Row, 1968. Uses concepts of social exchange, social role, and social learning to analyze a major sociological phenomenon, group cohesiveness.

CARTWRIGHT, D., AND ZANDER, A. (Eds.) *Group Dynamics: Research and Theory.* 3rd ed. New York: Harper and Row, 1968.

CATANIA, C. A. *Contemporary Research in Operant Behavior.* Glenview, Ill.: Scott, Foresman, 1968, 330–331.

CAUTELA, J. R. "Treatment of Compulsive Behavior by Covert Sensitization." *Psychological Record,* 1966, *16,* 33–41.

CAUTELA, J. R. "Covert Sensitization." *Psychological Record,* 1967, *20,* 459–468.

CAUTELA, J. R. "Behavior Therapy and Self-Control: Techniques and Implications." In C. M. Franks (Ed.), *Behavior Therapy: Appraisal and Status.* New York: McGraw-Hill, 1969.

CAUTELA, J. R. "Covert Reinforcement." *Behavior Therapy,* 1970, *1*(1), 33–50. Describes the implementation of covert behavior-modification techniques in clinical practice.

CAUTELA, J. R. "Covert Extinction." *Behavior Therapy,* 1971, *2*(2), 192–200.

CHURCHILL, S. R. "Prestructuring Group Content." *Social Work,* 1959, *4,* 52–59.

CHURCHILL, S. R. "Social Group Work: A Diagnostic Tool in Child Guidance." *American Journal of Orthopsychiatry,* 1965, *35,* 581–588. Explains how small groups can be used for behavioral diagnosis.

CICOUREL, A. V. *The Social Organization of Juvenile Justice.* New York: Wiley, 1967.

CLEMMER, D. *The Prison Community.* New York: Holt, Rinehart, and Winston, 1958.

CLOWARD, R. A. "Illegitimate Means, Anomie, and Deviant Behavior." *American Sociological Review,* 1959, 164–176.

CLOWARD, R. A., AND OHLIN, L. E. *Delinquency and Opportunity: A Theory of Delinquent Gangs.* New York: Free Press, 1960. The classic presentation of social-opportunity theory; describes its utility for analyzing the origins of delinquent behavior.

COHEN, A. K. *Delinquent Boys: The Culture of the Gang.* New York: Free Press, 1955.

COHEN, A. K. "The Sociology of the Deviant Act: Anomie Theory and Beyond." *American Sociological Review,* 1965, *30,* 5–14.

COHEN, D. J. "Justin and His Peers: An Experimental Analysis of a Child's Social World." *Child Development,* 1962, *33*(3), 697–717. Discussion of the use of behavior analysis to alter the behavior of one child.

COHEN, H. L., AND FILIPCZAK, J. *A New Learning Environment.* San Francisco: Jossey-Bass, 1971. A comprehensive description of the use of reinforcement contingencies to alter the behaviors of delinquents in a residential setting.

COHEN, H. L., FILIPCZAK, J., AND BIS, J. *Case One: An Initial Study of Contingencies Applicable to Special Education.* Silver Spring, Md.: Institute for Behavioral Research, 1967.

COLLINS, B. E., AND GUETZKOW, H. *A Social Psychology of Group Processes for Decision-Making.* New York: Wiley, 1964.

COMMOSS, H. H. "Source Characteristics Related to Social Isolation of Second-Grade Children." *Journal of Educational Psychology,* 1962, *53,* 38–42.

COSER, L. *The Functions of Social Conflict.* New York: Free Press, 1956. Essays that point to the possible utility of social conflict for groups, communities, and societies.

COYLE, G. L. *Group Experience and Democratic Values.* New York: Association Press, 1947. A classic contribution to the social work literature; refers particularly to the utility of group work for training in democratic decision making.

COYLE, G. L. *Group Work with American Youth.* New York: Harper and Row, 1948.

CRESSEY, D. R. "Contradictory Directives in Complex Organizations: The Case of the Prison." *Administrative Science Quarterly,* 1959, *4,* 1–19.

CRESSEY, D. R. "Epidemiology and Individual Conduct: A Case from Criminology." *Pacific Sociological Review,* 1960, *3,* 47–58.

CUTLER, B. R., AND DYER, W. G. "Initial Adjustment Processes in Young Married Couples." *Social Forces,* 1965, *44,* 135–142.

DAVIDS, A., AND PARENTI, A. N. "Personality, Social Choice, and Adults' Perception of Those Factors in Groups of Disturbed and Normal Children." *Sociometry,* 1958, *21,* 212–224.

DEASY, L. C. *Persons and Positions.* Washington, D.C.: Catholic University Press, 1969. An explication of basic social-role concepts.

DE LAMATER, J. "On the Nature of Deviance." *Social Forces,* 1968, *46* (4), 45–55.

DE LANGE, W. H. "Patient Role Conflict and Reactions to Hospitalization." *Journal of Health and Human Behavior,* 1963, *4*(2), 113–118.

DENTLER, R. A., AND ERIKSON, K. T. "The Functions of Deviance in Groups." *Social Problems,* 1959, *7,* 98–107.

DEUTSCH, M. "The Effects of Cooperation and Competition Upon Group Process." *Human Relations,* 1949, *2,* 129–152 and 199–231. A major experimental study of the differential behavioral consequences of cooperative and competitive group environments.

DEUTSCH, M., AND GERARD, H. B. "A Study of Normative and Informational Social Influences Upon Individual Judgment." In D. Cartwright and A. Zander (Eds.), *Group Dynamics: Research and Theory.* 2nd ed. Evanston, Ind.: Row, Peterson, and Co., 1960.

DEUTSCH, M., AND SOLOMON, L. "Reactions to Evaluations by Others as Influenced by Self-Evaluations." *Sociometry,* 1959, *22,* 93–112.

DIBNER, A. S. "Ambiguity and Anxiety." *Journal of Abnormal and Social Psychology,* 1958, *56,* 165–174.

DINGES, N. G., AND OETTING, E. R. "Interaction Distance Anxiety in the Counseling Dyad." *Journal of Counseling Psychology,* 1972, *19,* 146–149.

DINITZ, S., ANGRIST, S., LEFTON, M., AND PASAMANICK, B. "Instrumental Role Expectations and Posthospital Performance of Female Mental Patients." *Social Forces,* 1962, *40,* 248–254. Illustrates the positive relationship between role expectations and the posthospital performance of discharged female mental patients.

DINOFF, M. R., HORNER, F., KURPIEWSKI, B. S., RICKARD, H. C., AND TIMMONS, E. O. "Conditioning Verbal Behavior of Schizophrenics in a Group Therapy-Like Situation." *Journal of Clinical Psychology,* 1960, *16*(4), 371–372.

DITTES, J. E. "Attractiveness of Group as a Function of Self-Esteem and

Acceptance by Group." *Journal of Abnormal and Social Psychology*, 1959, *59*, 77–82.

DOUBROS, S. G., AND DANIELS, G. J. "An Experimental Approach to the Reduction of Overactive Behavior." *Behavior Research and Therapy*, 1966, *4*, 251–258.

DUNPHY, D. "The Social Structure of Urban Adolescent Peer Groups." *Sociometry*, 1963, *26*, 230.

DURKIN, H. E. *The Group in Depth*. New York: International Universities Press, 1965.

EDWARDS, J. M. "Familial Behavior as Social Exchange." *Journal of Marriage and the Family*, 1969, *31*(3), 518–526. A view of family functioning from a social exchange perspective.

EISENMAN, R. "Psychopathology and Sociometric Choice." *Journal of Abnormal Psychology*, 1966, *71*(4), 256–259.

EISNER, V. *The Delinquency Label: The Epidemiology of Juvenile Delinquency*. New York: Random House, 1969.

EMERSON, R. M. "Operant Psychology and Exchange Theory." In R. L. Burgess and D. Bushell, Jr. (Eds.), *Behavioral Sociology: The Experimental Analysis of Social Process*. New York: Columbia University Press, 1969. One of the few works that systematically examines the interrelationship between social exchange theory and concepts of operant psychology.

EMPEY, L. T., AND ERICKSON, M. *The Provo Experiment*. Toronto: D. C. Heath, 1972. The most comprehensive assessment of the well-known Provo Experiment; examines the effects of guided group interaction on community-based treatment for delinquents.

EMPEY, L. T., AND LUBECK, S. G. *The Silverlake Experiment*. Chicago: Aldine, 1971. Reports the findings of the Silverlake treatment programs for delinquents.

EMPEY, L. T., AND RABOW, J. "The Provo Experiment in Delinquency Rehabilitation." *American Sociological Review*, 1961, 679–695.

ENTWISLE, D. R., AND WEBSTER, M., JR. "Raising Children's Performance Expectations." *Social Science Research*, 1972, *1*, 147–158.

ERIKSON, K. T. "Patient Role and Social Uncertainty: A Dilemma of the Mentally Ill." *Psychiatry*, 1957, *20*, 263–274.

ERIKSON, K. T. "Notes on the Sociology of Deviance." *Social Problems*, 1962, *10*, 307–314.

EYNON, T. G., AND SIMPSON, J. E. "The Boy's Perception of Himself in a State Training School for Delinquents." *Social Service Review*, 1965, *39*, 31–37.

FANNIN, L. F., AND CLINARD, M. B. "Differences in the Conception of Self as a Male Among Lower- and Middle-Class Delinquents." *Social Problems*, 1965, *13*(2), 205–214.

FANSHEL, D. "Studying the Role Performance of Foster Parents." *Social Work*, 1961, *6*(1), 74–82.

FANSHEL, D. *Foster Parenthood: A Role Analysis*. Minneapolis, Minn.: University of Minneapolis Press, 1966. An analysis of foster parenthood from a role-theory perspective.

FELDMAN, R. A. "Determinants and Objectives of Social Group Work Interventions." In J. L. Roney (Ed.), *Social Work Practice*. New York: Columbia University Press, 1967, 34–57.

FELDMAN, R. A. "Interrelationships Among Three Bases of Group Integration." *Sociometry*, 1968, *31*(1), 30–46. Description of the interrelationships of normative integration, functional integration, and interpersonal integration in children's groups.

FELDMAN, R. A. "Group Integration and Intense Interpersonal Disliking." *Human Relations*, 1969a, *22*(5), 30–39.

FELDMAN, R. A. "Group Integration, Intense Interpersonal Dislike, and Social Group Work Intervention." *Social Work*, 1969b, *14*, 30–39. An experimental study that demonstrates the nature of scapegoating behavior in children's groups; delineates the interrelationship between group-level and individual-level determinants of such behavior.

FELDMAN, R. A. "Group Service Programs in Public Welfare: Patterns and Perspectives." *Public Welfare*, 1969c, *27*, 266–271.

FELDMAN, R. A. "Social Attributes of the Intensely Disliked Position in Children's Groups." *Adolescence*, 1969d, *4*(14), 181–198.

FELDMAN, R. A. "Role Theory for Social Group Work: A Conceptual Framework." Paper presented at 97th Annual Forum of the National Conference on Social Welfare, Chicago, 1970. A comprehensive explication of the utility of role-theory concepts for group-work treatment.

FELDMAN, R. A. "Power Distribution, Integration, and Conformity in Small Groups." *American Journal of Sociology*, 1973, *79*(3), 639–664. A field study that describes the interrelationships of group integration, power distribution, and conformity behavior in children's groups.

FELDMAN, R. A., AND SPECHT, H. "The World of Social Group Work." In J. L. Roney (Ed.), *Social Work Practice*. New York: Columbia University Press, 1968. Suggests the utility of group-work methods for social reform objectives.

FELDMAN, R. A., WODARSKI, J. S., FLAX, N., AND GOODMAN, M. "Treating Delinquents in 'Traditional' Agencies." *Social Work,* 1972, *17*(5), 72–78. Discusses rationales for integrating antisocial children into prosocial children's groups in order to facilitate rehabilitation.

FELDMAN, R. A., WODARSKI, J. S., FLAX, N., AND GOODMAN, M. "Delinquency Theories, Group Composition, Treatment Locus, and a Service-Research Model for 'Traditional' Community Agencies." *Journal of Sociology and Social Welfare,* 1973a, *1,* 59–74.

FELDMAN, R. A., WODARSKI, J. S., FLAX, N., AND GOODMAN, M. "Pro-Social and Anti-Social Boys Together." *Social Work,* 1973b, *18,* 26–36. A pretest study that examines the behavioral effects of integrating antisocial children into groups of prosocial children at a summer camp.

FERSTER, C. B. "Positive Reinforcement and Behavioral Defects of Autistic Children." *Child Development,* 1961, *32,* 437–456. Describes the application of reinforcement for the modification of behaviors exhibited by autistic children.

FISH, J. M. *Placebo Therapy.* San Francisco: Jossey-Bass, 1973. A recent discussion that views therapeutic change as one form of placebo, or expectation, effect.

FIXSEN, D. L., PHILLIPS, E. L., AND WOLF, M. M. "Achievement Place: The Reliability of Self-Reporting and Peer-Reporting and Their Effects on Behavior." *Journal of Applied Behavior Analysis,* 1972, *5,* 19–30.

FIXSEN, D. L., PHILLIPS, E. L., AND WOLF, M. M. "Achievement Place: Experiments in Self-Government with Pre-Delinquents." *Journal of Applied Behavior Analysis,* 1973, *6,* 31–47.

FIXSEN, D. L., WOLF, M. M., AND PHILLIPS, E. L. "Achievement Place: A Teaching-Family Model of Community-Based Group Homes for Youth in Trouble." In L. A. Hamerlynck, L. C. Handy, and E. J. Mash (Eds.), *Behavior Change: Methodology, Concepts, and Practice.* Champaign, Ill.: Research Press, 1973. Describes a well-known program for treating delinquent children through the use of behavior-modification principles; focuses on group treatment in community-based homes.

FLANNERY, R. B. "Use of Covert Conditioning in the Behavioral Treatment of a Drug-Dependent College Dropout." *Journal of Counseling Psychology,* 1972, *19,* 547–550.

FORMAN, M. "Conflict, Controversy, and Confrontation in Group Work with Older Adults." *Social Work,* 1967, *12*(1), 80–85.

FOXX, R. M., AND AZRIN, N. H. "Restitution: A Method of Eliminating Aggressive Disruptive Behavior of Retarded and Brain Damaged Patients." *Behavior Research and Therapy,* 1972, *10,* 15–27.

FRANK, J. D. "Some Determinants, Manifestations, and Effects of Cohesiveness in Therapy Groups." *International Journal of Group Psychotherapy,* 1957, *7,* 53–63.

FRANK, J. D. *Persuasion and Healing: A Comparative Study of Psychotherapy.* Baltimore: Johns Hopkins Press, 1961. One of the first books to discuss the relationship between therapeutic change and the role expectations of relevant others, including the therapist.

FREEMAN, H. E., AND SIMMONS, O. G. "Wives, Mothers, and the Posthospital Performance of Mental Patients." *Social Forces,* 1958, *37,* 153–159.

FREEMAN, H. E., AND SIMMONS, O. G. "Familial Expectations and Posthospital Performance of Mental Patients." *Human Relations,* 1959, *13*(3), 233–242. A study of discharged mental patients' responses to the role expectations of family members.

FRENCH, J. R. P., JR., AND RAVEN, B. "The Bases of Social Power." In D. Cartwright (Ed.), *Studies of Social Power.* Ann Arbor, Mich.: Institute for Survey Research, 1959. An important contribution to the literature of social power; views the concept in terms of five separate bases: reward power, coercive power, referent (attractive) power, legitimate power, and expert power.

FREUD, S. *Group Psychology and the Analysis of the Ego.* London: International Psychoanalytical Press, 1922. One of Freud's rare discussions of small-group behavior.

GALINSKY, M. J., AND SCHOPLER, J. H. "The Effects of Consensus and Latitude on Group Goal Formulation." Unpublished paper presented at National Conference on Social Welfare, Dallas, Tex., 1971.

GAMBRILL, E. D., THOMAS, E. J., AND CARTER, R. D. "Procedure for Socio-Behavioral Practice in Open Settings." *Social Work,* 1971, *16* (1), 51–62. Outlines steps for implementing behavior-modification techniques in open settings.

GARABEDIAN, P. G. "Social Roles and Processes of Socialization in the Prison Community." *Social Problems,* 1963, *11*(2), 139–152. A role-theory perspective of behavior in prisons.

GARLAND, J. A., AND FREY, L. A. "Application of Stages of Group Development to Groups in Psychiatric Settings." In S. Bernstein

(Ed.), *Further Explorations in Group Work*. Boston: Boston University Bookstores, 1970.

GARLAND, J. A., JONES, H., AND KOLODNY, R. "A Model of Stages of Development in Social Work Groups." In S. Bernstein (Ed.), *Explorations in Group Work*. Boston: Milford House, 1965.

GARVIN, C. D. "Complementarity of Role Expectations in Groups." *Social Work Practice, 1969*. New York: Columbia University Press, 1969.

GARVIN, C. D., AND GLASSER, P. H. "Social Group Work: The Preventive and Rehabilitative Approach." In R. Morris (Ed.), *Encyclopedia of Social Work*. Vol. 2. 16th issue. New York: National Association of Social Workers, 1971. Presents the main tenets of the traditional, or rehabilitative, model.

GAURON, E. F., AND DICKENSON, J. K. "Diagnostic Decision-Making in Psychiatry: Part I: Information Usage." *Archives of General Psychiatry*, 1966a, *14*, 225–232.

GAURON, E. F., AND DICKENSON, J. K. "Diagnostic Decision-Making in Psychiatry: Part II: Diagnostic Styles." *Archives of General Psychiatry*, 1966b, *14*, 233–237. A discussion of various approaches to the diagnosis of deviant behavior, focusing primarily on the inclusiveness and logical features of each approach.

GELFAND, D. M., AND HARTMAN, D. P. "Behavior Therapy with Children: A Review and Evaluation of Research Methodology." *The Psychological Bulletin*, 1968, *69*, 204–215. An excellent review of the early literature on behavior modification of hyperactive, autistic, antisocial, and retarded children.

GERGEN, K. J. *The Psychology of Behavior Exchange*. Reading, Mass.: Addison-Wesley, 1969. Discusses interrelationships between the basic postulates of behavioral theory and social-exchange theory.

GIBB, C. A. "Leadership." In G. Lindzey and E. Aronson (Eds.), *The Handbook of Social Psychology*. Vol. 4. 2nd Ed. Reading, Mass.: Addison-Wesley, 1968. A comprehensive review and analysis of the concept of leadership.

GIBBS, J. P. "Conceptions of Deviant Behavior: The Old and the New." *Pacific Sociological Review*, 1966, *9*, 9–14.

GLASSER, P. H. "Social Role, Personality, and Group Work Practice." *Social Work Practice, 1962*. New York: Columbia University Press, 1962.

GLASSER, P. H. "Group Methods in Child Welfare: Review and Preview." *Child Welfare*, 1963, *42*, 312–320.

GLASSER, P. H., AND GARVIN, C. "Social Group Work." *Encyclopedia of*

Social Work. New York: National Association of Social Workers, 1971.

GLASSER, P. H., AND NAVARRE, E. "Structural Problems of the One-Parent Family." *Social Issues,* 1965, *21*(1), 93–109.

GLASSER, P. H., SARRI, R., AND VINTER, R. (Eds.) *Individual Change Through Small Groups.* New York: Free Press, 1974. The most recent and up-to-date collection of readings concerning the traditional social group-work method.

GOLDBERG, M. H., AND MACCOBY, E. E. "Children's Acquisition of Skill in Performing a Group Task Under Two Conditions of Group Formation." *Journal of Personality and Social Psychology,* 1965, *2*(6), 898–902.

GOLDSTEIN, A. P. *Therapist-Patient Expectancies in Psycho-Therapy.* New York: Pergamon Press, 1962. Discusses the effects of different expectations on the outcomes of psychotherapy.

GOLDSTEIN, A. P. "Prognostic and Role Expectancies in Psychotherapy." *American Journal of Psychotherapy,* 1966, *20,* 35–44.

GOLDSTEIN, A. P., HELLER, K., AND SECHREST, L. B. *Psychotherapy and the Psychology of Behavior Change.* New York: Wiley, 1966. Excellent text, which applies empirically based concepts and techniques to psychotherapy; focuses on topics such as increasing interpersonal attraction and transferring therapeutic learning.

GOLDSTEIN, A. P., AND SIMONSON, N. R. "Social Psychological Approaches to Psychotherapy Research." In A. E. Bergin and S. L. Garfield (Eds.), *Handbook of Psychotherapy and Behavior Change: An Empirical Analysis.* New York: Wiley, 1971.

GOULDNER, A. W. "The Norm of Reciprocity: A Preliminary Statement." *American Sociological Review,* 1960, *25,* 161–178.

GROSSBERG, J. M. "Behavior Therapy: A Review." *Psychological Bulletin,* 1964, *62*(2), 83–84.

GROSSER, G. H. "The Role of Informal Inmate Groups in Change of Values." *Children,* 1958, *5,* 25–29.

GRUSKY, O. "Role Conflict in Organizations: A Study of Prison Camp Officials." *Administrative Science Quarterly,* 1959, *3,* 452–472.

GRUVER, G. G. "College Students as Therapeutic Agents." *Psychological Bulletin,* 1971, *76*(2), 111–127. Reviews the various settings, clients, and characteristics associated with college students who have worked as therapeutic agents.

GUMP, P. V., AND SUTTON-SMITH, B. "Activity-Setting and Social Interaction: A Field Study." *American Journal of Orthopsychiatry,* 1955a, *25,* 755–760. An early discussion of activity settings and their effects on behavior; considered a departure point for ceptions of programing denoted in the traditional social group-work method.

GUMP, P. V., AND SUTTON-SMITH, B. "The 'It' Role in Children's Games." *The Group*, 1955b, *17*, 3–8.

HALL, D. T. "A Model of Coping with Role Conflict: The Role of Behavior of College-Educated Women." *Administrative Science Quarterly*, 1972, *17*, 471–486.

HALL, R. V., PANYAN, M., RABON, D., AND BRODEN, M. "Instructing Beginning Teachers in Reinforcement Procedures Which Improve Classroom Control." *Journal of Applied Behavior Analysis*, 1968, *1*, 315–322. A classic article that describes how teachers can use reinforcement procedures to improve classroom control.

HALMOS, PAUL. *The Faith of the Counsellors*. New York: Schocken Books, 1966.

HAMBLIN, R. L., BUCKHOLDT, D. R., FERRITOR, D. E., KOZLOFF, M. A., AND BLACKWELL, L. J. *The Humanization Processes: A Social Behavioral Analysis of Children's Problems*. New York: Wiley, 1971. A text that describes various behavior-modification techniques implemented with hyperactive, autistic, and inner-city children with verbal, reading, and arithmetic deficiencies.

HAMBLIN, R. L., HATHAWAY, C., AND WODARSKI, J. S. "Group Contingencies, Peer Tutoring, and Accelerating Academic Achievement." In E. A. Ramp and B. L. Hopkins (Eds.), *A New Direction for Education: Behavior Analysis*. Lawrence: The University of Kansas Press, 1971. A description of two studies that evaluate the use of different reinforcement contingencies to increase various academic and social behaviors of inner-city children.

HARE, A. P. *Handbook of Small Group Research*. New York: Free Press, 1962.

HARRIS, T. A. *I'm OK—You're OK*. New York: Harper and Row, 1967. A widely known popular explication of the principles of transactional analysis.

HART, B. M., REYNOLDS, N. J., BAER, D. M., BRAWLEY, E. R., AND HOLLIS, F. R. "Effect of Contingent and Non-Contingent Social Reinforcement on the Cooperative Play of the Pre-School Child." *Journal of Applied Behavior Analysis*, 1968, *1*(1), 73–76.

HARTFORD, M. *Groups in Social Work*. New York: Columbia University Press, 1972. An important contribution to the group-work literature; discusses topics such as group development, group composition, group goals, and group influence from a social science perspective.

HARTMAN, D. P., AND ATKINSON, C. "Having Your Cake and Eating It Too: A Note on Some Apparent Contradictions Between Therapeutic Achievements and Design Requirements in N = 1 Studies." *Behavior Therapy*, 1973, *4*, 589–591.

HASTORF, A. H. "The Reinforcement of Individual Actions in a Group Situation." In L. Krasner and L. P. Ullmann (Eds.), *Research in Behavior Modification*. New York: Holt, Rinehart, and Winston, 1967. Describes the use of various individual reinforcement techniques to increase certain behaviors within a small-group context.

HAYES, D. P., AND MELTZER, L. "Interpersonal Judgments Based on Talkativeness: Fact or Artifact?" *Sociometry*, 1972, *35*, 538–561.

HEINE, R. W., AND TROSMAN, H. "Initial Expectations of the Doctor-Patient Interaction as a Factor in Continuance in Psychotherapy." *Psychiatry*, 1960, *23*, 275–278.

HELLER, K. "Ambiguity in the Interview Interaction." In J. M. Shlien (Ed.), *Research in Psychotherapy*. Vol. 3. Washington, D.C.: American Psychological Association, 1968.

HESLIN, R., AND DUNPHY, D. "Three Dimensions of Member Satisfaction in Small Groups." *Human Relations*, 1964, *17*, 99–112.

HINDELANG, M. J. "A Learning Theory Analysis of the Correctional Process." *Issues in Criminology*, 1970, *5*, 43–58.

HINZTGER, J. N., SANDERS, B. J., AND DE MEYER, M. K. "Shaping Cooperative Responses in Early Childhood Schizophrenics." In P. Ullmann and L. Krasner (Eds.), *Case Studies in Behavior Modification*. New York: Holt, Rinehart, and Winston, 1965.

HOBBS, D. F., JR. "Transition to Parenthood: A Replication and Extension." *Journal of Marriage and the Family*, 1968, *30*(3), 413–417.

HOFFMAN, L. R., AND MAIER, N. R. F. "Quality and Acceptance of Problem Solutions by Members of Homogeneous and Heterogeneous Groups." *Journal of Abnormal and Social Psychology*, 1961, *62*(2), 401–407.

HOLLANDER, E. P. "Conformity, Status, and Idiosyncrasy Credit." *Psychological Review*, 1958, *65*, 117–127.

HOLLIS, F. *Casework—Psycho-Social Therapy*. New York: Random House, 1965.

HOLMES, D. S. "Round Robin Therapy: A Technique for Implementing the Effects of Psychotherapy." *Journal of Consulting and Clinical Psychology,* 1971, 324–331. Describes how the systematic alternation of therapists can increase generalization effects in client behavior.

HOMANS, G. C. "Social Behavior as Exchange." *American Journal of Sociology,* 1958, *63,* 597–606. An early analysis of social behavior from a social exchange perspective.

HOMANS, G. C. *Social Behavior: Its Elementary Forms.* New York: Harcourt, Brace, Jovanovich, 1961. One of the first and most comprehensive discussions of the interrelationships of social-exchange, social-role, and social-learning theories.

HOMANS, G. C. "The Sociological Relevance of Behaviorism." In R. L. Burgess and D. Bushell, Jr. (Eds.), *Behavioral Sociology: The Experimental Analysis of Social Process.* New York: Columbia University Press, 1969. A major contribution to the convergence of microbehavioral and macrosociological perspectives.

JAHODA, M. *Current Concepts of Positive Mental Health.* New York: Basic Books, 1958.

JANSYN, L. R., JR. "Solidarity and Delinquency." *American Sociological Review,* 1966, *31,* 600–614.

JEFFREY, C. R. "Criminal Behavior and Learning Theory." *Journal of Criminal Law, Criminology, and Police Science,* 1965, *56,* 394–400.

JEFFREY, C. R. *Crime Prevention Through Environmental Design.* Beverly Hills, Calif.: Sage Publications, 1971. Discusses crime prevention procedures developed through systematic environmental design; draws largely upon social learning principles in order to deal with broader sociological concerns.

JESNESS, C. F. *The Fricot Ranch Study.* Sacramento: State of California Department of the Youth Authority, 1965.

JOHNSON, W. G. "A Behavioral Approach to Group Therapy." Paper presented at the Sixth Annual Meeting of the Association for the Advancement of Behavior Therapy, New York, N.Y., 1972.

JULIAN, J. W., AND STEINER, I. D. "Perceived Acceptance as a Determinant of Conformity Behavior." *Journal of Social Psychology,* 1961, *55,* 191–198.

KAHN, A. J. (Ed.) *Shaping the New Social Work.* New York: Columbia University Press, 1973.

KANFER, F. H., AND SASLOW, G. "Behavioral Diagnosis." In C. M. Franks (Ed.), *Behavior Therapy: Appraisal and Status.* New

York: McGraw-Hill, 1969. Describes various factors therapists should consider during behavioral diagnosis.

KANTOR, D., AND BENNETT, W. I. "Orientations of Street-Corner Workers and Their Effects on Gangs." In S. Wheeler (Ed.), *Controlling Delinquents*. New York: Wiley, 1968.

KARLINS, M., AND ABELSON, H. I. *Persuasion*. New York: Springer, 1970.

KAZDIN, A. E., AND BOOTZIN, R. R. "The Token Economy: An Evaluative Review." *Journal of Applied Behavior Analysis*, 1972, *5*, 343–372. Reviews research concerning the use of token economies to change behavior.

KELLER, F. S. *Learning: Reinforcement Theory*. New York: Random House, 1954.

KELLEY, H. H., AND THIBAUT, J. W. "Group Problem-Solving." In G. Lindzey and E. Aronson (Eds.), *Handbook of Social Psychology*. Vol. 4. Reading, Mass.: Addison-Wesley, 1968.

KELMAN, H. C. "Processes of Attitude Change." *Public Opinion Quarterly*, 1961, *25*, 57–78. Classic discussion concerning differences among the processes of compliance, conformity, and internalization.

KELMAN, H. C., AND PARLOFF, M. B. "Interrelationships Among Three Criteria of Improvement in Group Therapy: Comfort, Effectiveness, and Self-Awareness." *Journal of Abnormal and Social Psychology*, 1957, *54*, 281–288. Reports experimental findings that illustrate low correlations among clients' comfort, effectiveness, and self-awareness following group therapy.

KERCKHOFF, A. C., BACK, K. W., AND MILLER, N. "Sociometric Patterns in Hysterical Contagion." *Sociometry*, 1965, *28*, 2–15.

KIDNEIGH, J. "History of American Social Work." In H. L. Lurie (Ed.), *Encyclopedia of Social Work*. 15th issue. New York: National Association of Social Workers, 1965.

KIESLER, C. A. "Attraction to the Group and Conformity to Group Norms." *Journal of Personality*, 1963, *31*, 559–569.

KIMBLE, G. A. (Ed.) *Hilgard and Marquis' Conditioning and Learning*. New York: Appleton-Century-Crofts, 1961.

KINCH, J. W. "Self-Conceptions of Types of Delinquents." *Sociological Inquiry*, 1962, *32*, 228–234.

KINDELSPERGER, W. L. "Stages in Group Development." In W. L. Kindelsperger (Ed.), *The Use of Groups in Welfare Settings*. New Orleans: Tulane University, 1957.

KLAPP, O. E. "Heroes, Villains, and Fools as Agents of Social Control." *American Sociological Review*, 1954, *19*, 56–61.

KLEIN, A. F. *Society, Democracy, and the Group*. New York: Women's Press, 1953. A key discussion of the role of social group work in preparing individuals for democratic participation.

KLEIN, A. F. "Program as a Tool in Social Group Work with the Mentally Retarded." *Proceedings: Institute of Social Group Work with the Mentally Retarded*. New York: A.H.R.C., 1967.

KLEIN, A. F. *Social Work Through Group Process*. Albany: State University of New York Press, 1970.

KLEIN, M. W. "Juvenile Gangs, Police, and Detached Workers: Controversies About Intervention." *Social Service Review*, 1965, *39*, 183–190.

KLEIN, M. W., AND CRAWFORD, L. Y. "Groups, Gangs, and Cohesiveness." *Journal of Research in Crime and Delinquency*, 1967, *113*, 63–75.

KLEIN, W. H., LE SHAN, E. J., AND FURMAN, S. S. *Promoting Mental Health of Older People Through Group Methods*. New York: Manhattan Society for Mental Health, 1965.

KONOPKA, G. *Group Work in the Institution*. New York: Association Press, 1954. Discusses the use of group work for treating children in correctional and rehabilitative institutions.

KONOPKA, G. *Social Group Work: A Helping Process*. Englewood Cliffs, N.J.: Prentice-Hall, 1963. A classic contribution to the group-work literature; discusses theories of group process, the establishment of treatment objectives, and other features of the helping relationship.

KUNKEL, J. H. "Some Behavioral Aspects of Social Change and Economic Development." *Pacific Sociological Review*, 1966, *9*, 48–56.

KUNKEL, J. H. *Society and Economic Growth: A Behavioral Perspective of Social Change*. New York: Oxford University Press, 1970. An unusual effort to link social-learning concepts with an analysis of economic development and social change.

KVARECEUS, W. C., AND MILLER, W. B. *Delinquent Behavior, Culture, and the Individual*. Washington, D.C.: National Education Association, 1959.

LAUVER, P. J., KELLY, S. D., AND FROEHLE, T. C. "Client Reaction Time and Counselor Verbal Behavior in an Interview Setting." *Journal of Counseling Psychology*, 1971, *18*, 26–30.

LAWRENCE, H., AND SUNDEL, M. "Behavior Modification in Adult Groups." *Social Work*, 1972, *17*(26), 34–43.

LAZARUS, A. A. "Group Therapy of Phobic Disorders by Systematic Desensitization." *Journal of Abnormal and Social Psychology*, 1961, *63*, 504–510.

LEFTON, M. "Social Class, Expectations, and Performance of Mental Patients." *American Journal of Sociology*, 1962, *68*, 79–87.

LENTZ, W. P. "Delinquency as a Stable Role." *Social Work*, 1966, *11*, (4), 66–71. An analysis of delinquent behavior from a social-role perspective.

LERMAN, P. "Individual Values, Peer Values, and Subcultural Delinquency." *American Sociological Review*, 1968, *33*(2), 219–235.

LINDSLEY, O. R. "Experimental Analysis of Cooperation and Competition." In T. Verhave (Ed.), *The Experimental Analysis of Behavior: Selected Readings*. New York: Appleton-Century-Crofts, 1966.

LIPPITT, R., POLANSKY, N., REDL, F., AND ROSEN, S. "The Dynamics of Power." *Human Relations*, 1952, *5*, 37–64.

LITWAK, E. "Models of Bureaucracy Which Permit Conflict." *American Journal of Sociology*, 1961, *67*, 180–184.

LOGAN, F. A. "Experimental Psychology of Animal Learning and Now." *American Psychologist*, 1972, *11*, 1055–1062.

LONG, E. R., HAMMACK, J. F., MAY, F., AND CAMPBELL, B. J. "Intermittent Reinforcement of Operant Behavior in Children." *Journal of the Experimental Analysis of Behavior*, 1958, *1*(4), 315–339.

LOTT, A. J., AND LOTT, B. E. "Group Cohesiveness, Communication Level, and Conformity." *Journal of Abnormal and Social Psychology*, 1961, *62*, 408–412.

LOTT, A. J., AND LOTT, B. E. "Group Cohesiveness as Interpersonal Attraction: A Review of Relationships with Antecedent and Consequent Variables." *Psychological Bulletin*, 1965, *64*, 259–309. A comprehensive review of the antecedents and consequences of group cohesiveness; in this treatment the concept is interpreted as one form of interpersonal attraction.

LOVITT, T. C., GUPPY, T. E., AND BLATTNER, J. D. "The Use of a Free-Time Contingency with Fourth Graders to Increase Spelling Accuracy." *Behavior Research and Therapy*, 1969, *7*, 151–156. One of the first studies to use a group contingency to alter children's behavior.

LUBOVE, R. *The Professional Altruists: The Emergence of Social Work as a Career, 1880–1930*. Cambridge, Mass.: Harvard University Press, 1965.

LUCHINS, A. "Group Structures in Group Psychotherapy." *Journal of Clinical Psychology*, 1967, *3*, 269–272.

LUCKEY, E. B. "Marital Satisfaction and Congruent Self-Spouse Concepts." *Social Forces*, 1960, *39*, 153–156.

MC CORD, J., AND MC CORD, W. "A Follow-Up Report on the Cambridge-Somerville Youth Study." *The Annals of the American Academy of Political and Social Science*, 1959, *332*, 89–96.

MC CORD, W., AND MC CORD, J. *Origins of Crime: A New Evaluation of the Cambridge-Somerville Youth Study*. New York: Columbia University Press, 1959.

MC COY, J. "The Application of the Role Concept to Foster Parenthood." *Social Casework*, 1962, *43*(5), 252–256.

MC INTYRE, C. J. "Acceptance by Others and Its Relation to Acceptance of Self and Others." *Journal of Abnormal and Social Psychology*, 1952, *47*, 624–625.

MC LAUGHLIN, B. *Learning and Social Behavior*. New York: Free Press, 1971.

MC SALLY, B. F. "Finding Jobs for Released Offenders." *Federal Probation*, 1960, *24*, 12–17.

MAEHR, M. L., MENSING, J., AND NAFZGER, S. "Concept of Self and the Reaction of Others." *Sociometry*, 1962, *25*, 353–358.

MAIER, H. W. (Ed.) *Group Work as Part of Residential Treatment*. New York: National Association of Social Workers, 1965. Collected readings that analyze the application of group-work methods in residential treatment settings.

MARGULIES, M. S. "Classification of Activities to Meet the Psycho-Social Needs of Geriatric Patients." *The Gerontologist*, 1966, *6*, 207–211.

MATARAZZO, J. D., AND WIENS, A. N. *The Interview*. Chicago: Aldine-Atherton, 1972. A text that describes the effects of selected variables on the interview behavior exhibited by interviewees and interviewers.

MATARAZZO, R. G., AND SASLOW, G. "Speech and Silent Behavior in Clinical Psycho-Therapy." In J. L. Shlien, H. F. Hunt, J. D. Matarazzo, and C. Savage (Eds.), *Research in Psycho-Therapy*. Washington, D.C.: American Psychological Association, 1968.

MATZA, D. *Delinquency and Drift*. New York: Wiley, 1964.

MATZA, D., AND SYKES, G. M. "Juvenile Delinquency and Subterranean Values." *American Sociological Review*, 1961, *26*, 712–719.

MECHANIC, D. "Role Expectations and Communication in the Therapist-Patient Relationship." *Journal of Health and Human Behavior,* 1961, *2*(3), 190–198.

MEREI, F. "Leadership and Institutionalization." *Human Relations,* 1949, *2*, 23–29.

MERTON, R. "Conformity, Deviation, and Opportunity Structures." *American Sociological Review,* 1959, *24*, 177–189.

MEYER, H. J. "Profession of Social Work: Contemporary Characteristics." In R. Morris (Ed.), *Encyclopedia of Social Work.* Vol. 2. 16th issue. New York: National Association of Social Workers, 1971.

MEYER, H. J., BORGATTA, E. F., AND JONES, W. C. *Girls at Vocational High: An Experiment in Social Work Intervention.* New York: Russell Sage Foundation, 1965.

MIDDLEMAN, R. *The Non-Verbal Method in Working with Groups.* New York: Association Press, 1968.

MILLER, H., AND TRIPODI, T. "Information Accrual and Clinical Judgment." *Social Work,* 1967, *12*(3), 63–69.

MILLER, R., AND PODELL, L. *Role Conflict in Public Social Services.* New York: State of New York Office of Community Affairs, 1971.

MILLER, W. B. "Lower-Class Culture as a Generating Milieu of Gang Delinquency." *Journal of Social Issues,* 1958, *14*(3), 5–19.

MILLER, W. B. "The Mid-City Delinquency Control Project." In N. Johnston, L. Savitz, and M. E. Wolfgang (Eds.), *The Sociology of Punishment and Correction.* 2nd ed. New York: Wiley, 1970.

MITHAUG, D. E., AND BURGESS, R. L. "The Effects of Different Reinforcement Contingencies in the Development of Social Cooperation." *Journal of Experimental Child Psychology,* 1968, *5*, 441–454.

MORSE, W. H. "Intermittent Reinforcement." In W. K. Honig (Ed.), *Operant Behavior: Areas of Research and Application.* New York: Appleton-Century-Crofts, 1966.

National Council on Crime and Delinquency. *Task Force Report: Corrections.* Appendix A, "Corrections in the United States: Data Summary." Prepared for the Task Force on Corrections of the President's Committee on Law Enforcement and Administration of Justice. Washington, D.C.: U.S. Government Printing Office, 1967.

NORMAN, R. D. "The Interrelationships Among Acceptance-Rejection, Self-Other Identity, Insight Into Self, and Realistic Perception of Others." *Journal of Social Psychology,* 1953, *37,* 205–235.

NORTHEN, H. *Social Work with Groups.* New York: Columbia University Press, 1969. An examination of the social worker's role in group-work treatment; describes planning and intake processes, orientation, exploration and testing of the group, use of the group for problem solving, and termination.

O'BRIEN, F., BUGLE, C., AND AZRIN, N. H. "Training and Maintaining a Retarded Child's Proper Eating." *Journal of Applied Behavior Analysis,* 1972, *5*(1), 67–72.

OHLIN, L. E. "The Reduction of Role Conflict in Institutional Staff." *Children,* 1958, *5,* 65–69.

OHLIN, L. E., PIVEN, H., AND PAPPENFORT, D. M. "Major Dilemmas of the Social Worker in Probation and Parole." *National Probation and Parole Association Journal,* 1956, *2*(3), 211–225.

O'LEARY, K. D. "Behavior Modification in the Classroom: A Rejoinder to Winett and Winkler." *Journal of Applied Behavior Analysis,* 1972, *5,* 505–511. Discusses rationales for choosing particular behaviors for systematic modification.

O'LEARY, K. D., AND KENT, R. "Behavior Modification for Social Action: Research Tactics and Problems." In L. A. Hamerlynck, L. C. Hardy, and E. J. Mash (Eds.), *Behavior Change: Methodology, Concepts, and Practice.* Champaign, Ill.: Research Press, 1973.

O'LEARY, K. D., POULOUS, R. W., AND DEVINE, V. T. "Tangible Reinforcers: Bonuses or Bribes?" *Journal of Consulting and Clinical Psychology,* 1972, *38,* 1–8.

OLSEN, K. M., AND OLSEN, M. "Role Expectations and Perceptions for Social Workers in Medical Settings." *Social Work,* 1967, *12*(3), 70–78.

OLSON, D. H. "Empirically Unbinding the Double Bind: Review of Research and Conceptual Definitions." *Family Process,* 1972, *11*(1), 69–94.

ORLANDO, R., AND BIJOU, S. W. "Single and Multiple Schedules of Reinforcement in Developmentally Retarded Children." *Journal of Experimental Analysis of Behavior,* 1960, *3*(4), 339–348.

OXLEY, G. B. "The Caseworker's Expectations and Client Motivation." *Social Casework,* 1966, *47,* 432–438.

PAPELL, C. P., AND ROTHMAN, B. "Social Group Work Models: Possession and Heritage." *Journal of Education for Social Work,* 1966,

2(2), 66–67. A comparison of three major group-work models, including the traditional, or rehabilitative, approach.

PARSONS, T. *The Social System.* New York: Free Press, 1951.

PASTORE, N. "A Note on Changing Attitudes Toward Liked and Disliked Persons." *Journal of Social Psychology,* 1960, *52,* 173–175.

PATTERSON, G. R. "An Application of Conditioning Techniques to the Control of a Hyperactive Child." In L. P. Ullmann and L. Krasner (Eds.), *Case Studies in Behavior Modification.* New York: Holt, Rinehart, and Winston, 1965.

PATTERSON, G. R. "Changes in Status of Family Members as Controlling Stimuli: A Basis for Describing Treatment Process." In L. A. Hamerlynck, L. C. Hardy, and E. J. Mash (Eds.), *Behavior Change: Methodology, Concepts, and Practice.* Champaign, Ill.: Research Press, 1973. Specifies how the behaviors of various family members can shape the aggressive behaviors of children.

PATTERSON, G. R., JONES, R., WHITTIER, J., AND WRIGHT, M. A. "A Behavior Modification Technique for the Hyperactive Child." *Behavior Research and Therapy,* 1965, *2,* 217–226.

PAUL, G. L. "Behavior Modification: Research Design and Tactics." In C. M. Franks (Ed.), *Behavior Therapy: Appraisal and Status.* New York: McGraw-Hill, 1969. An excellent discussion of behavior-modification research designs and procedures.

PERLMAN, H. H. *Persona: Social Role and Personality.* Chicago: University of Chicago Press, 1968. Explains the utility of social-role theory for understanding personality and interpersonal behavior.

PHILLIPS, E. L. "Achievement Place: Token Reinforcement Procedures in a Home-Style Rehabilitation Setting for 'Pre-Delinquent' Boys." *Journal of Applied Behavior Analysis,* 1968, *1,* 213–223. An excellent portrayal of how behavior modification can be implemented in an open community setting to change the behavior of antisocial children.

PHILLIPS, E. L., PHILLIPS, E. A., FIXSEN, D. L., AND WOLF, M. M. "Achievement Place: Modification of the Behaviors of Pre-Delinquent Boys Within a Token Economy." *Journal of Applied Behavior Analysis,* 1971, *4,* 45–59.

PHILLIPS, E. L., PHILLIPS, E. A., WOLF, M. M., AND FIXSEN, D. L. "Achievement Place: Development of the Elected Manager System." *Journal of Applied Behavior Analysis,* 1973, *6*(5).

PHILLIPS, H. V. *Essentials of Social Group Work Skill.* New York: Association Press, 1957.

PHILLIPS, H. V., AND DUNPHY, D. "Developmental Trends in Small Groups." *Sociometry*, 1959, *22*, 162–174.

PILIAVIN, I. "The Reduction of Custodian-Professional Conflict in Correctional Institutions." *Crime and Delinquency*, 1966, *12*(2), 125–134.

PILIAVIN, I. "Restructuring the Provision of Social Work Services." *Social Work*, 1968, *13*, 34–41.

PILIAVIN, I., AND BRIAR, S. "Police Encounters with Juveniles." *American Journal of Sociology*, 1964, *70*, 206–214.

PILNICK, S., ELIAS, A., AND CLAPP, N. W. "The Essexfields Concept: A New Approach to the Social Treatment of Juvenile Delinquents." *Journal of Applied Behavioral Science*, 1966, *2*(1), 109–125.

PIVEN, H., AND PAPPENFORT, D. "Strain Between Administrator and Worker: A View From the Field of Corrections." *Social Work*, 1960, *5*(4), 37–45.

PLATT, A. M. *The Child Savers: The Invention of Delinquency.* Chicago: University of Chicago Press, 1969.

POLSKY, H. W. *Cottage Six.* New York: Russell Sage Foundation, 1962.

POSER, E. G. "The Effect of Therapists' Training on Group Therapeutic Outcome." *Journal of Consulting Psychology*, 1966, *30*, 283–289.

POWERS, E., AND WITMER, H. *An Experiment in the Prevention of Delinquency: The Cambridge-Somerville Youth Study.* New York: Columbia University Press, 1951.

PRATT, L. "Level of Sociological Knowledge Among Health and Social Workers." *Journal of Health and Social Behavior*, 1969, *10*, 59–65.

PRENTICE, N. M., AND KELLY, F. J. "The Clinician in the Juvenile Correctional Institution: Frictions in an Emerging Collaboration." *Crime and Delinquency*, 1966, *12*, 49–54.

PSATHAS, G. "Phase Movement and Equilibrium Tendencies in Interaction Process in Psychotherapy Groups." *Sociometry*, 1960, *23*(2), 177–194.

PUMPHREY, R. E., AND PUMPHREY, M. W. *The Heritage of American Social Work.* New York: Columbia University Press, 1961.

RECKLESS, W. G., AND DINITZ, S. "Pioneering with Self-Concept as a Vulnerability Factor in Delinquency." *Journal of Criminal Law, Criminology, and Police Science*, 1967, *58*(4), 515–523.

REDL, F. "Group Emotion and Leadership." In A. P. Hare, E. F. Borgatta, and R. F. Bales (Eds.), *Small Groups: Studies in Social Interaction.* New York: Knopf, 1955.

REDL, F. "The Impact of Game Ingredients on Children's Play Behavior." In B. Schaffner (Ed.), *Group Processes: Transactions of the Fourth Conference.* New York: Josiah Macy, Jr., Foundation, 1959.

REDL, F., AND WINEMAN, D. *Children Who Hate—Controls From Within.* New York: Free Press, 1951.

REDL, F., AND WINEMAN, D. *The Aggressive Child.* New York: Free Press, 1957. A classic contribution that describes antecedents and concomitants of aggressive behavior by children; includes suggestions for treatment; focuses on both intrapsychic and small-group factors.

REESE, E. P. *The Analysis of Human Operant Behavior.* Dubuque, Iowa: William C. Brown, 1966.

REESE, H. W. "Relationships Between Self-Acceptance and Sociometric Choice." *Journal of Abnormal and Social Psychology,* 1961, *62,* 472–474.

REID, W. J., AND EPSTEIN, L. *Task-Centered Casework.* New York: Columbia University Press, 1972.

REISS, A. J., JR. "Systematic Observation of Natural Social Phenomena." In H. L. Costner (Ed.), *Sociological Methodology.* San Francisco: Jossey-Bass, 1971.

REISS, A. J., JR., AND RHODES, A. L. "The Distribution of Juvenile Delinquency in the Social Class Structure." *American Sociological Review,* 1961, *26,* 720–732.

REYNOLDS, N. J., AND RISLEY, T. R. "The Role of Social and Material Reinforcers in Increasing Talking of a Disadvantaged Pre-School Child." *Journal of Applied Behavior Analysis,* 1968, *1*(3), 253–262.

RICHARDS, C. V. "Discontinuities in Role Expectations of Girls." In H. C. Richey (Ed.), *Social Deviancy Among Youth.* Chicago: University of Chicago Press, 1966.

RICHER, S. "The Economics of Child Rearing." *Journal of Marriage and the Family,* 1968, *30*(3), 462–466.

RICHMOND, M. E. *Social Diagnosis.* New York: Free Press, 1965.

ROETHLISBERGER, E. J., AND DICKSON, W. J. *Management and the Worker.* Cambridge, Mass.: Harvard University Press, 1939.

ROGERS, C. R. *Client-Centered Therapy: Its Current Practice, Implications, and Theory.* Boston: Houghton Mifflin, 1951. The classic explication of client-centered therapy from a Rogerian perspective.

ROGERS, C. R., AND DYMOND, R. F. *Psychotherapy and Personality Change.* Chicago: University of Chicago Press, 1954.

ROGERS, C. R., AND STEVENS, B. *Person to Person: The Problem of Being Human.* Menlo Park, Calif.: Real People Press, 1967.

ROGERS, E. M. *The Diffusion of Innovations.* New York: Free Press, 1962.

ROLDE, E., MACK, J., SCHERL, D., AND MACHT, L. "The Maximum Security Institution as a Treatment Facility for Juveniles." In J. E. Teele (Ed.), *Juvenile Delinquency: A Reader.* Itasca, Ill.: Peacock Publishers, 1970.

ROSE, S. D. "A Behavioral Approach to Group Treatment of Children." In E. J. Thomas (Ed.), *The Socio-Behavioral Approach and Applications to Social Work.* New York: Council on Social Work Education, 1967.

ROSE, S. D. "A Behavioral Approach to the Group Treatment of Parents." *Social Work,* 1969, *14*(3), 21–29.

ROSE, S. D. "Counseling in a Correctional Institution: A Social Learning Approach." Unpublished paper presented at National Conference on Social Welfare, May 1971.

ROSE, S. D. *Treating Children in Groups.* San Francisco: Jossey-Bass, 1972. A behavioral approach to treating children in groups; discusses behavioral assessment, monitoring and charting, treatment plans, contracts, and interventions to alter member behaviors and group structures.

ROSEN, A. "The Treatment Relationship: A Conceptualization." *Journal of Consulting and Clinical Psychology,* 1972, *38*(3), 329–337. Discusses variables in the formation and continuance of the psychotherapeutic relationship.

ROSEN, A., AND LIEBERMAN, D. "The Experimental Evaluation of Interview Performance of Social Workers." *Social Service Review,* 1972, *46*(3), 395–412.

ROSENBLATT, A., AND MAYER, J. L. "Client Disengagement and Alternative Treatment Resources." *Social Casework,* 1966, *47*(1), 3–12.

ROSENFELD, J. M. "Strangeness Between Helper and Client: A Possible Explanation of Non-Use of Available Professional Help." *Social Service Review,* 1964, *38*(1), 17–25.

ROSENTHAL, R. *Experimenter Effects in Behavioral Research.* New York: Appleton-Century-Crofts, 1966. Comprehensive discussion of experimenter effects upon behavioral research.

ROSENTHAL, R., AND FODE, K. L. "The Effect of Experimenter Bias on the Performance of the Albino Rat." *Behavioral Science,* 1963, *8,* 88–189.

ROSENTHAL, R., AND JACOBSON, L. "Teachers' Expectancies as Determinants of Pupils' I.Q. Gains." *Psychological Reports,* 1966, *19,* 115–118.

ROSENTHAL, R., AND ROSNOW, R. L. (Eds.) *Artifact in Behavioral Research.* New York: Academic Press, 1969. Excellent collection of readings on problems of behavioral research, particularly those pertaining to experimenter and to expectation effects.

RUBEIZ, G. "Program Activities: A Critical Analysis and Study." Unpublished doctoral dissertation. Washington University, St. Louis, Mo., 1972.

SABATH, G. "The Effect of Disruption and Individual Status on Person Perception and Group Attraction." *Journal of Social Psychology,* 1964, *64,* 119–130.

SALZINGER, K. "The Place of Operant Conditioning of Verbal Behavior in Psycho-Therapy." In C. M. Franks (Ed.), *Behavior Therapy: Appraisal and Status.* New York: McGraw-Hill, 1969.

SAPOLSKY, A. "Relationship Between Patient-Doctor Compatibility, Mutual Perception, and Outcome of Treatment." *Journal of Abnormal Psychology,* 1965, *70,* 70–76.

SARBIN, T. "Schizophrenic Thinking: A Role Theoretic Analysis." *Journal of Personality,* 1969, *37*(2), 190–206.

SARRI, R. C., AND GALINSKY, M. J. "A Conceptual Framework for Group Development." In R. D. Vinter (Ed.), *Readings in Group Work Practice.* Ann Arbor, Mich.: Campus Publishers, 1967. Presents a seven-phase model of group development, along with concomitant phases of the treatment sequence in social group work.

SARRI, R. C., AND VINTER, R. D. "Group Treatment Strategies in Juvenile Correctional Programs." *Crime and Delinquency,* 1965, *11,* 326–340.

SARRI, R. C., AND VINTER, R. D. "Organizational Requisites for a Socio-Behavioral Technology." In E. J. Thomas (Ed.), *A Social Behavioral Approach and Application to Social Work.* New York: Council on Social Work Education, 1967. Outlines items practitioners should review prior to implementing behavior-modification programs in an open setting.

SCHACHTER, S. "Deviation, Rejection, and Communication." In D. Cartwright and A. Zander (Eds.), *Group Dynamics: Research and Theory.* 2nd ed. New York: Harper and Row, 1960.

SCHAFER, W. E. "Deviance in the Public School: An Interactional

View." In E. J. Thomas (Ed.), *Behavioral Science for Social Workers*. New York: Free Press, 1967.

SCHEIDLINGER, S. *Psychoanalysis and Group Behavior*. New York: Norton, 1952. Discusses application of the psychoanalytic perspective in small-group treatment.

SCHOPLER, J. H., AND GALINSKY, M. J. "Goals in Social Group Work Practice: Formulation, Implementation, and Evaluation." In P. H. Glasser and others (Eds.), *Individual Change Through Small Groups*. New York: Free Press, 1974. Explains how goals can be elaborated, differentiated, and applied for effective group-work treatment.

SCHRAG, C. "Leadership Among Prison Inmates." *American Sociological Review*, 1954, *19*, 37–42.

SCHRAG, C. "Delinquency and Opportunity: Analysis of a Theory." *Sociology and Social Research*, 1962, *46*, 167–175.

SCHUR, E. M. *Labeling Deviant Behavior*. New York: Harper and Row, 1971.

SCHWARTZ, M., AND TANGRI, S. S. "A Note on Self-Concept as an Insulator Against Delinquency." *American Sociological Review*, 1965, *30*, 922–926.

SCHWARTZ, R. D., AND SKOLNICK, J. H. "Two Studies of Legal Stigma." *Social Problems*, 1962, *10*, 133–142.

SCHWARTZ, W. "The Social Worker in the Group." In *New Perspectives on Services to Groups*. New York: National Association of Social Workers, 1961.

SCHWARTZ, W. "Toward a Strategy of Group Work Practice." *Social Service Review*, 1962, *36*(3), 268–279.

SCHWARTZ, W. "Small Group Science and Group Work Practice." *Social Work*, 1963, *8*(4), 39–46.

SCHWARTZ, W. "Group Work in Public Welfare." *Public Welfare*, 1968, *26*, 322–370.

SCHWARTZ, W. "Social Group Work: The Interactionist Approach." In R. Morris (Ed.), *Encyclopedia of Social Work*. Vol. 2. 16th issue. New York: National Association of Social Workers, 1971. Brief description of an important group-work method that focuses primarily upon the worker's mediating and interacting roles within the group.

SCHWARTZ, W., AND ZALBA, S. *The Practice of Group Work*. New York: Association Press, 1972. Collection of readings focusing on use of group work in various settings, such as schools, settlement houses, hospitals, trade unions, and prisons.

SCHWITZGEBEL, R., AND KOLB, D. A. "Inducing Behavior Change in Adolescent Delinquents." *Behavior Research and Therapy*, 1964, *1*(4), 297–304.

SEABURY, B. A. "Arrangement of Physical Space in Social Work Settings." *Social Work*, 1971, *16*(3), 43–49.

SHAH, S. A. "Treatment of Offenders: Some Behavioral Concepts, Principles, and Approaches." *Federal Probation*, 1966, *30*, 29–38. A discussion of the application of behavior-modification techniques to criminal offenders.

SHALINSKY, W. "Group Composition as a Factor in Assembly Effects." *Human Relations*, 1969a, *22*(5), 379–478.

SHALINSKY, W. "Group Composition as an Element of Social Group Work Practice." *Social Service Review*, 1969b, *43*(1), 42–49. Using Schutz's work as an organizing framework, this discussion represents one of the few extensive treatments of the relationship between group composition and group-work practice.

SHAPIRO, A. K. "Placebo Effects in Medicine, Psychotherapy, and Psychoanalysis." In A. E. Bergin and S. L. Garfield (Eds.), *Handbook of Psychotherapy and Behavior Change*. New York: Wiley, 1971. An extensive review of placebo and expectation effects in a variety of rehabilitative settings.

SHAPIRO, D. "The Reinforcement of Disagreement in a Small Group." *Behavior Research and Therapy*, 1963, *1*(3), 267–272.

SHAW, M. E. "A Note Concerning Homogeneity of Membership and Group Problem-Solving." *Journal of Abnormal and Social Psychology*, 1960, *60*(3), 448–450.

SHERIDAN, W. H. "Juveniles Who Commit Non-Criminal Acts—Why Treat in a Correctional System?" *Federal Probation*, 1967, *31*(1), 26–30.

SHERIF, M. "Experiments in Group Conflict." *Scientific American*, 1956, *195*(5), 54–58.

SHERIF, M., WHITE, J., AND HARVEY, O. J. "Status in Experimentally Induced Groups." *American Journal of Sociology*, 1955, *60*, 370–379.

SHERWOOD, J. J. "Self-Identity and Referent Others." *Sociometry*, 1965, *28*, 66–81.

SHORT, J. F., JR. "Differential Association and Delinquency." *Social Problems*, 1957, *4*, 233–239.

SHORT, J. F., JR. "Social Structure and Group Processes in Gang Delinquency." In M. B. Clinard and R. Quinney (Eds.), *Criminal Behavior Systems: A Typology*. New York: Holt, Rinehart, and

Winston, 1967. An examination of the relationship between group structure and members' behavior in delinquent gangs.

SHORT, J. F., JR., RIVERA, R., AND TENNYSON, R. A. "Perceived Opportunities, Gang Membership, and Delinquency." *American Sociological Review,* 1965, *30*(1), 56–67.

SHULMAN, L. "Scapegoats, Group Workers, and Pre-Emptive Intervention." *Social Work,* 1967, *12*(2), 37–43. Examines scapegoating in small groups; intervention is approached from a transactional perspective.

SHULMAN, L. *A Casebook of Social Work with Groups: The Mediating Model.* New York: Council on Social Work Education, 1968. Case examples of intervention using the mediating model of social group work.

SILVERMAN, M. "Knowledge in Social Group Work: A Review of the Literature." *Social Work,* 1966, *11*(3), 56–62.

SIMMONS, J. L. "Public Stereotypes of Deviants." *Social Problems,* 1965, *13*(2), 223–232.

SIMMONS, R. G. "The Role Conflict of the First-Line Supervisor: An Experimental Study." *American Journal of Sociology,* 1968, *73*(4), 482–495.

SKINNER, B. F. *Science and Human Behavior.* New York: Macmillan, 1953.

SKINNER, B. F. "Contingencies of Reinforcement in the Design of a Culture." *Behavioral Science,* 1966, *11,* 159–166.

SKINNER, B. F. *Contingencies of Reinforcement.* New York: Appleton-Century-Crofts, 1969.

SKINNER, B. F. *Beyond Freedom and Dignity.* New York: Bantam, 1971. Discusses the possible application of reinforcement theory to a broad variety of societal problems.

SOYIT, C. M. "The Double Bind Hypothesis and the Parents of Schizophrenics." *Family Process,* 1971, *10*(1), 53–75.

SPERGEL, I. "Selecting Groups for Street Work Service." *Social Work,* 1965, *10,* 47–55.

SPERGEL, I. *Street Gang Work: Theory and Practice.* Reading, Mass.: Addison-Wesley, 1966. Discussion of group-work theory and intervention programs for application with street gangs.

SPERGEL, I. "Deviant Patterns and Opportunities of Pre-Adolescent Negro Boys in Three Chicago Neighborhoods." In M. W. Klein (Ed.), *Juvenile Gangs in Context: Theory, Research, and Action.* Englewood Cliffs, N.J.: Prentice-Hall, 1967.

SPOHN, H. E., AND WOLK, W. P. "Social Participation in Homogeneous and Heterogeneous Groups of Chronic Schizophrenics." *Journal of Abnormal Psychology*, 1966, *61*(3), 335–340.

STAATS, A. W. "Social Behaviorism, Human Motivation, and the Conditioning Therapies." In B. Maher (Ed.), *Progress in Experimental Personality Research*. Vol. 5. New York: Academic Press, 1970.

STAATS, A. W., AND BUTTERFIELD, W. H. "Treatment of Non-Reading in a Culturally Deprived Juvenile Delinquent: An Application of Reinforcement Principles." *Child Development*, 1965, *36*, 925–942.

STAATS, A. W., MINKE, K. A., AND BUTTS, P. "A Token Reinforcement Remedial Reading Program Administered by Black Therapy Technicians to Problem Black Children." *Behavior Therapy*, 1970, *1*, 331–353.

STAATS, A. W., AND STAATS, C. K. *Complex Human Behavior*. New York: Holt, Rinehart, and Winston, 1964. Basic text that discusses behavior-modification procedures in a variety of clinical settings.

STEINZOR, B. "The Spatial Factor in Face-to-Face Discussion Groups." *Journal of Abnormal and Social Psychology*, 1950, *45*, 552–555.

STEPHENSON, R. M., AND SCARPITTI, F. R. "Essexfields: A Non-Residential Experiment in Group-Centered Rehabilitation of Delinquents." *American Journal of Corrections*, 1969, *31*(1), 12–18.

STOTLAND, E., COTTRELL, N. S., AND LAING, G. "Group Interaction and Perceived Similarity of Members." *Journal of Abnormal and Social Psychology*, 1960, *61*(3), 335–340.

STREAN, H. S. "Role Theory, Role Models, and Casework: A Review of the Literature and Practice Applications." *Social Work*, 1967, *12*(2), 77–89. A brief review of social-role concepts, with particular reference to their application in social casework.

STREET, D. "The Inmate Group in Custodial and Treatment Settings." *American Sociological Review*, 1965, *30*, 40–55.

STREET, D., VINTER, R. D., AND PERROW, C. B. *Organization for Treatment: A Comparative Study of Institutions for Delinquents*. New York: Free Press, 1966. Compares various models of custodial and treatment institutions for juveniles, paying particular attention to their potential for rehabilitation.

STRODTBECK, F. L., AND SHORT, J. F., JR. "Aleatory Risks versus Short-Run Hedonism: An Explanation of Gang Action." *Social Problems*, 1964, *12*, 2, 127–140.

STUART, R. B. "Casework Treatment of Depression Viewed as an Interpersonal Disturbance." *Social Work*, 1967, *12*(2), 27–36.

SUTHERLAND, E. H., AND CRESSEY, D. R. *Principles of Criminology.* 7th ed. Philadelphia: Lippincott, 1966.

SYKES, G., AND MATZA, D. "Techniques of Neutralization: A Theory of Delinquency." *American Sociological Review,* 1957, *22,* 664–670.

SYKES, G., AND MESSINGER, S. L. "Inmate Social System." In R. Cloward and others (Eds.), *Theoretical Studies in the Social Organization of the Prison.* New York: Social Science Research Council, 1960.

TALLAND, G. A. "Task and Interaction Process: Some Characteristics of Therapeutic Group Discussion." *Journal of Abnormal and Social Psychology,* 1955, *50*(1), 105–109. A study of developmental patterns and phases in treatment groups.

TANGRI, S. S., AND SCHWARTZ, M. "Delinquency Research and the Self-Concept Variable." *Journal of Criminal Law, Criminology, and Police Science,* 1967, *58*(2), 182–190. Discussion of the relevance of "self-concept" in delinquent behavior and for delinquency research.

TATE, B. G. "Case Study: Control of Chronic Self-Injurious Behavior by Conditioning Procedures." *Behavior Therapy,* 1972, *3*(11), 72–78.

THARP, R. G., AND WETZEL, R. J. *Behavior Modification in the Natural Environment.* New York: Academic Press, 1969. A behavior-modification text for the treatment of antisocial children in natural settings.

THELEN, H. A. *Dynamics of Groups at Work.* Chicago: University of Chicago Press, 1954. Presentation of six technologies for group treatment, including the laboratory method.

THEODORSON, G. A. "The Function of Hostility in Small Groups." *Journal of Social Psychology,* 1962, *56,* 57–66. Shows how hostile behavior in small groups can be functional, as well as dysfunctional, for group development.

THIBAUT, J. W., AND KELLEY, H. H. *The Social Psychology of Groups.* New York: Wiley, 1959. Classic explication of social-exchange concepts and principles.

THOMAS, E. J. "Effects of Facilitative Role Interdependence on Group Functioning." *Human Relations,* 1957, *10,* 347–366. Experimental study of the effects of members' facilitative interdependence upon mutual trust, cooperation, and other behaviors.

THOMAS, E. J. "Problems of Disability from the Perspective of Role Theory." *Journal of Health and Human Behavior,* 1966, *7*(1),

2–13. Uses role-theory concepts to examine various types of disability.

THOMAS, E. J. *The Socio-Behavioral Approach and Applications to Social Work.* New York: Council on Social Work Education, 1967a.

THOMAS, E. J. "Themes in Small Group Theory." In E. J. Thomas (Ed.), *Behavioral Science for Social Workers.* New York: Free Press, 1967b.

THOMAS, E. J. "Selected Socio-Behavioral Techniques and Principles: An Approach to Interpersonal Helping." *Social Work,* 1968, *13*(1), 12–26.

THOMAS, E. J., AND CARTER, R. D. "Instigative Modification with a Multi-Problem Family." *Social Casework,* 1971, *52,* 444–454.

THOMAS, E. J., AND FELDMAN, R. A. "Concepts of Role Theory." In E. J. Thomas (Ed.), *Behavioral Science for Social Workers.* New York: Free Press, 1967. Presentation of basic social-role concepts, using a programed instruction format and case illustrations.

THOMAS, E. J., AND FINK, C. F. "Effects of Group Size." *Psychological Bulletin,* 1963, *60*(4), 371–384. Reviews effects of differences in group size on member behavior.

THOMAS, E. J., KOUNIN, J., AND POLANSKY, N. A. "The Expected Behavior of a Potentially Helpful Person." In E. J. Thomas (Ed.), *Behavioral Science for Social Workers.* New York: Free Press, 1967.

THOMPSON, J., AND TUDEN, A. "Strategies, Structures, and Processes of Organizational Decisions." In *Comparative Studies of Administration.* Pittsburgh, Pa.: University of Pittsburgh Press, 1959.

TITTLE, C. R. "Inmate Organization: Sex Differentiation and the Influence of Criminal Subcultures." *American Sociological Review,* 1969, *34*(4), 492–505.

TOREN, N. "Semi-Professionalism and Social Work: A Theoretical Perspective." In A. Etzioni (Ed.), *The Semi-Professions and Their Organization.* New York: Free Press, 1969.

TRECKER, H. B. *Social Group Work: Principles and Practice.* New York: Association Press, 1955. An early discussion of basic social group-work methods and principles, with case illustrations.

TRECKER, H. B. *Social Group Work: Principles and Practices.* rev. ed. New York: Association Press, 1972. Extensively revised version of the earlier book; discusses group-work purposes, agency policies, worker roles, program development, evaluation procedures, basic principles, and application in a broad variety of settings.

TRIESCHMAN, A. E., WHITTAKER, J. K., AND BRENDTRO, L. K. *The Other 23 Hours.* Chicago: Aldine, 1969. Comprehensive discussion of methods and procedures relevant to the residential treatment of children.

TRIPODI, T., AND MILLER, H. "The Clinical Judgment Process: A Review of the Literature." *Social Work,* 1966, *11*(3), 63–69.

TROPP, E. "Group Intent and Group Structure: Essential Criteria for Group Work Practice." *Journal of Jewish Communal Service,* 1965, *61*(3), 229–250.

TROPP, E. *A Humanistic Foundation for Group Work Practice.* New York: Selected Readings, 1969. An application of the humanistic perspective to group-work theory and practice.

TROPP, E. "Social Group Work: The Developmental Approach." In R. Morris (Ed.), *Encyclopedia of Social Work.* Vol. 2. 16th issue. New York: National Association of Social Workers, 1971. Presents major facets of an important group-work method that focuses primarily upon members' social development.

TUCKMAN, B. "Developmental Sequences in Small Groups." *Psychological Bulletin,* 1965, *63,* 384–399. A review of group-development studies along socioemotional and instrumental dimensions; posits a sequence of developmental phases that progress through forming, storming, norming, and performing.

TURK, H., AND SIMPSON, R. L. *Institutions and Social Exchange.* Indianapolis, Ind.: Bobbs-Merrill, 1971. Examines basic social institutions from a social-exchange perspective.

TWARDOSZ, J., AND SAJWAJ, T. "Multiple Effects of a Procedure to Increase Sitting in a Hyperactive, Retarded Boy." *Journal of Applied Behavior Analysis,* 1972, *5*(11), 73–78.

TYLER, V. O., AND BROWN, G. D. "The Use of Swift, Brief Isolation as a Group Control Device for Institutionalized Delinquents." *Behavior Research and Therapy,* 1967, *5*(1), 1–11. Describes the use of isolation techniques to modify the behavior of delinquents.

ULLMANN, L. P. "Making Use of Modelling in the Therapeutic Interview." In I. Rubin and C. Franks (Eds.), *Advances in Behavior Therapy.* New York: Academic Press, 1969.

ULLMANN, L. P., AND KRASNER, L. (Eds.) *Case Studies in Behavior Modi-*

fication. New York: Holt, Rinehart, and Winston, 1965. One of the early texts in behavior modification.

VERPLANCK, W. S. "The Control of the Content of Conversation: Reinforcement of Statement of Opinion." *Journal of Abnormal and Social Psychology,* 1955, *51,* 668–676.

VIDEBECK, R. "Self-Conception and the Reaction of Others." *Sociometry,* 1960, *23,* 351–359.

VINTER, R. D. "Social Group Work." In H. L. Lurie (Ed.), *Encyclopedia of Social Work.* 15th issue. New York: National Association of Social Workers, 1965. A brief explication of major facets of the traditional social group-work method.

VINTER, R. D. (Ed.) *Readings in Group Work Practice.* Ann Arbor, Mich.: Campus Publishers, 1967. First collection of readings concerning the traditional social group-work method, contributed primarily by present or former faculty members of The University of Michigan School of Social Work.

VINTER, R. D., AND JANOWITZ, M. "Effective Institutions for Juvenile Delinquents: A Research Statement." *Social Service Review,* 1959, *33,* 118–130.

VINTER, R. D., AND SARRI, R. C. "Malperformance in the Public School: A Group Work Approach." *Social Work,* 1965, *10*(1), 3–14. Discussion of group-work problems and methods, with particular reference to public school settings.

VOGEL, E. F., AND BELL, N. W. "The Emotionally Disturbed Child as the Family Scapegoat." In N. W. Bell and E. F. Vogel (Eds.), *A Modern Introduction to the Family.* New York: Free Press, 1960. Discussion of the scapegoating of emotionally disturbed children, focusing upon its functions in family stability and spouse relations.

VOSS, H. L. "Differential Association and Containment Theory: A Theoretical Convergence." *Social Forces,* 1969, *47,* 381–391.

VUKELICH, R., AND HAKE, D. F. "Reduction of Dangerously Aggressive Behavior in a Severely Retarded Resident Through a Combination of Positive Reinforcement Procedures." *Journal of Applied Behavior Analysis,* 1971, *4*(3), 215–225.

WAHLER, R. G. "Selling Generality: Some Specific and General Effects of Child Behavior Therapy." *Journal of Applied Behavior Analysis,* 1969, *2*(4), 239–248. Discusses factors that must be considered by those attempting to generalize newly learned behaviors to other social environments.

WALKER, H. M., AND BUCKLEY, N. K. "Programming Generalization and Maintenance of Treatment Effects Across Time and Across Settings." *Journal of Applied Behavior Analysis*, 1972, *5*, 209–224. Discusses the generalization and maintenance of learned behavior in new social settings.

WARREN, M. Q. *Correctional Treatment in Community Settings: A Report of Current Research.* Paper presented at Sixth International Congress on Criminology, Madrid, 1970. Review of successes and failures in a broad variety of community-based correctional settings.

WASIK, B. H., SENN, K., WELCH, R. H., AND COOPER, B. R. "Behavior Modification with Culturally Deprived School Children: Two Case Studies." *Journal of Applied Behavior Analysis*, 1969, *2* (3), 181–194.

WATERS, F. W., AND MC CALLUM, R. N. "The Basis of Behavior Therapy: Mentalistic or Behavioristic? A Reply to E. A. Locke." *Behavior Research and Therapy*, 1973, *11*, 157–163. Discusses the relevance of cognitive variables for behavior modification.

WEBER, G. H. "Conflicts Between Professional and Non-Professional Personnel in Institutional Delinquency Treatment." *Journal of Criminal Law, Criminology, and Police Science*, 1957, *48*, 26–43.

WEBER, G. H., AND HABERLEIN, B. J. *Residential Treatment of Emotionally Disturbed Children.* New York: Behavioral Publications, 1972. Collection of readings concerning a number of variables important for successful residential treatment.

WERTHMAN, C. "The Function of Social Definitions in the Development of Delinquent Careers." In President's Commission on Law Enforcement and Administration of Justice, *Task Force Report: Juvenile Delinquency and Youth Crime.* Washington, D.C.: U.S. Government Printing Office, 1967.

WETZEL, R. "The Use of Behavioral Techniques in a Case of Compulsive Stealing." *Journal of Consulting Psychology*, 1966, *30*, 367–374.

WHEELER, L. "Toward a Theory of Behavioral Contagion." *Psychological Review*, 1966, *73*(2), 179–192.

WHEELER, L., AND COTTRELL, L. S., JR. *Juvenile Delinquency: Its Prevention and Control.* New York: Russell Sage Foundation, 1966.

WHEELER, L., AND LEVINE, L. "Observer-Model Similarity in the Contagion of Aggression." *Sociometry*, 1967, *30*, 41–49.

WHITE, R., AND LIPPITT, R. *Autocracy and Democracy.* New York:

Harper and Row, 1960. Classic study of autocratic and democratic decision-making processes in small groups.

WHITMAN, T. L., MERCURIO, J. R., AND CAPONIGRI, V. "Development of Social Responses in Two Severely Retarded Children." *Journal of Applied Behavior Analysis,* 1970, *3,* 133–138.

WHITTAKER, J. K. "Models of Group Development: Implications for Social Group Work Practice." *Social Service Review,* 1970, *44* (3), 308–322.

WIDGERY, R., AND STACKPOLE, C. "Desk Position, Interviewee Anxiety, and Interviewer Credibility: An Example of Cognitive Balance in a Dyad." *Journal of Counseling Psychology,* 1972, *19,* 173–177.

WIGGINS, J. A. "Interaction Structure, Frustration, and the Extensiveness and Intensity of Aggression." *Sociometry,* 1965, *28*(1), 89–99.

WILENSKY, H. L., AND LEBEAUX, C. N. *Industrial Society and Social Welfare.* New York: Russell Sage Foundation, 1958.

WILLIAMS, J. R., AND GOLD, M. "From Delinquent Behavior to Official Delinquency." *Social Problems,* 1972, *20*(2), 209–229. Through the use of interview data, delineates critical differences between the delinquent behavior of youth and official records of delinquency; discusses implications for labeling of juveniles.

WILSON, G., AND RYLAND, G. *Social Group Work Practice: The Creative Use of the Group Process.* Boston, Mass.: Houghton Mifflin, 1949. A classic contribution to the group-work literature; discusses program media, professional leadership, program supervisory processes, and draws upon case records for illustration.

WINETT, R. A., AND WINKLER, R. C. "Current Behavior Modification in the Classroom: Be Still, Be Quiet, Be Docile." *Journal of Applied Behavior Analysis,* 1972, *5,* 499–504. A review of important issues in selecting target behaviors to be increased or decreased during treatment.

WODARSKI, J. S., FELDMAN, R. A., AND FLAX, N. "Social Learning Theory and Group Work Practice with Anti-Social Children." *Clinical Social Work Journal,* 1973, *1*(2), 78–93. Brief explication of social-learning principles and their relevance for group-work practice with antisocial children.

WODARSKI, J. S., HAMBLIN, R. L., BUCKHOLDT, D. R., AND FERRITOR, D. E. "The Effects of Low Performance Group and Individual Contingencies on Cooperative Behaviors Exhibited by Fifth Graders." *Psychological Record,* 1972, *22,* 359–368.

WODARSKI, J. S., HAMBLIN, R. L., BUCKHOLDT, D. R., AND FERRITOR, D. E. "Individual Contingencies Versus Different Shared Consequences Contingent on the Performance of Low-Achieving Group Members." *Journal of Applied Social Psychology,* 1973, *3,* 276–290. An evaluation of the effects of various reinforcement contingencies on the cooperative and academic behaviors of children.

WOLF, M. M., GILES, D. K., AND HALL, R. V. "Experiments with Token Reinforcement in a Remedial Classroom." *Behavior Research and Therapy,* 1968, *6,* 51–64. Shows how different token systems influence social and academic behaviors of children.

WOLF, M. M., RISLEY, T. R., AND MEES, H. L. "Application of Operant Conditioning Procedures to the Behavior Problems of an Autistic Child." *Behavior Research and Therapy,* 1964, *1,* 305–312.

WOLFE, D., AND SNOEK, J. "A Study of Tensions and Adjustments Under Role Conflict." *Social Issues,* 1962, *18,* 102–121.

WOLFGANG, M. E., FIGLIO, R. M., AND SELLIN, T. *Delinquency in a Birth Cohort.* Chicago: University of Chicago Press, 1972. Longitudinal cohort analysis of delinquent behavior in a major American city.

WOLKEN, G. H., AND HALDEMAN, R. B. "Role Position Salience and Social Functioning of Psychiatric Patients." *Journal of Social Psychology,* 1969, *78,* 113–119.

YATES, A. J. *Historical Development of Behavior Therapy.* New York: Wiley, 1970. An introductory text to behavior therapy.

ZALD, M. N. "Power Balance and Staff Conflict in Correctional Institutions." *Administrative Science Quarterly,* 1962, *6,* 22–49.

ZELEN, S. L. "Acceptance and Acceptability: An Examination of Social Reciprocity." *Journal of Consulting Psychology,* 1954, *18,* 316.

Index